The Life of the Real
Brigadier Gerard

The Colonel
of Chasseurs

The Life of the Real
Brigadier Gerard

The Colonel
of Chasseurs

Volume 3:
A French Cavalryman of the Napoleonic Wars
in the Retreat from Moscow, Lutzen, Bautzen,
Katzbach, Leipzig, Hanau & Waterloo

1811 – 1815

Jean–Baptiste de Marbot

LEONAUR

The Life of the Real Brigadier Gerard: The Colonel of Chasseurs
Volume 3:
A French Cavalryman of the Napoleonic Wars
in the Retreat from Moscow, Lutzen, Bautzen, Katzbach,
Leipzig, Hanau & Waterloo
1811 - 1815
by Jean-Baptiste de Marbot

Published by Leonaur Ltd

First Edition

ISBN (10 digit): 1-84677-050-5 (hardcover)
ISBN (13 digit): 978-1-84677-050-0 (hardcover)

ISBN (10 digit): 1-84677-046-7 (softcover)
ISBN (13 digit): 978-1-84677-046-3 (softcover)

http://www.leonaur.com

Publisher's Notes

In the interests of authenticity, the spellings, grammar and place names used have been retained from the original editions.

The opinions of the authors represent a view of events in which he was a participant related from his own perspective, as such the text is relevant as an historical document.

The views expressed in this book are not necessarily those of the publisher.

Contents

Chapter 1
I Become Major, Chasseurs á Cheval

My brother and the rest of Masséna's aides-de-camp made haste to leave Spain and come to join us in Paris, where I remained all summer and the following autumn. I went each month to spend some days at the Château de Bonneuil, the home of M. and Mme. Desbrières. During my absence the Desbrières had been most friendly towards my mother, and on my return the affection I had felt for a long time for their daughter was increased, and I was shortly permitted to ask for her hand in marriage. The marriage was agreed, and I even had, for a time, the hope of being promoted to colonel before this important ceremony took place.

It was the accepted thing for the Emperor to sign the marriage contract of any of the colonels in the army, but he only very rarely accorded this favour to officers of lower rank, and they were required to inform the minister for war of the reasons which led them to ask for this distinction. I based my request on what the Emperor had said to me when I saw him on the eve of the battle of Marengo. He had said to me, speaking of my father who had died during the siege of Genoa, "If you behave yourself and follow in his footsteps, I, myself, will be your father." I added that since that day I had been wounded eight times, and was conscious that I had always done my duty.

The minister, Clarke, a very stern character, who almost always rejected requests of this sort, agreed that mine merited consideration, and promised me that he would submit it to his majesty. He kept his word, for a few days later I was ordered to report to the Emperor at the château of Compiègne, and to bring with me the notary who held the contract of marriage; this was the good M. Mailand, with whom I set off in a post carriage.

When we arrived, the Emperor had gone hunting: not that he much enjoyed the sport, but he thought that he should copy the former kings of France. The signing was therefore put off until the next day, which greatly upset M. Mailand who was awaited in Paris. But what could one do?

On the following day we were presented to the Emperor, whom we found in the apartment where, twenty years later, I have so often served as aide-de-camp to princes of the House of Orléans. My contract was signed in the salon where later was signed that of the King of Belgium with Princess Louise, the daughter of King Louis-Phillipe of France.

During these short interviews, Napoleon was always very affable. He addressed some questions to the notary, asked me if my fiancée was pretty, what was her dowry, etc. etc. On dismissing me he said that he would like to see me in a good position, and that he would soon reward me for my good services. For a moment I saw myself as a colonel, and this hope was reinforced when, on leaving the Imperial presence, I was accosted by General Mouton, Comte de Lobau, who assured me confidentially that the Emperor had put my name on a list of officers to whom he wished to give the command of a regiment. My pleasure on hearing this was increased by my knowledge that the Comte de Lobau, an aide-de-camp to Napoleon, was responsible under the minister for war, for military promotions. I returned to Paris full of joy and hope! I was married on the 14th November following.

I was happy in the bosom of my family, and expected every day my brevet as colonel, when I was told by the minister for war that I was to be posted as Major to the 1st regiment of Chasseurs á Cheval, then in garrison in the depths of Germany. I was much downcast at this news, for it seemed to me most hurtful that I should be sent once more to serve as a simple squadron commander, a rank in which I had been wounded three times and had campaigned from Wagram to Portugal. I could not understand why I was being treated like this, after what the Emperor and the Comte de Lobau had said to me. It was the latter who gave me the key to this puzzle.

Masséna, on his entry into Portugal, had fourteen aides-de-camp, of whom six were senior officers. Two of these, MM. Pelet and Casabianca, were made colonels during the campaign; they were senior to me and had amply fulfilled their duties. Their promotion seemed to make mine the more certain since I now became the most senior squadron commander on the staff. The man in the fifth place was M. Barain, who was a captain when I joined the staff. M. Barain had lost a hand at Wagram, and was promoted to major, which was fair; however, the Emperor in advancing him to this rank had designated him for work in the arsenals, work which can easily be done with an arm missing. Masséna had expected that M. Barain would remove himself, but the latter insisted on going with him to Portugal, although he could not carry out any mission in such difficult country. No one thought therefore that he would get any further promotion.

It so happened, however, that M. Barain was a nephew of M. Francois de Nantes, the director of legal codification, who had found numerous positions for members of Masséna's family. M. Francois de Nantes demanded in return that his nephew, Barain, should be recommended for the rank of colonel. The marshal, forced to choose between me and Barain, chose Barain. I learned from the Comte de Lobau that the Emperor was reluctant to sign, but that he eventually yielded to the insistence of the worthy director who had come to add weight personally to the only request he had yet made on the behalf of his family. So Barain was promoted to colonel.

I have perhaps dwelt a little overmuch on this regrettable affair, but to assess my disappointment it is necessary to think back to the period in question and recall the important position occupied by battalion commanders in the imperial army, which resulted in several instances of colonels who refused promotion to general and asked only to be left in command of their regiments.

Masséna sent me the following letter, the only reward for three campaigns fought and three wounds recieved under his command.

Paris. 24th November. 1811

My dear Marbot, I send you the service order which I have received on your behalf. I asked for promotion for you, as you are aware, and I am doubly disappointed that you did not obtain this and that I am also to lose you. I have been very satisfied with your services; a satisfaction which you are entitled to feel, regardless of any rewards which this may bring. Your record will always do you credit in the eyes of those under whose orders you may find yourself. Please be-

lieve, my dear Marbot, in my appreciation, my regrets and my sincere good wishes for you.
Masséna.

I had not expected to meet Masséna again, but his wife wrote to me saying that she wished to meet my wife, and inviting us both to dinner. I had always had the highest regard for the conduct of Madame Masséna, particularly at Antibes, her home territory, where I met her for the first time, on my return from Genoa. So I accepted the invitation. Masséna came up to me and once more expressed his regrets, and suggested that he might ask for my nomination as an officer of the Legion of Honour. I replied that as he had been unable to do anything for me when I was on his staff, and wounded before his eyes, I would not like to expose him to any further embarrassment, and that I would now seek advancement by my own efforts; then I lost myself in the crowd of guests.

This was my last contact with Masséna, though I continued to visit his wife and his son, both of them my firm friends.

Chapter 2
I Move to the 23rd Chasseurs á Cheval

At the beginning of 1812, I was in Paris, with my young wife and our families. But the happiness which I enjoyed was lessened by the thought of my imminent departure. I was due to join the 1st Chasseurs à Cheval as a squadron commander with the rank of Major. The chagrin which I felt at not having been promoted to Colonel, which I thought I deserved, was somewhat relieved when, having gone to the Tuileries to pay my new year respects, the Emperor sent an aide-de-camp to command my presence in his private quarters, where I found General Mouton, Comte de Lobau, who had always been on my side.

Napoleon appeared and told me in the most friendly manner that he had intended to give me a regiment, but that there were certain reasons which had led him to nominate Major Barain. He said that having promoted three of Masséna's aides to Colonel he could not accord any more promotions to one general staff, but that he had not forgotten me and although he could not give me the nominal command, he would put me in the position of being, in effect, a regimental commander. "The commanding officer of the 23rd Chasseurs á Cheval, M. de La Nougarède, has become so afflicted by gout that he can hardly mount a horse", the Emperor said, "but he is an excellent officer who has fought several campaigns with me, and I have a high regard for him. He has begged me to let him try to go once more on campaign and I do not wish to remove him from his regiment. However, I hear that this fine unit is going down hill in his hands so I am sending you as "Co-adjutor" to M. de La Nougarède. You will be working for yourself, for if the Colonel recovers his health I shall promote him to general, and if not I shall transfer him to the gendarmes. In either case he will leave his regiment and you will become their colonel; so I repeat you will be working for your own benefit." This promise gave me renewed hope, and I was making ready to leave when the minister for war extended my leave until the end of March, which I found very acceptable.

The 23rd Chasseurs were stationed in Swedish Pomerania, so I had an enormous distance to travel, and as I wished to arrive before the expiration of my leave, I left Paris on the 15th of March, parting with much regret from my dear wife. I had bought a good barouche, in which, at the request of Marshal Mortier, I gave a seat to his nephew, Lieutenant Durbach, who belonged to the regiment which I was about to join. As my former servant, Woirland, had asked if he might stay in Spain, where he hoped to make his fortune running a canteen, I had replaced him, on my leaving Salamanca, by a Pole named Lorentz Schilkowski. This man, at one time an Austrian Uhlan, was not lacking intelligence, but, like all Poles he was a drunkard, and unlike the soldiers of that nation, he was as timid as a hare. Lorentz, however, as well as his native language, spoke passable French and fluent German and Russian, and for this reason he was most valuable to me in my travelling and campaigning in the north. I was nearing the Rhenish provinces, when on leaving Kaiserslauten at night, the postilion tipped my barouche into a pothole, where it was damaged. No one was hurt, but both M. Durbach and I agreed that this was a bad omen for soldiers who were about to face the enemy. However, after spending a day waiting for repairs to be made, we were able to get under way once more. Unfortunately the accident had so weakened the springs and the wheels that they broke six times during our journey, which delayed us considerably, and on occasions forced us to walk for several leagues in the snow. We arrived at last at the shores of the Baltic sea, where the 23rd Chasseurs were in garrison at Stralsund and Greifswald.

I found Colonel de La Nougarède to be an excellent officer, well-informed and capable, but so prematurely aged by gout that he was hardly able to sit on a horse, and went everywhere in a carriage, a most unsuitable method of transport for the commander of a regiment of light cavalry! He gave me an enthusiastic welcome, and after explaining the reasons which, in the interest of his career, made him stay with the regiment, he showed me a letter in which the Comte de Lobau informed him of the motives which had led the Emperor to attach me to him. M. de La Nougarède, far from being offended, saw this as another kindness on the part of the Emperor, and looked forward to being promoted to general or heading the gendarmerie. He counted, with my help, on completing at least part of the campaign, and on the realisation of his hopes at the first imperial revue. To make it clear that I shared the command, which was not in keeping with my rank as Major, he called together all the officers, in front of whom he provisionally delegated all his powers to me, until such time as he recovered his health, and instructed them to obey my orders without referring to him, since his illness often made it impossible for him to follow the regiment sufficiently closely to command it in person. An order of the day was issued along these lines, and from that day forward, except for the rank, I was virtually the commander of the regiment, and the regiment soon got into the habit of looking on me as their real leader.

Since that time, I have commanded several cavalry regiments, either as colonel or general. And I was for a long time inspector of this branch of the service; I can say with certainty that if I have seen units as good as the 23rd Chasseurs, I have never seen one better. It was not that the unit contained any outstanding personalities, such as I have seen sometimes in other regiments, but if there was not in the 23rd any one of remarkable talents, there was no one who did not maintain a high standard in carrying out his duties. There were no peaks, but there were no troughs; everyone kept in step. The officers were intelligent, well trained and well behaved. They lived together as true brothers-in-arms. The same applied to the N.C.O.s. And the troopers followed this good example. They were almost all old soldiers, veterans of Austerlitz, Jena, Friedland, Wagram, a fine body of men who came mostly from Normandy, Alsace, Lorraine and Franche-comte, provinces known for their martial spirit and their love of horses. The build and strength of these men was noticed by General Bourcier, who was in charge of remounts, and he supplied the regiment with horses which were bigger and more lively than the usual issue. A period of several years spent in the fertile land of Germany, had left both men and horses in splendid condition, and the regiment, when I took over, consisted of a thousand officers and men, well disciplined, calm and quiet in the face of the enemy.

I did not yet have a horse, so I went to Stralsund in the isle of Rugen, where they have excellent horses, and I bought several; I got some others from Rostock and ended with a stable of seven good beasts, which was not too many, as war with Russia appeared imminent. I had already forecast this during the summer of 1811, when I saw the great number of old soldiers whom the Emperor was taking from the regiments in the peninsula to reinforce his Old Guard. I had been confirmed in this opinion during my stay in Paris. There were, at first, some distant rumours of a rupture, which vanished quickly amid the entertainments and festivities of winter, but these soon returned with increased insistence; and became almost certainties.

Chapter 3
The Background to War

The principal reason which led the Emperor to declare war on Russia was his desire to see the implementation of the treaty of Tilsit, whereby the Emperor Alexander agreed to close all the ports of his country to English traders, an undertaking which had never been properly carried out. Napoleon thought, rightly, that he could ruin the English, a manufacturing and trading nation, by preventing their commerce with the European continent; but the execution of this gigantic project offered so much difficulty, that it was only in France that the restrictions were enforced, and there the use of licences, to which I have referred above, made an enormous breach in the regulations. As for Italy, Germany and the Adriatic provinces, although the continental system was established by imperial decree, it was only implemented in theory, partly because of the extent of the coastline, and partly because of connivance and lack of surveillance by those responsible for the administration of these vast areas. So the Russian Emperor replied to the demands made by France by pointing to the state of affairs which was almost universal in Europe. The true cause, however, of the refusal of Alexander to accede to the demands of Napoleon, was that he feared that he would be assassinated in the same manner as his father, the Emperor Paul, who was accused firstly of having sullied the nation's reputation by allying himself to France and secondly of having destroyed Russian trade by declaring war on Britain. Alexander was aware that he had already given offence by the deference and friendliness which he had shown towards Napoleon at Tilsit and Erfurt, and he was anxious not to arouse more anger by cutting off all trade with England, the sole outlet whereby the Russian nobility could dispose of the products of their vast estates, and acquire a monetary income. The death of the Emperor Paul clearly showed the danger faced by Alexander, if he followed his father's example. An additional cause of fear was the fact that he was surrounded by the same officers who had surrounded his father, amongst whom was his chief-of-staff, Benningsen.

Napoleon did not take sufficiently into consideration these difficulties, when he threatened Alexander with war, unless he fell in with his wishes; although, when he learned of the losses and reverses suffered in Spain and Portugal, he seemed hesitant to engage in a conflict the outcome of which he deemed uncertain.

According to General Bertrand, Napoleon, on St. Helena said repeatedly that his only intention, to begin with, was to frighten Alexander into carrying out the terms of the treaty: "We were" he said, "like two opponents of equal ability, who are well able to fight, but being reluctant to do so, menace each other by threats and sabre-rattling, edging slowly forward, each hoping that his adversary will retreat rather than do battle"; but the Emperor's comparison was not exact, for one of these swordsmen had behind him a bottomless pit, ready to engulf him at the first backward step, so that having to choose between an ignominious death and a combat in which he might be successful he had to choose the latter. This was the situation in which Alexander found himself, a situation made worse by the influence exerted by the Englishman Wilson on General Benningsen and the officers of his staff. The Emperor Napoleon was still hesitant and seemed anxious to consult the sage opinions of Caulincourt, his former ambassador at St. Petersburg and those of a group of French officers who had lived for some time in Russia.

Among the latter was Lieutenant-colonel de Ponthon, who had been among a number of engineer officers who, after the Treaty of Tilsit had been posted, at the request of Alexander, to Russia, where they had spent several years. De Ponthon was a highly competent, but withal a very modest officer, he was attached to the topographic service, and did not think it was his place to offer his advice unasked, on the problems which would face an army at war in the Russian empire; but when he was questioned by the Emperor he felt it was his duty to tell the whole truth to the head of state, even at risk of displeasing him, so he described all the obstacles which would face this enterprise. The principal ones were the apathy and lack of co-operation between the Lithuanian states, subject for many years to Russia; the fanatical resistance to be expected from the people of Moscow; the scarcity of food and forage; the almost uninhabited areas which would have to be crossed; roads impassable for artillery after several hours of rain; but above all he stressed the rigour of the winter and the physical impossibility of conducting a war once the snow had begun to fall, which might be as early as the first days of October. Finally, at risk of giving offence and jeopardising his career, he begged Napoleon, for the sake of France and his own reputation, not to undertake this dangerous expedition, the calamitous outcome of which he now predicted. Having listened quietly to M. de Ponthon, the Emperor dismissed him without making any comment. For some days he appeared withdrawn and contemplative, and the rumour spread that the undertaking was off, but then M. Maret, Duc de Bassano, persuaded him to go back to his original intention, and assured him that Marshal Davout would be happy to move his large army of Germany to the banks of the Nieman, on the frontier of the Russian empire, in order to galvanise Alexander into action.

From this time on, although M. de Ponthon was in constant attendance as a member of the cabinet, the Emperor did not address a word to him during the advance from the Nieman to Moscow, and when, during the retreat, Napoleon was forced to admit to himself that the predictions of this admirable officer had been only too accurate, he avoided catching his eye. Nevertheless, he promoted him to the rank of colonel.

To return to the preparations which Napoleon was making to force the Russians, by hook or by crook, to comply with his wishes: from the month of April, the French troops stationed in Germany, as well as those of various princes of the Germanic confederation allied to France, were put into motion, and their march towards Poland was delayed only by the difficulty of finding forage for their numerous horses; the grass, and even the corn being scarcely out of the ground at this time in these northern countries. However, the Emperor left Paris on the 9th of May, and accompanied by the Empress, went to Dresden, where, awaiting him, were his father-in-law the Emperor of Austria, and almost all the German princes; attracted there, in some cases by the hope of having their domains extended, and in others by the fear of displeasing the arbiter of their destiny. The only absentee was the King of Prussia, who, not being included in the confederation of the Rhine, was not invited to this reunion and dared not turn up without the permission of Napoleon. He humbly requested this, and when it was obtained he hurried to Dresden to pay court to the all-powerful conqueror of Europe.

The protestations of fidelity and devotion which were lavished on Napoleon misled him into making a most serious error in the organisation of the contingents which were to make up the great army destined for the war against Russia. Instead of weakening the governments of Austria and Prussia, his former enemies, by demanding from them the greater part of their available troops, which, prudence would suggest should be placed in the van, not only to spare French lives, but to allow a watch to be kept on these new and undependable allies, Napoleon required no more than 30,000 men from each of these powers, and placed them on the two wings of his force. The Austrians under Prince Schwartzenberg on the right in Volhynie, and the Prussians, to whom he appointed as commander the French Marshal Macdonald, on the left, near the mouth of the Nieman. The centre was composed of French troops and those members of the German federation whose loyalty had been proved at Jena and Wagram.

There were discerning observers who were dismayed to see the wings of the army made up of foreigners, who, in the event of a reverse, could form two hostile armies in our rear, while the centre was embroiled in the heart of Russia. Not only that, Austria who had an army of 200,000, placed only 30,000 at the disposal of Napoleon, and had 170,000 left with which to attack us in the event of failure, while Prussia, though less powerful, still had 60,000 men in reserve.

One is astonished that the Emperor was so little concerned about what he was leaving behind him; but his confidence was so great that when the King of Prussia requested him to allow his eldest son to join in the campaign as an imperial aide-de-camp, Napoleon turned him down, although the young prince would have been a valuable hostage to ensure the fidelity of his father.

While there was a succession of entertainments at Dresden, Napoleon's troops were wending their way through northern Germany. Already the army of Italy, having crossed the mountains of the

Tyrol, was heading for Warsaw. The 1st, 2nd and 3rd Corps commanded by Davout, Oudinot and Ney, were passing through Prussia on their march to the Vistula. The states comprising the confederation of the Rhine had supplied their contingents, as had Austria and Prussia; it was noticeable, however that although the Austrian generals were happy to unite their flags with ours, the junior officers and the soldiers were reluctant to attack Russia, while the situation was reversed in the Prussian army, where the generals and Colonels felt humiliated by being compelled to serve under the command of their conqueror, while officers of lower rank and the soldiers, were pleased to have the opportunity of fighting alongside the French, and hoped to show that if they were defeated at Jena, it was not through any lack of courage on their part, but due to poor leadership by their superiors.

Napoleon had not only taken into the "Grande Armée" the troops of Austria and Prussia, but he had lowered the morale of the French forces by intermingling them with foreign contingents, so that the various Corps commanded by his marshals contained bodies of men from every part of Europe, Italians, Poles, Spaniards, Portuguese, Germans and Croatians. This admixture of races with different languages, cultures and interests, worked very poorly, and often hindered the efforts of the French troops. It was one of the principal causes of the reversals which we suffered.

Chapter 4
We Cross the Border into Russia

Having left Dresden on the 29th of May, the Emperor made his way towards Poland via Danzig and the old Prussia, through which his troops were passing, whom he reviewed whenever he encountered them.

The army was now organised so that the 23rd Chasseurs á Cheval were brigaded with the 24th. This brigade was commanded by General Castex and formed part of the 2nd Army Corps, commanded by Marshal Oudinet. I had known General Castex for a long time, an excellent officer, who treated me very well throughout the campaign. Marshal Oudinet had seen me at the siege of Genoa when I was with my father and also in Austria when I was aide-de-camp to Marshal Lannes, and was well disposed towards me.

On the 20th June, 2nd Corps was given the order to stop at Insterberg in order to be reviewed by the Emperor. These military ceremonies were awaited with impatience by those people who hoped to benefit from the awards distributed on the occasion by Napoleon. I was among this number. I felt sure that I would be promoted to the command of the regiment of which I was the acting commander, for apart from the promises given me by the Emperor, General Castex and Marshal Oudinothad had told me that they intended to propose me officially, and that Colonel Nougarède was to be posted, as general, to command of one of the huge remount depots, which would have to be set up in the rear of the army; but the bad luck which had, a few months earlier delayed my promotion to major, also held up my promotion to colonel.

At these reviews, the commanders of regiments were subjected to a rigourous cross-examination by the Emperor, particularly on the eve of a campaign; for apart from the usual questions about their strength in men and horses, their arms etc., he would suddenly ask a number which were unforeseen and not always easy to answer. For example: "How many men from such and such a department have you received in the last two years? How many of your carbines come from Tulle and how many from Charleville? How many of your horses are from Normandy, from Brittany, from Germany? What is the average age of your men, your officers, your horses? How many men in this company have long-service chevrons? etc...etc."

These questions, which were always posed in an abrupt and demanding manner, and accompanied by a piercing look, disconcerted many colonels; but woe to him who hesitated to reply, he went into Napoleon's bad books. I was so well briefed that I was able to reply to all his questions, and, after complementing me on the fine turnout of the regiment, it looked as if the Emperor was going to promote me to colonel and M. de La Nougarède to general, when the latter, who with his limbs wrapped in flannel, had been hoisted onto horseback to follow from afar the movements of his regiment, which I commanded, hearing himself called for, came to Napoleon, and unwisely angered him by making a request on behalf of an officer, a member of his family, who was wholly undeserving. This roused a storm of which I suffered the consequences. The Emperor flew into a rage and ordered the Gendarmerie to clear the officer in question out of the army, and leaving M. de La Nougarède in dismay, he went off at the gallop. So M. de La Nougarède was not made a general.

Marshal Oudinot followed the Emperor to find out what was to happen to the 23rd, and was told "Major Marbot will continue to command them." Before reaching the rank of colonel I was destined to suffer yet another serious wound.

In fairness to M. de La Nougarède, I have to say that he expressed the liveliest remorse at having been the involuntary cause of the delay in my advancement. I was sorry for the difficult position in which this worthy man found himself, for he felt that he had forfeited the Emperor's confidence, and owing to his disability he had little hope of restoring himself by his conduct in the battles which were about to take place.

I was comforted by the fact that the Emperor, on the day of the review, had awarded all the promotions and the decorations which I had requested for the officers and other ranks of the 23rd, and as the gratitude for these favours is always directed to the commanding officer who has obtained them, the influence which I was beginning to have in the regiment was greatly increased and went some way to calm my regrets at not having been awarded substantive rank for the position which I occupied.

At about this time, I received a letter from Marshal Masséna and another from his wife, the first recommending a M. Renique, and the second her son, Prosper. I was touched by this double approach and I responded by accepting the two captains into my regiment. However, Madame Masséna did not carry out her intention, and Prosper Masséna did not go to Russia. In any case he would not have been able to stand the harsh climate.

The army was soon to reach the frontier of the Russian empire, and see once more the river Nieman, where we had stopped in 1807. The Emperor positioned his troops on the left bank of this river as follows: on the extreme right was the Austrian Corps of Prince Schwartzenberg, on the border of Galicia near Drogitchin. On Schwartzenberg's left was King Jérôme with two considerable army corps, between Bialystok and Grodno. Next to them was Prince Eugène de Beauharnais, with 80,000 men, at Prenn. The Emperor was in the centre, facing Kovno, with 220,000 men commanded by Murat, Oudinot, Ney, Lefebvre and Bessières. The Guard formed part of this immense body of troops. Finally, at Tilsit, Marshal Macdonald with 35,000 Prussians formed the left wing. Across the Nieman was the Russian army of about 400,000 men, commanded by the Emperor Alexander, or rather by Benningsen, his chief-of-staff. This force was divided into three parts, commanded by Generals Bagration, Barclay de Tolly and Wittgenstein.

I have no intention of writing a history of the campaign of 1812, but I think I should relate the principal events, since they form an essential part of my life and times and several of them have a bearing on what happened to me.

At a time when the two powerful European empires were about to come to blows, England, a natural ally of Russia, had a duty to make every effort to help her to repel the invasion projected by Napoleon. By disbursing money to the Turkish ministers, the English cabinet was able to arrange a peace between the Sultan and Russia, which allowed the latter to recall the army which was on the frontier of Turkey, an army which played a highly important rôle in the war. The English had also contrived a peace between the Emperor Alexander and Sweden, an ally of France, on whose goodwill Napoleon counted, the more so because Bernadotte had just been nominated as the heir apparent, and governed the country for the King, his adoptive father.

I have already explained how, through a bizarre sequence of events, Bernadotte was raised to the rank of heir presumptive to the crown of Sweden. The new Swedish prince, after announcing that he would always remain French at heart, allowed himself to be seduced or intimidated by the English, who could have easily overthrown him. He sacrificed the true interests of his adoptive country by submitting to the domination of England and allying himself with Russia in an interview with the Emperor Alexander. This meeting took place in Abo, a little town in Finland. The Russians had recently seized this province and they promised to compensate Sweden by the gift of Norway, which they intended to take from Denmark, which was a faithful ally of France. So Bernadotte, far from relying on our army to restore to him his provinces, accepted these Russian encroachments by ranging himself with her allies.

If Bernadotte had been willing to support us, the geographical position of Sweden could have been of great assistance to our common cause. The new prince did not, however, openly state his position, as he wanted to see who was going to be the victor, and he did not declare himself until the following year. Deprived of the aid of Turkey and Sweden, on whom he had relied to keep the Russian army occupied, Napoleon's only possible allies in the north were the Poles, but these turbulent people, whose forefathers had been unable to agree when they were an independent state, offered neither moral nor physical support.

In fact, Lithuania and the other provinces which formed more than a third of the former Poland, having been in Russian hands for almost forty years, had mostly forgotten their ancient constitution and had for a long time thought of themselves as Russian. The nobility sent their sons to join the army of the Czar, to whom they were too much attached by long custom to permit any hope that they would join the French. The same considerations applied to other Poles who in various divisions of their country had found themselves under the rule of Austria or Prussia. They were willing to march against Russia, but it was under the flags and under the command of their new sovereigns. They had neither love nor enthusiasm for the Emperor Napoleon, and feared to see their country devastated by war. The grand duchy of Warsaw, ceded in 1807 to the King of Saxony under the Treaty of Tilsit, was the only province of the ancient Poland which retained a spark of national spirit and was somewhat attached to France, but what was the use of this little state to the Grande Armée of Napoleon?

Napoleon, however, full of confidence in his army and in his own ability, decided to cross the Nieman, and so on the 23rd of June, accompanied by General Haxo and dressed in the uniform of a Polish soldier of his guard, he rode along its bank, and that same evening at ten o'clock, set in motion the crossing of the river by the pontoon bridges, the most important of which had been laid across the river opposite the little Russian town of Kovno, which our troops occupied without encountering any resistance.

Chapter 5
I Lead the 23rd Against the Russians

At sunrise on the 24th we witnessed a most impressive spectacle. On the highest part of the left bank were the Emperor's tents. Around them, on the slopes of the hills and in the valleys, glittered the arms of a great concourse of men and horses. This mass, consisting of 250,000 soldiers split into three huge columns, streamed in perfect order towards the three bridges which had been thrown across the river, over which the different corps crossed to the right bank in a prearranged manner. On this same day the Nieman was crossed by our troops at other points, near Grodno, Pilony and Tilsit. I have seen a situation report, covered by notes written in Napoleon's hand, which gives the official strength of the force which crossed the Nieman as 325,000 men, of whom 155,400 were French and 170,000 allies, accompanied by 940 guns.

The regiment which I commanded formed part of 2nd Corps, commanded by Marshal Oudinot, which having crossed the bridge at Kovno headed immediately for Ianovo. The heat was overpowering. This, close to nightfall, led to a tremendous storm, and torrential rain, which drenched the roads and the countryside for more than fifty leagues around. Happily the army did not see this as a bad omen, as the soldiers considered violent thunder-storms were something to be expected in summer. The Russians too, every bit as superstitious as some of the French, had an unpropitious omen, for during the night of 23rd-24th of June the Emperor Alexander escaped with his life when, at a ball in Wilna, the floor of a room collapsed under the chair on which he was sitting, at the very hour when the first French boat, carrying a detachment of Napoleon's troops, reached the right bank of the Nieman and Russian soil. Be that as it may, the storm had made the air much cooler and the horses in bivouac suffered from this and also from eating wet grass and lying on muddy ground. So that the army lost several thousand from acute colic.

Beyond Kovnow there runs a little river called the Vilia, the bridge over which had been cut by the Russians. The storm had so swollen this tributary of the Nieman that Oudinot's scouts were held up. The Emperor arrived at the same moment as I did at the head of my regiment. He ordered the Polish lancers to see if the river was fordable, and in this process, one man was drowned; I took his name, it was Tzcinski. I mention this because the losses suffered by the Polish lancers in the crossing of the Vilia have been grossly exaggerated.

The Russians, however, retreated without waiting for the French army, which shortly occupied Wilna, the capital of Lithuania. It was near here that there took place a cavalry encounter in which Octave de Ségur, who had been with me on Masséna's staff, was captured by the Russians while leading a squadron of the 8th Hussars which he commanded, he was the elder brother of General the Comte de Ségur. On the same day that the Emperor entered Wilna, Marshal Oudinot's troops came up against Wittgenstein's Russians at Wilkomir, where the first serious engagement of the campaign took place. I had not previously served under Oudinot, and this début confirmed the high opinion I had of his courage, without convincing me of his intelligence.

One of the greatest faults of the French at war, is to go, without reason, from the most meticulous caution to limitless confidence. Now, since the Russians had allowed us to cross the Nieman, invade Lithuania and occupy Wilna without opposition, it had become the done thing, amongst certain officers to say that the enemy would always retreat and would never stand and fight. Oudinot's staff and the marshal himself frequently stated this, and treated as fairy tales the information given by the peasants that there was a large body of Russian troops positioned in front of the little town of Wilkomir. This incredulity nearly resulted in disaster, as you will see.

The light cavalry, being the eyes of the army, while on the march, is always in front and on the flanks. My regiment then was less than a league ahead of the infantry, when, having gone a little way beyond Wilkomir without seeing any sign of the enemy, we were confronted by a forest of huge pine trees, through which the mounted men could move with ease but whose branches obscured the distant view. Fearing an ambush, I sent a single squadron, commanded by a very capable captain, to investigate. In about 15 minutes he came back and reported that he had seen an enemy army. I went to the edge of the forest from where I could see, at about a cannon shot from Wilkomir, behind a stream, a hill on which drawn up in battle order were 25 to 30 thousand Russian infantry, with cavalry and artillery.

You may be surprised that these troops did not have in front of them any outposts, pickets or scouts, but that is how the Russians operate when they are determined to defend a strong position. They allow the enemy to approach without any warning of the resistance they are about to meet, and it is only when the main body of their opponents comes within range that they open a ferocious fire with musketry and cannon, which can shatter the columns of their adversaries. It is a method which has often produced good results for the Russians; so General Wittgenstein had prepared this welcome for us.

The situation seemed to me to be so serious that to keep my regiment out of sight, I ordered them to go back into the forest while I myself hurried to warn Marshal Oudinot of the danger which lay ahead.

I found him in some open country, where having dismounted and halted his troops, he was peacefully eating his lunch in the midst of his staff. I expected that my report would shake him out of this false security, but he treated it with an air of disbelief, and clapping me on the shoulder he called out "Let's go! Marbot here has discovered thirty thousand men for us to thump." General Lorencez, the marshal's son-in-law and his chief-of-staff was the only one to take me seriously; he had once been aide-de-camp to Augereau and he had known me for a long time. He came to my defence saying that when the commander of a unit says "I have seen" he should be believed, and that to take no notice of information brought by an officer of the light cavalry was to court disaster. These observations made by his chief-of-staff caused the marshal to think, and he had started to question me about the enemy presence, which he still seemed to doubt, when a staff-captain by the name of Duplessis arrived, all out of breath, and announced that he had searched the whole area and had even been into the forest, and had seen not a single Russian. At this the marshal and his staff began laughing at my fears, which greatly upset me. Nevertheless I kept my mouth shut, certain that before very long the truth would become apparent.

Luncheon being over, the march got under way once more and I returned to my regiment, which formed the advance-guard. I led them through the trees as I had done previously, for I could see what was going to happen the moment we emerged opposite the enemy positions. In spite of what I had told him, the marshal decided to go down a wide, dead straight road which ran through the forest; but he had scarcely reached the edge of the trees when the enemy, seeing the large group formed by his staff, opened a running fire from their cannons which, placed opposite the road, could fire directly along it, throwing into disorder the gilded squadron, recently so full of themselves. Fortunately no one was hit by this fire, but the marshal's horse was killed, as was that of M. Duplessis and a number of others. I had been amply avenged, and I must confess, to my shame, that I had difficulty in hiding my satisfaction at seeing those who had scoffed at my report and treated as fantasy what I had said about the enemy presence, taking to their heels under a hail of shot and scrambling over ditches as best they could to seek shelter behind the great pine trees! The worthy General Lorencez, whom I had warned to stay in the forest, laughed heartily at this scene. In fairness to Oudinot, I must say that once remounted, he came and apologised for for his behaviour at luncheon, and asked me to brief him on the Russian positions, and point out a route through the forest which the infantry might take without being too much exposed to the enemy's guns.

Several officers of the 23rd who, like me, had been through the woodland in the morning, were detailed to guide the infantry divisions. Nevertheless, on their emerging from the trees they were subjected to a terrible cannonade, which could have been avoided if, having been warned of the Russian presence, there had been an attempt to turn one of their flanks, instead of making a frontal approach. As it was, we were now committed, once we emerged from the wood, to attacking the most heavily defended point and taking the bull by the horns.

However, our gallant soldiers engaged the enemy with such determination that they drove them from all their positions, and after two hours of fighting they began to retreat. This operation was not without danger, for, to carry it out, they had to go through the town and cross the bridge over a very steep-sided stream. This manoeuvre, always difficult to execute under fire, started off in an orderly fashion, but our light artillery, having taken up a position on a height which overlooked the town, by means of its gunfire soon produced disorder among the enemy columns, which broke ranks and rushed to the bridge. Once they had crossed the stream, instead of regrouping they fled helter-skelter over the open ground of the opposite bank, where the retreat soon became a rout! Only one regiment, that of Toula, stood its ground on the town side of the bridge. Marshal Oudinot very much wanted to force a passage across the bridge to complete his victory by pursuing the fugitives on the other side of the stream; but our infantry had hardly reached the suburbs, from where it would take them at least 15 minutes to reach the bridge, and time was precious.

My regiment, which had made a successful charge at the entrance to the town, had re-formed on the promenade, a short distance from the stream. The marshal sent word to me to bring them at the gallop and we had hardly arrived before he ordered me to charge the enemy battalions which were covering the bridge, then to cross the bridge and pursue the fugitives on the open ground of the opposite side. Experienced soldiers know how difficult it is for cavalry to overcome infantry, who are determined to defend themselves in the streets of a town. I was well aware of the dangers of the task which I had been given, but it had to be done, and without hesitation. I knew also that it is by his conduct in his first action that a commanding officer gains a good or a bad reputation amongst his men. My regiment was composed of battle-hardened troopers: I raised them to the gallop and, with me at their head, we fell on the Russian Grenadiers, who stood firm behind their bayonets. They were, however, overwhelmed by our first impetuous charge, and once their ranks had been penetrated, my terrible chasseurs, using the points of their sabres inflicted a frightful slaughter. The enemy retreated to the causeway of the bridge, where we followed them so closely that, on reaching the other side, they were unable to re-form, and our men got amongst them, killing all whom they could reach. When the Russian colonel was killed, his regiment, without leadership, lost heart and, seeing that the French skirmishers had now reached the bridge, they surrendered. I lost seven men killed and some twenty wounded, but captured a flag and two thousand prisoners. After this action, we advanced onto the open ground where we took a great number of fugitives, several guns and many horses.

Marshal Oudinot had watched this action from a vantage point in the town, and he came to congratulate the regiment, for which he henceforth had a particular regard, which it well merited. I was proud to be in command of such men and when the marshal told me that he intended to recommend me for promotion to colonel, I was afraid that the Emperor would go back on his original plan, and post me to the first regiment which became vacant. How strange are the twists of fortune! The successful action at Wilkomir, where the 23rd earned such a fine reputation, nearly led on a later occasion to its destruction, because the courage which it had displayed at the time resulted in its being chosen to carry out a mission which was virtually impossible, which I shall describe shortly.

Although the concentration of French troops on their frontiers should have warned the Russians that hostilities were about to commence, they were nonetheless taken by surprise by the crossing of the Nieman, which they nowhere opposed. Their army began a retreat towards the Duna (Dvina) on the left bank of which they had prepared, at Drissa, an immense entrenched camp. From all parts the different French Corps followed the Russian columns. Prince Murat was in command of the cavalry of the advance-guard, and every evening he caught up with the Russian rear-guard; but after some skirmishing they made off during the night by forced marches, without it being possible to bring them to a decisive action.

Chapter 6
Campaigning with the 23rd

During the first days of our invasion of Russia, the enemy had made the very serious mistake of allowing Napoleon to split their forces, so that the greater part of their army, led by the Emperor Alexander and Marshal Barclay, had been driven back to the Duna, while the remainder, commanded by Bagration, was on the upper Nieman around Mir, eighty leagues from the main body. Cut off in this way, Bagration tried to join the Emperor Alexander by going through Minsk; but Napoleon had entrusted the protection of Minsk to Marshal Davout, who vigourously repelled the Russians and drove them back to Bobruisk, which he knew was supposed to be guarded by Jérôme Bonaparte, at the head of two corps, amounting to 60,000 men. Bagration was about to be forced to surrender when he was saved by the foolishness of Jérôme, who had not accepted the advice which Davout had given him, and failing to recognise the superior wisdom of the experienced and successful marshal, had decided to go his own way, whereupon he manoeuvred his troops so ineptly that Bagration was able to escape from this first danger. Davout, however, followed him with his usual tenacity, and caught up with him on the road to Mohilew, where, although he had no more than 12,000 men, he attacked the 36,000 Russians and defeated them; though admittedly the Russians were surprised on an area of very broken ground which prevented them from making the best use of their superior numbers. Bagration was compelled to cross the Borysthenia much lower down at Novoi-Bychow, and being now out of reach of Davout he was able to rejoin the main Russian army at Smolensk.

During the marches and countermarches which Bagration undertook in his efforts to evade Davout, he surprised the brigade of French cavalry comannded by General Bordesoulle, and captured from him the whole of the 3rd Regiment of Chasseurs, whose colonel was my friend Saint-Mars.

The elimination of Bagration's force would have been of tremendous benefit to Napoleon, so his fury with King Jérôme was unbounded. He ordered him to quit the army immediately and return to Westphalia, a rigourous but necessary measure, which had the effect of greatly damaging King Jérôme's reputation in the army. However, one has to ask if he was entirely to blame? His major mistake was to think that his dignity as a sovereign should not permit him to accept the advice of a simple marshal, but Napoleon knew perfectly well that the young prince had never in his life commanded so much as a single battalion, nor taken part in the most minor skirmish, and yet he confided to his care an army of 60,000 men, and this at a somewhat critical juncture. General Junot, who replaced Jérôme, was, before long, also guilty of a serious blunder.

It was around this time that the Russian emperor sent one of his ministers, Count Balachoff, to parley with Napoleon, who was still in Wilna. The purpose of this discussion has never been entirely clear; there were those who believed it was to arrange an armistice, but they were quickly disabused by the departure of the Count, and it appeared later that the English, who had a tremendous influence in the Russian court and the army, had taken umbrage at this mission, and fearing that Alexander might be considering coming to terms with Napoleon, they had loudly insisted that he should leave the army and return to St.Petersburg. Alexander accepted this proposal, but ensured that his brother, Constantine came with him. Left to themselves, and egged on by the Englishman Wilson, the Russian generals sought to wage war with a ferocity which might shake the French morale, so they ordered their troops to lay waste the country behind them as they withdrew, by burning all the houses and everything else which they could not carry away.

While Napoleon, from the central point of Wilna, was directing the various units of his army, the columns led by Murat, Ney, Montbrun, Nansouty and Oudinot had, on the 15th of July, reached the river Dvina. Oudinot, who had probably misunderstood the Emperor's orders, took the unusual step of going down the left bank of the river, while Wittgenstein and his men were going up the river on the other side. He arrived opposite Dvinaburg, an old walled town whose fortifications were in bad repair, where he hoped to capture the bridge and, having crossed to the other bank, to attack Wittgenstein from the rear. Wittgenstein, however, on leaving Dvinaburg, had left behind a strong garrison with numerous pieces of artillery. My regiment, as usual, constituted the advance-guard, which on this day was led by Marshal Oudinot himself.

The town of Dvinaburg is on the right bank of the river. We arrived on the left bank, where there is a considerable fortification which protects the bridge which links it to the town, from which it is separated by the river, which is very wide at this point. A quarter of a league from the fortifications, which Marshal Oudinot claimed were not equipped with cannon, I came on a Russian battalion, whose left flank was protected by the river and whose front was covered by the planks and hutments of an abandoned camp. In such a position the enemy was very difficult for cavalry to attack; however the Marshal ordered me to attack them. After I had left it to individual officers to make their way through the gaps between the huts, I ordered the charge, but the regiment had hardly gone a few paces, amid a shower of bullets from the Russian infantry, when the artillery, whose existence the Marshal had denied, thundered from the battlements, to which we were so close that the canisters of grape-shot were going over our heads before they had time to burst. A stray ball from one of them went through a fisherman's hut and broke the leg of the trumpeter who was sounding the charge by my side...I lost several men there. Marshal Oudinot, who had made a serious mistake in attacking a position which was protected by cannon, hoped to flush out the Russian infantry by sending in a Portuguese battalion which was ahead of our infantry; but these foreigners, former prisoners of war, who had been enlisted, somewhat unwillingly, into the French army, made little headway and we remained exposed. Seeing that Oudinot bore the enemy fire with courage but without giving any orders, I thought that if this state of affairs continued for a few minutes more, my regiment was going to wiped out, so I told my men to spread out and attack the enemy infantry in open order, with the double aim of driving them out of their position and preventing the gunners from firing for fear of hitting their own men who were intermingled with ours. Cut down by my troopers the defenders of the camp fled towards the bridgehead, but the garrison of this outpost was composed of recent recruits, who, fearing that we would follow the fugitives into the fortifications, hurriedly closed the gates; which compelled them to make for the pontoon bridge in an attempt to reach the other bank and the shelter of the town of Dvinaburg itself.

The bridge had no guard-rail. The pontoons wobbled. The river was deep and wide and I could see the armed garrison on the other side trying to close the gates. It seemed to me to be folly to advance any further. Thinking that the regiment had done enough, I had halted them when the Marshal arrived, shouting "Forward the twenty-third! Do as you did at Wilkomir! Cross the bridge! Force the gates! Seize the town!" General Lorencez tried in vain to persuade him that the difficulties were too great, and that a regiment of cavalry could not attack a fortress, however badly defended, if to get there they had to cross, two abreast, a third-rate pontoon bridge; but the Marshal persisted, "They will be able to take advantage of the disorder and fears of the enemy" he said, and repeated his order to me to attack the town. I obeyed; but I was scarcely on the first span of the bridge, at the head of the leading section of my men, when the garrison, having managed to close the gates which led to the river, mounted the ramparts, from where they opened fire on us. The slender line which we presented offered a poor target for these inadequately trained men, so that their musket and cannon fire caused us fewer casualties than I had feared, but on hearing the fortress firing on us, the defenders of the bridgehead recovered their nerve and joined in the fray. Oudinot, seeing the 23rd caught between two fires, at the start of an unstable bridge across which it was impossible to advance, conveyed to me the order to retreat. The large gap which I had left between each section allowed them to turn round without too much confusion, however, two men and their horses fell into the river and were drowned. In order to regain the left bank we had to pass once more under the ramparts of the bridgehead, when we were exposed to a rolling fire which, fortunately, was aimed by unskilled militia, for if we had been up against trained marksmen, the regiment could have been wholly destroyed.

This unsuccessful action, so imprudently undertaken, cost me thirty men killed and many wounded, and it was to be hoped that the Marshal would be content with this fruitless effort, especially in view of the fact that the Emperor had not ordered him to take Dvinaburg; but, as soon as the infantry had arrived, he made a new assault on the bridgehead, which had now been reinforced by a company of Grenadiers, who, at the sound of firing had hurried from nearby billets, so that our troops were once more repelled with much greater losses than those suffered by the 23rd. When the Emperor heard of this abortive attack he placed the blame squarely on Marshal Oudinot.

At this time, my regiment was brigaded with the 24th Chasseurs, and General Castex, who commanded this brigade, had instituted an admirable routine in our method of operation. Each of the two regiments took it in turn to form, for twenty-four hours, the advance-guard if we were approaching the enemy, or the rear-guard if we were retreating, and to provide all the sentries, pickets and so on, while the other regiment marched peacefully along, recovering from the fatigues of the day before and preparing for those of the morrow, which did not prevent it from going to the aid of the unit on duty, if they came in contact with the enemy. This system, which was not in the regulations, had the great advantage of never separating the men from their officers or their comrades, or placing them under the orders of unknown commanders and mingling them with troopers of another regiment. Moreover, during the night, half of the brigade slept, while the other half watched over them. However, since no system is without its shortcomings, it could so happen, by chance, that it was the same regiment which was more often on duty when a serious engagement occurred, as happened to the 23rd at Wilkomir and Dvinaburg. It was the sort of luck which we had throughout the campaign, but we never complained. We came out of all these events well and were often envied by the 24th, who had fewer occasions on which to distinguish themselves.

While Oudinot was making his assault on Dvinaburg, the corps commanded by Ney, as well as the immense body of cavalry commanded by Murat, were proceeding up the left bank of the Dvina towards Polotsk, while Wittgenstein's Russian army followed the same route on the right bank. Being separated from the enemy by the river, our troops grew careless, and pitched their bivouacs in the French manner, much too close to its bank. Wittgenstein had noticed this and he allowed the bulk of the French force to draw ahead. The last unit in the line of march was Sébastiani's division, which had as its rear-guard the brigade commanded by General Saint-Geniès, who had served as an officer in the army of Egypt, and who, although courageous, was not very bright. When he had reached a some way beyond the little town of Drouia, General Saint-Geniès, on the orders of Sébastiani, put his troops into bivouac some two hundred paces from the river, which was believed to be uncrossable without boats. Wittgenstein, however, knew of a ford, and during the night he made use of it to send across the river a division of cavalry, which fell on the French troops and captured almost the entire brigade, including General Saint-Geniès. This forced Sébastiani to hurry upstream with the rest of his division to make contact with the Corps commanded by Montbrun. After this swift raid, Wittgenstein recalled his troops and continued his march up the Dvina. The affair did Sébastiani's reputation a great deal of harm and drew down on his head the reproaches of the Emperor.

Shortly after this regrettable incident, Oudinot having been ordered to leave Dvinaburg and go up the river to rejoin Ney and Montbrun, his army corps took the same route as they had done and passed the town of Drouia. The Marshal intended to encamp his force some three leagues further on, but he feared that the enemy might use the ford to send across large parties of men to harass the great convoy which trailed behind him, so he decided that while he made off into the distance, with the main body of the troops, he would leave behind a regiment of General Castex's brigade in the position which had been occupied by General Saint-Geniès, to watch the ford. As my regiment was on duty, there fell to it the dangerous task of remaining behind at Drouia on their own until the following morning. I knew that the greater part of Wittgenstein's force had gone up the river, but I could see that he had left behind, not far from the ford, two strong regiments of cavalry, a force more than sufficient to overcome me.

However much I might have wished to carry out the order to set up my bivouac on the spot used two days previously by Saint-Geniès, this was impossible, for the ground was littered with more than two hundred bodies in a state of putrefaction, and to this major reason was linked another not less important. What I had seen and what I had learned about war had convinced me that the best means of defending a river against an enemy whose aim is not to establish himself on the bank which one occupies, is to keep the main body of one's troops well back from the river edge; firstly to have timely warning of the enemy's approach, and secondly, because, as it his intention to make a sudden raid and then retire smartly, he dare not go too far from the spot where he can cross back to the other side. So I settled the regiment half a league from the Dvina, on some slightly undulating ground. I left only some two-man sentinels on the bank, because, when it is purely a matter of observation, two men can see as much as a large picket. Several lines of troopers were placed one after the other between these sentinels and our bivouac, where, like a spider at the bottom of its web, I could be rapidly informed by these threads about what was going on in the area which it was my duty to guard. I had forbidden all fires and even the lighting of pipes, and had ordered complete silence.

The nights are extremely short in Russia in the month of July, but this one seemed very long to me, so afraid was I that I might be attacked during the hours of darkness by a force superior in strength to my own. Half of the men were in the saddle, the remainder were allowing their horses to graze but were ready to mount if given the signal. All seemed quiet on the opposite bank, when my Polish servant, who spoke Russian fluently, came to tell me that he had heard one old Jewish woman who lived in a nearby house say to another, "The lantern has been lit in the clock tower at Morki. The attack is going to begin." I had the two women brought to me, and questioned by Lorentz. They said that, as they were afraid of their village becoming a battleground for the two enemies, they had been alarmed to see the lamp lit in the bell tower of the church at Morki, which, the night before last had been the signal for the Russian troops to cross the ford and attack the French camp.

Although I was prepared for any eventuality, this was a piece of very useful information. At once the regiment was on horse, sabres in their hands. The sentinels by the river and the string of horsemen stretched across the plain passed from man to man, in low voices, the orders to come back. Two of the boldest sous-officiers,

Prud'homme and Graft, went with Lieutenant Bertin to see what the enemy was doing. He came back shortly to say that a large column of Russian cavalry was crossing the ford, and that already there were some squadrons on our side of the river; but seemingly taken aback at not finding us camped at the same place as Saint-Geniès they had halted, fearing, no doubt to go too far from their only means of retreat; then, having decided to go on, they were now approaching at a walk, and were not far off.

I immediately set fire to a huge haystack and to several barns which stood on some high ground, and by the light of the flames I could easily distinguish the enemy column, consisting of Grodno Hussars. I had with me about a thousand brave men, and with a cry of "Vive L'Emperor!" we charged at the gallop towards the Russians who, taken by surprise by this fierce and unexpected attack, turned tail and rushed in disorder to the ford. There they came face to face with a regiment of dragoons who, being part of their brigade had followed them and were just emerging from the river. This resulted in the most fearful confusion which enabled our men to kill many of the enemy and take many horses. The Russians tried to recross the ford in a mob to escape from the fire which my men aimed at them from the bank and a number of them were drowned. Our surprise attack had so startled the enemy who had thought to find us asleep, that they put up no resistance, and I was able to return to our bivouac without having to regret the death or wounding of any of our number. The break of day disclosed the field of battle covered by some hundreds of dead or wounded Russians. I left the wounded in the care of the inhabitants of the village near which we had spent the night, and took to the road to rejoin Marshal Oudinot, with whom I caught up that same evening. The Marshal gave me a hearty welcome and complemented the regiment on their conduct.

2nd Corps continued its march up the left bank of the Dvina and in three days arrived opposite Polotsk. There we learned that the Emperor had at last left Wilna, where he had spent twenty days, and was heading for Vitepsk, a town of some size, which he intended to make his new centre of operations.

On quitting Wilna, the Emperor had left the Duc de Bassano as governor of the province of Lithuania and General Hogendorp as military commander. Neither of these two officials was suited to organising the rear echelons of an army. The Duc de Bassano, a former diplomat and private secretary, knew nothing about administration, while the Dutchman Hogendorp, who spoke little French and had no idea of our military regulations and customs, was not likely to make much impression on those French who passed through Wilna or on the local nobility. So the resources available in Lithuania were of no help to our troops.

The town of Polotsk is situated on the right bank of the Dvina. Its houses are built of wood and it is dominated by a very large and splendid college, at that time occupied by the Jesuits, almost all of whom were French. It is surrounded by an earthwork fortification, having at one time undergone a siege during the war waged by Charles XII against Peter the Great. The corps commanded by Ney, Murat and Montbrun, in order to get from Drissa to Witepsk, had built a pontoon bridge across the Dvina, opposite Polotsk, which they left for Oudinot's corps, which was going to take the road for St.Petersburg. It was from here that 2nd Corps took a different direction to that of the Grande Armée, which we did not see again until the following winter, at the crossing of the Beresina.

It would require several volumes to describe the manoeuvres and the battles of that part of the army which followed the Emperor to Moscow. I shall therefore limit myself to describing the salient events as they occur.

On the 25th of July, there took place near to Ostrovno an advance-guard action, in which our infantry were successful, but where several regiments of cavalry were too hastily engaged by Murat. The 16th Chasseurs was amongst this number, and my brother, who commanded a squadron, was captured. He was taken far beyond Moscow to Sataroff, on the Volga, where he joined Colonel Saint-Mars and Octave de Ségur. They helped each other to bear the boredom of captivity, to which my brother was already accustomed, as he had spent several years in the prisons and hulks of Spain. The fortunes of war treated us both differently: Adolphe was captured three times but never wounded, while I was often wounded but never captured.

While the Emperor, now in control of Wilna, tried in vain to manoeuvre the Russian army into a decisive battle, Oudinot's corps, having crossed the Dvina at Polotsk, established itself in front of this town, facing the numerous troops of General Wittgenstein who formed the enemy right wing. Before I describe the events which took place on the banks of the Dvina, I should, perhaps, acquaint you with the composition of 2nd Corps.

Marshal Oudinot, who commanded the Corps, had under his orders no more than 44,000 men, divided into three divisions of infantry, commanded by Generals Legrand, Verdier and Merle. There were two brigades of light cavalry. The first, composed of the 23rd and the 24th regiments of Chasseurs, was commanded by General Castex, an excellent officer on all counts. The second was formed of the 7th and 20th Chasseurs and the 8th Polish Lancers, commanded by General Corbineau, a brave but dull-witted officer. These brigades were not combined into a single division, but were employed wherever the Marshal thought necessary.

The 24th Chasseurs, with which my regiment was brigaded, was a first class unit which would have done very well if there had been a bond of sympathy between the men and their commander. Unfortunately Colonel A... was very hard on his subordinates, who, for their part, disliked him. This state of affairs led General Castex to travel and camp with the 23rd, and to unite his field kitchen with mine, even though he had once served in the 24th. Colonel A..., big, skillful and always perfectly mounted, showed up well in engagements featuring the "arme blanche", but was thought not to be so keen on those in which fire-arms and artillery were involved. In spite of this, the Emperor recognised in him qualities which made him undoubtedly the best light cavalry officer in our European armies. No one had a better eye for country. Before he set out, he could predict where there would be obstacles not shown on the map, and where streams, roads and even paths would lead to, and deduce from enemy movements forecasts which were almost always correct. In all the aspects of war, great or small, he was remarkably adept. The Emperor had often used him for reconnaissance in the past and had recommended him to Marshal Oudinot, who frequently called him into consultation; with the result that many of the laborious and dangerous jobs fell to my regiment.

Chapter 7
We Charge and I am Wounded

Hardly had the various army corps which had preceded us into Polotsk left to join the Emperor at Witepsk, when Oudinot, collecting his troops into a single immense column on the road to St.Petersburg, marched to attack Wittgenstein's army, which we believed was in a position some ten leagues from us, between two little towns named Sebej and Newel. At the end of the day we made our bivouac on the banks of the Drissa. This tributary of the Dvina is no more than a rivulet at the coaching inn of Siwotschina, where it is crossed by the main road to St.Petersburg and where, as there is no bridge, the Russian government has instead cut back the steep banks between which the stream runs to make a gently sloping approach and has paved its bed to the same width as the road, thus creating a passable ford. To the right and left of the ford, however, troops and vehicles cannot cross, because of the steepness of the banks. I mention this because, three days later this spot was the scene of a brisk engagement.

The next day, the 30th, my regiment being on duty, I took my place at the head of the advance-guard and followed by the whole army corps I crossed the ford through the Drissa. The heat was most oppressive, and in the dust-covered corn fields at the side of the road one could see two large areas where the grain had been flattened and crushed, as if a roller had been dragged over it, indicating the passage of a large column of infantry. Suddenly, near the coaching inn of Kliastitsoui these signs disappeared from the main road, and could be seen to the left on a wide side-road which led to Jacoubovo. It was evident that the enemy had turned off the road to Sebej at this point and was preparing to attack our left flank. This seemed to me to be a serious matter, so I halted our troops and sent a message to warn my general. The Marshal however, who usually kept in view of the advance-guard, had seen that I had halted. He came along at the gallop and in spite of the opinions of Generals Castex and Lorencez, he ordered me to continue up the main road. I had scarcely gone a league when I saw coming towards me a calische drawn by two post-horses....I stopped it and I saw a Russian officer who, overcome by the heat, was lying full-length on its floor. This young man, the son of the nobleman who owned the coaching inn of Kliastitsoui which I had just passed, was one of Wittgenstein's aides-de-camp, and was returning from St.Petersburg with the reply to some despatches which the general had sent to the government. You may imagine his surprise when, startled out of his sleep, he found himself surrounded by our bearded chasseurs, and saw not far away the numerous columns of French soldiers. He could not understand why he had not encountered Wittgenstein's army, or at least some of his scouts, between Sebej and the spot where we were; but his astonishment confirmed the opinion held by General Castex and me that Wittgenstein, to lay a trap for Oudinot, had suddenly quitted the road to St.Petersburg to attack the left flank and the rear of the French force. In fact, it was not long before we heard the sound of artillery and musket-fire.

Marshal Oudinot, although taken by surprise by this unexpected attack, extricated himself quite well from the tight spot in which he had landed himself. Ordering his columns to left face, he presented a line to the attacker, who was repulsed so vigourously that he did not care to renew the attack that day, and retired to Jakoubovo. Wittgenstein's cavalry had, however, enjoyed a considerable success, for they had captured, in the French rear, some thousand men and some of our equipment, amongst other things all our mobile forges. This was a serious loss, which was felt badly by the cavalry of 2nd Corps throughout the whole of the campaign. After this engagement, Oudinot's troops having taken up their position, Castex was ordered to return to Kliastitsoui to guard the point at which the road branched, where we were joined by General Maison's infantry. The Russian officer held prisoner in the house belonging to his father did us the honours with good grace.

In expectation of a major battle on the following day, the commanders of both armies had made their dispositions, and, at daybreak, the Russians attacked the inn at Kliastitsoui, which constituted the French right wing. Although in these circumstances both our regiments would be in action, the regiment on duty would be in the first rank, and it was the turn of the 24th Chasseurs. To avoid any possibility of hesitation, General Castex placed himself at the head of the regiment, and falling rapidly on the Russians, he overran them and took 400 prisoners without suffering many casualties. He was in the forefront of the attack, and his horse was killed by a bayonet thrust. In the resultant fall his foot had been trodden on, and he was unable for several days to lead the brigade. His place was taken by Colonel A....

The Russian battalions which the 24th had just defeated were immediately replaced by others which, emerging from Jacoubovo, marched rapidly towards us. The Marshal ordered A...to attack them, and we were told to advance, which we did without delay. Having arrived at the front line, we arranged ourselves in battle order and approached the Russians, who awaited us resolutely. As soon as we were within range, I ordered the charge... It was carried out with the greatest vigour, for my troopers, as well as displaying their usual courage, were aware that their comrades of the 24th were watching their every move. The Russians made what I consider to be the fatal mistake of discharging all their weapons at once by firing a volley, which, badly aimed, killed only a few men and horses. Continuous fire would have been much more devastating. They then needed to reload, but we did not give them time; our excellent horses, galloping at full speed, hit them with such force that many of them were knocked to the ground. A good number got to their feet and attempted to defend themselves with their bayonets against the sabres of our Chasseurs, but after suffering a great many casualties they fell back, then broke ranks, and a good number were killed or captured as they fled towards a cavalry regiment which had come to their aid. This was the Grodno Hussars.

I have noticed that when a unit has defeated another, it always maintains its superiority. I saw here a further proof of this, for the Chasseurs of the 23rd hurled themselves on the Grodno Hussars, as if they were easy prey, having previously beaten them soundly in a night battle at Drouia, and the Hussars, having recognised their enemy, took to their heels. This regiment, during the rest of the campaign, invariably faced the 23rd, who always retained their ascendancy. While these events were taking place on our right wing, the infantry on the left and in the centre had attacked the Russians who, defeated everywhere, abandoned the field of battle and at nightfall went to take up a position about a league away. Our army settled itself in the area which it occupied, between Jakoubovo and the road junction at Kliastitsoui. There was much celebration that night in the brigade bivouacs, on account of our victory. My regiment had captured the flag of the Tamboff infantry, and the 24th had also taken that of the Russian unit which they had overcome; but their satisfaction was diminished by the knowledge that two of their squadron commanders had been wounded, both of whom however, made a rapid recovery and served throughout the rest of the campaign.

When a unit endeavours to outflank an enemy it risks being itself outflanked. This is what happened to Wittgenstein, for on the night of the 29th, having left the St. Petersburg road to attack the left and rear of the French army, he had compromised his line of communication, which Oudinot could have cut completely if he taken full advantage of the victory achieved on the 30th. The Russian situation was made worse by the fact that while facing a victorious army which barred its line of retreat it learned that Marshal Macdonald, having crossed the Dvina and taken the fort of Dvinaberg, was advancing on the Russian rear. To get out of this difficulty, Wittgenstein had, during the night after the battle, made a cross-country detour which took his army back on to the St.Petersburg road at a point beyond the inn at Kliastitsoui. Since, however, he was afraid that the French troops who were in that area might fall on his force during this flank move, he decided to prevent them from doing so by himself attacking them with superior strength, while the bulk of his army regained the route to St.Petersburg and reopened his communications with Sebej.

The next day, the 31st of July, my regiment came on duty at dawn, when it could be seen that part of the army which we had defeated the day before had avoided our right wing and was in full flight towards Sebej, while the remainder were about to attack us at Kliastitsoui. All of Marshal Oudinot's troops were immediately stood to, but while the generals were arranging them in battle order, a strong column of Russian Grenadiers attacked our allies, the Portuguese, and reduced them to complete disorder; they then turned on the large and solid coaching inn, an important point which they were about to take, when Marshal Oudinot, always in the forefront of any action, hurried to my regiment, which was already at the outposts, and ordered me to try to stop or at least slow down the enemy advance until the arrival of our infantry which was approaching rapidly. I took my regiment off at the gallop, and ordering the trumpeter to sound the charge, I struck the right of the enemy line obliquely, which greatly hindered the ability of their infantry and Grenadiers to fire on us, and they were about to be cut down, for they were already in disorder, when either spontaneously or under the orders of their officers, they made an about turn and ran for a large ditch which they had behind them. They all scrambled into it and from its cover they directed a continuous fire at us. Immediately I had six or seven men killed and some twenty wounded and I was hit by a stray ball in the left shoulder. My troopers had their blood up, but they could not attack men whom it was physically impossible to reach. At this moment Generak Maison arrived with his infantry and having ordered me to withdraw behind his columns, he attacked the ditch from both ends and all its defenders were either killed or made prisoner.

As for me, with a painful wound I was taken back to the inn and removed with difficulty from my horse. The good Dr. Parot, the regimental surgeon, came to dress my injury, but he had scarcely started this when he was forced to break off. There was a new Russian assault and a hail of ball fell about us, so that we had to remove ourselves out of range of the fire. The doctor found that my injury was serious and could have been fatal if the thick braiding of my epaulet, through which the ball had passed, had not deflected it and lessened its force. The blow had been sufficiently heavy to knock me back almost onto my horse's crupper, so that the officers and troopers who were following me thought I had been killed, and I would have fallen if my orderlies had not supported me. The dressing was very painful for the ball was embedded in the bone at the point where the upper arm joins the collar-bone. To get it out the wound had to be enlarged.

If I had been already a colonel, I would have joined the many wounded who were being sent back to Polotsk, and after crossing the Dvina I would have sought some Lithuanian town where I might be cared for; but I was only a squadron commander and at any time the Emperor could arrive at Witepsk and hold a revue, at which he would award nothing except to those who were present bearing arms. This custom which at first may seem cruel, was based nevertheless on the interest of the service, for it encouraged the wounded not to remain in hospital any longer than was necessary, and to rejoin their units as soon as they were fit enough to do so. In view of the above, my success in action against the enemy, my recent wound received in combat and my devotion to the regiment, all compelled me not to go away; so I stayed in spite of the severe pain which I was suffering, and having put my arm in a sling as well as I could, and had myself hoisted onto horseback, I rejoined my regiment.

Chapter 8
Action at the Guns

Since I had been wounded, things had changed considerably; our troops had defeated those of Wittgenstein and taken a great number of prisoners, but the Russians had reached the St. Petersburg road and were continuing their retreat to Sebej.

To get to this town from the inn at Kliastitsoui, one must cross the enormous marsh of Khodanui, in the middle of which the main road is raised on an embankment made of huge pine trees laid one next to another. On each side of this causeway is a ditch or rather a wide and deep canal, and there is no other route except by making an exceedingly long detour. The embankment is almost a league long, but of considerable width, so that, it being impossible to put flank guards in the marsh, the Russians marched in dense columns along this artificial road, beyond which our maps showed open country. Marshal Oudinot, aiming at further victory, had decided to follow them, and for this reason he had already despatched on the road to the marsh General Verdier's infantry, which was to be followed first by Castex's brigade of cavalry, then the whole army corps. My regiment had not yet joined the line when I returned to it.

When, in spite of my injury, I took up my place at their head, I received a general acclamation from both officers and men, which showed the affection and esteem in which these brave people held me; I was deeply touched by this, and even more so by the welcome I received from Major Fontaine. This officer, although both courageous and competent, was so unambitious that he had remained a captain for eighteen years, having refused promotion three times, which he had finally accepted only on a direct order from the Emperor.

So I once more took command of the 23rd, and began to cross the marsh behind General Verdier's division, at which the rear unit of the enemy column fired only a few long range shots while they were still on the causeway. When, however, our infantry reached the open country, they saw the Russian army deployed in battle formation, and were treated to a devastating barrage of artillery fire. Nevertheless, in spite of their losses the French battalions continued to advance. Soon they were all off the embankment and it was the turn of my regiment, at the head of the brigade, to reach the open ground. Colonel A... who was the temporary brigade commander was not there to give me orders, so I thought it right to remove my regiment from this dangerous spot and I led them off at the gallop as soon as the infantry gave me room; however I had seven or eight men killed and a greater number wounded. The 24th, who followed me, also suffered many casualties. The same happened to General Legrand's infantry division; but as soon as they were formed up on the plain, Marshal Oudinot attacked the enemy lines, and they directed their artillery fire at several different points so that the exit from the marsh would have become less perilous for the remainder of the army, if Wittgenstein had not at that moment attacked with all his force the units which we had in the open. His superiority in numbers compelled us to give ground and we were driven back towards the causeway of the Khodanui. Fortunately the track was very wide, which allowed us to proceed by platoons. As soon as we left the plain the cavalry became more of a hindrance than a help. The marshal put us in front of the retreat; we were followed by Verdier's division, whose general had been very seriously wounded, and General Legrand's division made the rear-guard. The last brigade of this division, commanded by General Albert, had to fight a very sharp action while its last battalions were getting onto the causeway, but once they were formed into columns General Albert put eight artillery pieces at the tail end which kept up a continuous fire during the retreat, so it was the turn of the enemy to suffer heavy casualties. By contrast, the Russian artillery rarely discharged a shot because the guns had to be turned round to fire at us and then turned back to continue the pursuit, a lengthy and difficult operation on the causeway, so that they did us little damage.

The day was ending when the French troops, having crossed the marsh, repassed Kliastitsoui and found themselves once more on the banks of the Drissa, at the ford of Sivotschina which they had crossed in the morning to follow the Russians who had been defeated at Kliastitsoui. The Russians had their revenge, for having caused us seven or eight hundred casualties on the plain beyond the marsh they now had a sword at our backs. To put an end to the fighting and allow the army some rest, Marshal Oudinot led it across the ford to set up camp at Bieloe.

Night was falling when the outposts which had been left to watch the Drissa, reported that the enemy were crossing the river. The Marshal went there at once, and could see that eight Russian battalions with a battery of fourteen guns were setting up their bivouac on our side of the river, while the remainder of the army stayed on the other side, preparing no doubt to cross over and attack us on the morrow. This advance party was commanded by General Koulnieff, an enterprising officer but one who, like most of the Russian officers of the period drank to excess. It would seem that on this evening he had drunk more than usual, for it is otherwise difficult to explain why he made the grave error of coming, with no more than eight battalions to set up camp a short distance from an army of forty thousand men, and that in a most unfavourable position; for he had, some two hundred paces behind him, the Drissa, which could not be crossed except by the ford; not because of the depth of the water but because it ran between very steep banks fifteen to twenty feet high. Koulnieff had therefore no other line of retreat but the ford. Could it be that he hoped that his eight battalions and fourteen canons would be able, if defeated, to withdraw smartly across this one passage, in the face of an attack which might be launched at any moment by the French army from nearby Bieloe? The answer must be no, but general Koulnieff was in no state to consider the matter when he put his camp on the left bank of the river. It is perhaps surprising that Wittgenstein should have entrusted the command of his advance guard to Koulnieff, of whose intemperate habits he must have been aware.

While the head of the Russian column approached rashly to within such a short distance of us, a great confusion reigned, not among the troops, but among their leaders. Marshal Oudinot, although the bravest of men, lacked consistency, and passed rapidly from a plan of attack to one of a withdrawal. The losses which he had suffered towards the end of the day on the other side of the great marsh had thrown him into a state of perplexity, and he could not think how he was to carry out the Emperor's orders, which were to push Wittgenstein back at least as far as Sebej and Newel. He was therefore delighted to receive, during the night, a despatch informing him of the imminent arrival of a Bavarian corps commanded by General Saint-Cyr, which the Emperor was placing under his orders; but instead of awaiting this powerful reinforcement in his present sound position, Oudinot, advised by the general of artillery Dulauloy, wished to make contact with the Bavarians by withdrawing his army as far as Polotsk. This inexplicable notion was warmly opposed by the group of generals summoned by the Marshal. General Legrand said that although our success of the morning had been counter-balanced by the losses of the evening, the army was still in good heart and ready to advance, and that to retreat to Polotsk would damage their morale and present them to the Bavarians as a defeated force coming to seek refuge amongst them; an idea which would arouse indignation in all French bosoms. This vigourous speech by Legrand was acclaimed by all the generals and the Marshal then gave up the project of a retreat.

There remained the question of what to do the next day. General Legrand, with the authority of his seniority, long service and experience in warfare, proposed that they should take advantage of the serious error made by Koulnieff by attacking the advance-guard so imprudently placed without support on the bank which we occupied, and drive them back into the Drissa which they had behind them. This advice having been accepted by the Marshal and all the group, the execution of it was confided to General Legrand.

Oudinot's army was encamped in a forest of huge, widely spaced pines, beyond which there was a very extensive clearing. The boundaries of the wood took the form of a bow, the two ends of which reached the Drissa, which formed as it were the bow-string. The Russians had set up their bivouac very close to the river, opposite the ford. Their frontage was protected by fourteen artillery pieces. General Legrand wanted to take the enemy by surprise, so he ordered General Albert to send a regiment of infantry to each of the ends of the wood from where they could attack the camp from the flank, as soon as they heard the approach of the cavalry who, emerging from the woods in the centre of the bow would go bald-headed for the Russian battalions and drive them into the ravine. The task given to the cavalry was plainly the most dangerous, for not only had they to make a frontal attack on an enemy armed with 6000 muskets but would also be exposed to the fire of fourteen artillery pieces before they could reach their objective. It was, however, hoped that by a surprise attack, the Russians might be caught asleep, and put up little resistance.

You have seen that my regiment having come on duty on the morning of the 31st July at Kliastitsoui, had continued to serve for the whole of that day, and should, according to the regulations, have been relieved by the 24th at 1 A.M. on the 1st August, and it was this regiment whose duty it was to carry out the attack, while mine remained in reserve. There being only enough space in the clearing between the woods and the stream for one regiment of cavalry. However, Colonel A... went to Oudinot and suggested to him that there was a danger that while we were preparing to attack the troops in front of us, General Wittgenstein might send a strong column to our right which could cross the Drissa at another ford which probably existed some three leagues upstream from where we were, and gaining our rear could capture our wounded and our equipment; and that it would be a good idea to send a regiment of cavalry to keep an eye on this ford. The Marshal fell in with this suggestion and Colonel A... whose regiment had just come on duty, quickly ordered his men into the saddle and led them off on this expedition which he had thought up, leaving to the 23rd the dangers of the battle which was about to take place.

My regiment received with calm the news of the perilous mission which had been thrust upon them and welcomed the appearance of the Marshal and General Legrand when they came to supervise the preparations for this important attack which we were about to carry out.

At this time all the French regiments, with the exception of the Cuirassiers, had a company of Grenadiers known as the élite company, whose customary position was on the right of the line, a position which they held in the 23rd. General Legrand observed to the Marshal that as the enemy had placed their artillery in front of their centre, it was there that most danger would lie, and in order to avoid any hesitation which might compromise the whole operation, it would be advisable to attack this point with the élite company, which was composed of the most seasoned soldiers mounted on the best horses. It was in vain that I assured the Marshal that the regiment was in all respects as solid in one part as in another, he ordered me to put the élite company in the centre, which I then did. I next gathered the officers together and explained to them in low tones what we were to do, and warned them that, the better to surprise the enemy, I would give no preparatory commands and would simply order the charge when we were within close range of the enemy guns. Once everything had been arranged, the regiment left its bivouac, in complete silence, at the first faint light of dawn, and made its way without difficulty through the wood, the great trees of which were widely spaced, and arrived at the level clearing in which was the Russian encampment. I alone in the regiment had no sabre in my hand, for having only one hand which I could use, I needed that to hold the reins of my horse. You will understand that this was a very unpleasant situation for a cavalry officer about to engage the enemy.

However, I had chosen to go with my regiment and so I placed myself in front of the élite company, having beside me their gallant captain, M. Courteau, one of the finest of officers and one whom I valued most highly.

All was quiet in the Russian camp, towards which we advanced slowly and in silence, and my hopes of achieving a total surprise were increased by the fact that General Koulnieff not having brought any cavalry across the ford, we saw no mounted outposts, and could distinguish by the feeble light of their fires only a few infantry sentries, posted so close to the camp that between their warning and our sudden arrival the Russians would have little chance to prepare themselves for defence. Suddenly, however, two prowling and suspicious Cossack peasants appeared on horseback, some thirty paces from our line, and after regarding it for a moment they fled towards the camp, where it was obvious that they intended to give warning of our presence. This mischance was very unfortunate, because had it not been for that we would certainly have reached the Russians without losing a man; however since we were now discovered and were in any case nearing the spot where

I had decided to increase the speed of our advance, I urged my horse into a gallop; the regiment did the same, and shortly I gave the order to sound the charge.

At this signal my gallant troopers and I launched ourselves at the enemy, upon whom we fell like a thunderbolt. The two Cossacks had, however, raised the alarm. The gunners, sleeping beside their guns, grabbed their slow matches, and fourteen canons belched grapeshot at the regiment. Thirty-seven men, of whom nineteen belonged to the élite company, were killed outright. The brave Captain Courteau was amongst them, as was Lieutenant Lallouette. The Russian gunners were attempting to reload their guns when they were cut down by our men. We had few wounded, almost all the injuries having been fatal. We had some forty. horses killed, mine was maimed by a heavy bullet but was able to carry me to the Russian camp where the soldiers, rudely awakened from their sleep, were rushing to take up their arms, but were being sabred by our troopers, whom I had ordered to get between them and the rows of muskets, so that few were able to reach one and fire at us. Then, alerted by the sound of gunfire, General Albert's two regiments of infantry ran from the wood to attack the two sides of the camp, bayoneting all who resisted. The Russians, in disorder, were unable to withstand this triple attack. Many of them, who having arrived at night had not been able to see the height of the river banks, tried to escape by this route and falling fifteen or twenty feet onto the rocks were injured and in many cases killed.

General Koulnieff, hardly awake, joined a group of two thousand men of whom about one third had muskets, and following mechanically this disorganised crowd he arrived at the ford, but I had given orders that this important spot should be occupied by five or six hundred horsemen, amongst whom were the élite company who, enraged at the loss of their captain, massacred most of the Russians. General Koulnieff, who had already been drinking, attacked Sergeant Legendre, who, thrusting his sabre into the Russian's neck, laid him dead at his feet. The victory achieved by General Albert's infantry and the 23rd was complete. The enemy had at least 2000 men killed or wounded and we took around 4000 prisoners. The remainder perished by falling on the sharp rocks of the river. Some of the most agile Russians managed to rejoin

Wittgenstein who, when he heard of the sanguinary defeat of his advance-guard, began a retreat toward Sebej.

Marshal Oudinot, encouraged by the resounding success which he had just gained, decided to pursue the Russians, and took his army, as on the previous day, back across the Drissa to the right bank; but in order to give General Albert's infantry brigade and the 23rd Chasseurs an opportunity to recover from the effects of the fighting, he left them to keep watch on the field of battle at Sivotschina. I took advantage of this period of rest to carry out a ceremony rarely seen in war. This was to pay my last respects to those of our brave comrades who had lost their lives. They were laid, arranged by rank, in a large pit, with Captain Courteau and his lieutenant at their head. Then the fourteen canons, so gallantly captured by the 23rd, were placed before this military tomb.

Having completed this act of piety, I wished to dress my wound of the previous day, which was causing me a great deal of pain, and to do this I went to sit apart under a huge pine tree. There I saw a young battalion commander, who with his back against the trunk and held up by two Grenadiers, was painfully closing a little package on which a name was traced in his blood. This officer, who belonged to Albert's brigade, had suffered, during the attack on the Russian camp, an appalling bayonet wound which had slit open his abdomen from which the intestines were protruding, pierced in several places. Although some dressing had been applied the blood still flowed and the wound was mortal. The doomed man, who was well aware of this, had wished, before he died, to take leave of a lady whom he loved but did not know to whom he might entrust this precious message, when chance brought me there. We knew each other only by sight, but nonetheless, urged by the approach of death, he asked me, in a voice now faint, to do him two favours, then motioning the Grenadiers to one side he gave me the package, and saying, with tears in his eyes, "It is a portrait," he made me promise to deliver it secretly, with my own hands, if I was fortunate enough to return one day to Paris. "In any case" he added "there is no hurry, for it would be better if this was received long after I am gone". I promised to carry out this sad task which I was unable to do until two years later in 1814. The second request which he made I was able to carry out within some two hours. He was distressed to think that his body would be devoured by the wolves which abounded in the country and asked to be put beside the captain and the troopers of the 23rd, whose burial he had seen. This I promised, and when he died, not long after our unhappy meeting, I carried out this last wish.

Chapter 9
Action Around Polotsk

Deeply moved by this unhappy event, I was meditating with much sadness, when I was awakened from my reveries by the distant sound of a sustained cannonade. The two armies were once more in action. Marshal Oudinot, after passing the inn at Kliastitsoui where I had been wounded the day before, had contacted the Russian rear-guard at the beginning of the marsh, the exit from which had been so disastrous for us on the previous day. He was determined to drive the enemy back, but they were not prepared to pass through this dangerous defile, and mounted a counter-offensive against the French troops who after suffering considerable losses retreated, followed by the Russians. One might have thought that Oudinot and Wittgenstein were playing a game of prisoner's base, advancing and retreating by turn. The news of this fresh retreat by Oudinot was given to us on the battlefield of Sivotschina by an aide-de-camp, who brought to General Albert the order to take his brigade together with the 23rd Chasseurs, two leagues to the rear, in the direction of Polotsk.

When it came to leaving, I was unwilling to part with the fourteen artillery pieces captured that morning by my regiment, and as the horses which pulled them had also fallen into our hands, they were harnessed up and we took the guns to our next bivouac, and on the night following to Polotsk, where it was not long before they played an effective part in the defence of that town.

Oudinot withdrew that same day to the ford at Sivotschina, which he had crossed in the morning in pursuit of Wittgenstein who bearing in mind the disaster which had overwhelmed his advance-guard at this place on the occasion, did not risk sending any isolated unit across to the bank which we occupied. So the two armies, separated by the Drissa, settled themselves for the night.

On the following day, the 2nd August, Oudinot having joined his units at Polotsk, hostilities ceased for a few days, as both sides were in need of a rest. We were rejoined by the good General Castex and also by the 24th Chasseurs, who were very angry with their Colonel for leading them away when it was their turn to attack the Russian camp. On their trip up the Drissa they had seen no sign of the enemy nor had they found any trace of the supposed ford.

After several days rest Wittgenstein led part of his troops towards the lower Dvina, from where Macdonald was threatening his right. When Marshal Oudinot followed the Russian army in that direction it turned to face him, and for a week or ten days there was a series of marches and countermarches, and several minor engagements which it would be too long and wearisome to describe, and which resulted only in the useless killing of men and the demonstration of the indecision of both commanders.

The most serious engagement during this short period took place on the 13th August near the magnificent monastery of Valensoui, built on the bank of the Svolna. This little river which has very muddy banks separated the French and the Russians, and it was obvious that whichever general attempted to force a crossing on such unfavourable terrain would come to grief. Neither Oudinot nor Wittgenstein had any intention of crossing the Svolna at this point; but instead of going to look for some other place where they could meet in combat, they took up positions on either side of this watercourse, as it were in mutual despite. Soon there was from both banks a lively cannonade which was totally useless as the troops on neither side could attack their adversaries and was no credit to either party.

However Wittgenstein, to protect the lives of his men, had restricted himself to posting some battalions of unmounted Chasseurs among the willows and reeds which bordered the stream, and had kept the bulk of his force out of the range of the French guns, whose brisk fire hit only some of his sharpshooters, while Oudinot, who had insisted, in spite of the sensible advice of several generals, on bringing his first line up to the Svolna suffered losses which he could have and should have avoided. The Russian artillery is nowhere as good as ours, but they used pieces called licornes, which had a range exceeding that of the French guns of the period, and it was these licornes which did the most damage among our troops.

Marshal Oudinot, in his belief that the enemy were going to

cross the river, not only kept a division of infantry in position to repel them, but supported them with General Castex's cavalry, an unnecessary precaution, since a crossing of even a small river takes more time than is needed for the defenders to hurry into a position to oppose it. Nonetheless my regiment was exposed for twenty-four hours to the Russian fire, which killed or wounded several of my men.

During this confrontation in which the troops remained stationary for a long period, there arrived the aide-de-camp whom Oudinet had sent to Witepsk to report to the Emperor the result of the battles at Kliastitsoui and at Sivotschina. Napoleon who wanted to make it clear to the troops that he did not blame them for the lack of success in our operations, loaded 2nd Corps with rewards in the way of decorations and promotions, and then, turning to the cavalry, he awarded four Crosses of the Legion of Honour to each of the cavalry regiments. In the despatch announcing this news, Major-general the Prince Berthier added that in order to show his satisfaction with the conduct of the 23rd Chasseurs at Wilkomir, the bridge of Dvinaburg, the night battle at Drouia, Kliastitsoui and above all in the attack on the Russian camp at Sivotschina, the Emperor was awarding them, in addition to the four decorations given to the other regiments, fourteen decorations, one for each of the guns captured by them from Koulnieff's advance-guard, so that I had now eighteen crosses to distribute among my brave soldiers. The aide-de-camp had not brought the awards themselves, but the Major-general had added to his letter the request that the regimental commanders should draw up a list of recipients and forward it to him.

I assembled all the captains, and after taking their advice, I drew up my list, and presented it to Marshal Oudinot, asking at the same time if I might be allowed to announce the awards immediately to my regiment: "What, here, under fire?" "Yes, marshal, under fire. That enhances their value."

General Lorencez, who as chief of staff had written the report of the various actions, in which he had highly praised the 23rd, agreed with my suggestion and so the Marshal consented. The decorations would not arrive until later, but I had my servant look in my baggage for a piece of ribbon which I had in my portmanteau, and when it was found, and after it had been cut into eighteen pieces, I announced to the regiment the awards which the Emperor had presented, and calling out of the ranks each of the recipients in turn, I gave them a piece of the red ribbon, then so keenly wished for and so proudly worn, and which has since then been so diminished in value, almost prostituted, by handing it out indiscriminately to all and sundry.

This ceremony, conducted in the field and under fire, had a great effect, and the enthusiasm of the regiment was at its height when I announced the name of Sergeant Prud'homme, reputed justly to be the most intrepid and unassuming of the warriors of the 23rd. This brave survivor of many a fierce encounter, accepted with modesty his piece of ribbon, to the sound of loud acclamation from all the squadrons. A moment of well earned triumph. I shall never forget this moving scene which took place, as you know, within range of the enemy guns.

Sadly, there is no rose without its thorn. Two of the men who were included in my list had just been severely wounded. Sergeant Legendre, who had killed General Koulnieff, had an arm carried away, and Corporal Griffon had a leg smashed. The injured limbs were being amputated when I went to the dressing station to give them their decorations. At the sight of the ribbons they forgot for a moment their pain, but unhappily, Sergeant Legendre did not long survive his injury, though Griffon recovered and was sent back to France, where I saw him some years later in Les Invalides.

The 24th Chasseurs, who received only four decorations as opposed to the eighteen awarded to the 23rd, conceded that this was fair, but nevertheless they regretted that they had been deprived of the honour of taking the fourteen Russian guns at Sivotschina, even at the cost of suffering such casualties as ours, "We are soldiers" they said, "and must take our chances for better or worse." They blamed their colonel for providing them with what they called this let-out. Here was an army whose men actually clamoured for action.

You will doubtless wonder what I got out of all this, and the answer is nothing. The Emperor, before he removed Colonel de La Nougarède from the command of the regiment and either made him a general or head of a legion of gendarmes, wanted to know if his health would permit him to carry out the duties of either of these two ranks. As a consequence Marshal Oudinot was ordered to bring Colonel de La Nougarède before a medical board, whose conclusion was that he would never be able to mount a horse. In view of this, the Marshal authorised the Colonel's return to France, where he was given the command of a minor fortress. The unfortunate Colonel, before leaving Polotsk, where his infirmities had forced him to remain, wrote me a very touching letter in which he took his leave of the 23rd, and although he had never led the regiment into action, an event which increases the men's regard for their commander, his departure was justifiably regretted.

The regiment now being without a colonel, the Marshal expected to receive at any moment the order for my promotion to that rank, and quite frankly so did I. The Emperor had however moved away, and had left Witepsk to take Smolensk and from there to march on Moscow, and the work of his cabinet had been slowed by their preoccupation with military operations to such an extent that I was not gazetted Colonel until three months later.

Let us now return to the banks of the Svolna, which the French left hurriedly, after depositing some of their wounded in the monastery of Valensoui. Amongst those whom we lost was M. Casabianca, Colonel of the 11th light infantry regiment, who had served with me as aide-de-camp to Masséna. He was a very fine officer whose promotion had been rapid; but his career was ended by a head injury received when he was visiting some of his men on the bank of the Svolna. He was dying when I saw him on a stretcher carried by some sappers. He recognised me and shaking my hand he observed that he was sorry to see our army corps so poorly managed. The poor fellow died that evening.

His last words were only too well founded, for our leader seemed to proceed without method or plan. After a success, he pursued Wittgenstein regardless of any obstacles and spoke of nothing less than driving him back as far as St.Petersburg, but at the least check he retreated swiftly and started seeing enemies everywhere. It was in this last state that he took his troops back to Polotsk, although they were displeased at being made to fall back before the Russians whom they had recently defeated in almost every encounter.

On the 15th of August, the Emperor's birthday, 2nd Corps arrived dejectedly at Polotsk, where we met with 6th Corps, formed of the two fine Bavarian divisions of General Wrède, which had a French general, Gouvion Saint-Cyr in overall command. The Emperor had sent this reinforcement of 8 to 10,000 men to Marshal Oudinot, who would have received it with more pleasure if he had not been afraid of the man in command.

Saint-Cyr was one of the most competent soldiers in Europe. A contemporary and rival of Moreau, Hoche, Kleber and Desaix, he had successfully commanded one wing of the French army of the Rhine at a time when Oudinot was scarcely a colonel or a brigade commander. I do not know anyone who could command troops in the field better than Saint-Cyr.

One could not imagine anyone more self-controlled. The greatest dangers, setbacks, successes, or defeats, failed to rouse him to any show of emotion. He maintained an icy calm in all situations. It is obvious how useful such a temperament coupled with a taste for study and meditation, might be to a general officer, but Saint-Cyr had also some serious faults. Jealous of his comrades, he had been known to hold his troops back while, close to him, other divisions were decimated in a desperate struggle. He would then advance and profiting from the exhaustion of the enemy he would overcome them, and thus appear to have won the victory single-handed. Secondly, if Saint-Cyr was one of the best officers in the employment of troops in the field, he was without doubt the one who took the least interest in their welfare. He never inquired if the men had food, clothing or footwear, or if their arms were in proper repair. His fellow officers dreaded working with him and the various governments which had taken power in France had employed him only out of necessity. The Emperor did the same, but he so much disliked Saint-Cyr that when he created the rank of marshal he left his name off the list of promotions, even though he had seen more service and shown more skill than most of those to whom Napoleon awarded the baton. Such was the man whom the Emperor had just placed under Oudinet's orders, to the great regret of the latter, who feared that he would be shown up by comparison with Saint-Cyr's superior talents.

On the 16th of August, the day on which my eldest son Alfred was born, the Russian army of some sixty thousand men attacked

Oudinot, who, including the Bavarian unit led by Saint-Cyr, had fifty two thousand men under his command. In any other circumstances an engagement between one hundred and twelve thousand men would have been called a battle; but in 1812 the when the total number of combatants amounted to some six or seven hundred thousand, a fight involving one hundred thousand men was no more than an action, and it is this description which is given to the struggle at Polotsk between the Russian troops and those of Marshal Oudinot.

The town of Polotsk, built on the right bank of the Dvina, is surrounded by old earthen ramparts. Before the main frontage of the town the fields are divided by a large number of little ditches between which vegetables are grown. Although these obstacles are not impassable for artillery and cavalry, they hinder their movement. These gardens extend for less than half a league in front of the town, but on their left, on the bank of the Divna there is a large area of level ground. It is here that the Russian general should have attacked Polotsk, for it would have given him command of the frail and only pontoon bridge, which was our communication with the left bank from which we drew our ammunition and food supply. But Wittgenstein chose to make a frontal attack and directed his main force towards the gardens from where he hoped to scale the ramparts which, to tell the truth, were no more than easily climbed embankments, whose height, however, allowed them to dominate the ground in front of them. The attack was pressed home vigourously, but our infantry put up a stout defence among the gardens, while from the height of the ramparts the guns, among which were the fourteen captured by the 23rd at Sivotschina, ravaged the enemy ranks. The Russians fell back in disorder to reform themselves on the plain. Oudinot, instead of staying sensibly where he was, went after them and was in turn driven off with casualties. The greater part of the day was spent in this way, the Russians returning repeatedly to the attack, only to be driven back beyond the gardens by the French.

During these blood-stained comings and goings, what was General Saint-Cyr doing? He was following Oudinot about in silence, and when asked for his opinion he merely bowed and said "Monseigneur le Marachal" as if meaning since you have been made marshal, you must know more than me, a simple general. So you can sort this out for yourself.

Wittgenstein, having lost a great many men and despairing of gaining victory by continued attacks in the area of the gardens, ended up where he should have begun, by marching his troops towards the meadows which bordered the Dvina. Up until this time Oudinot had kept his twelve pounders and all his cavalry at this spot, as if they had nothing to do with the fighting; but the artillery general, Dulauloy, anxious about his guns, suggested to the Marshal that he should send not only the large calibre guns but also all the cavalry over to the left bank, on the pretext that they got in the way of the infantry. When Oudinot asked Saint-Cyr what he thought, instead of offering the sound advice that the artillery and the cavalry should stay where they were, on ground which allowed them to manoeuvre with ease and support the infantry, he only repeated his endless "Monseigneur le Marachal". In the end, Oudinot, in spite of the opinion of General Lorencez, his chief-of-staff, ordered the artillery and the cavalry to withdraw to the other side of the river. This ill-advised movement which looked like the prelude to a retreat and the total abandonment of Polotsk and the right bank, greatly displeased the troops who were involved, and lowered the morale of the infantry whose job it was to defend that part of the town which faced the open ground. The spirits of the Russians were, on the contrary, raised when they saw ten regiments of cavalry and several batteries of guns leaving the field of battle. In an effort to create confusion in this huge mass as it departed they brought forward and fired their licornes, the hollow ammunition of which acts first as a cannon-ball and then explodes like a mortar bomb. The regiments next to mine had several men killed or wounded. I was lucky enough to have none of my men hit though I lost some horses. My own horse was hit in the head and as it fell I went down with it and my injured shoulder struck hard on the ground, which was very painful. If the Russian gun had been elevated a bit more, it would have been I who was hit, fair and square, and my son would have been an orphan a few hours after first seeing the light of day.

The enemy now resumed their attack, and when, after crossing the bridge, we looked back to see what was happening on the bank which we had just left, we saw a disturbing spectacle. The French, Bavarian and Croatian infantry were fighting bravely and holding their own, but the Portuguese legion and the two Swiss regiments fled before the Russians, and did not stop until, having been driven into the river, they were in the water up to their knees. Then, forced to face the enemy or drown, they at last struck back, and by a constant barrage of fire they compelled the Russians to draw back a little. The commander of the French artillery, who had just crossed the Dvina with the cavalry, skillfully made use of the opportunity to be useful by bringing his guns to the river bank and directing a heavy fire across the stream at the enemy battalions drawn up on the opposite bank.

This powerful intervention having stopped Wittgenstein's men at this point, while the French, Bavarians and Croats drove them back elsewhere, the fighting eased up and an hour before the end of the day had degenerated into random firing. The Marshal, however could not escape the fact that he would have to continue fighting the next day; and so, preoccupied by a situation the outcome of which he could not predict, and ruffled by the obstinate silence of Saint-Cyr, he was walking his horse slowly, followed by only one aide-de-camp, among musketeers of his infantry, when enemy marksmen, seeing a rider with a plumed hat, took aim and put a ball through his arm.

The Marshal at once informed Saint-Cyr of the injury and handing to him the command of the army left him to sort matters out. He himself left the field, crossed the bridge, stopped for a few moments at the cavalry bivouac and quitting the army went to Lithuania in our rear, to have his wound cared for. We did not see him again for two months.

Chapter 10
A Great Cavalry Battle

Saint-Cyr took up with a firm and skillful hand the reins of command, and in a few hours completely changed the look of things. Such is the influence of a man who is competent and who inspires confidence. Marshal Oudinot had left the army in a perilous state: part of his force driven back to the edge of the river, and the rest scattered amongst the gardens where they were firing at random: an inadequate lay-out of guns on the ramparts: the streets of the town cluttered with wagons, baggage, sutlers and wounded, all in complete confusion, while the troops had no means of retreat, should they be overcome, other than the pontoon bridge across the Dvina, a bridge which was very narrow and in such a bad state that the water was six inches over the planking of its platform. Finally, night was approaching and it was feared that the shooting would lead to a general action which might be disastrous in view of the disorder which ruled amongst the regiments of different nationalities.

General Saint-Cyr's first act was to order the withdrawal of those infantrymen who were in action, in the certainty that the tired enemy would do the same, as soon as they were no longer under attack.

The result was that soon the firing ceased on both sides. The troops were able to re-form and to have some rest, and further fighting was postponed until the next day. In order to put himself in a more favourable position, Saint-Cyr used the night to make preparations for the repulse of the enemy and to ensure a line of retreat, should it be necessary. With this aim, he gathered together all the corps commanders and after making clear to them the dangers of the situation, one of the more serious of which was the obstruction of the streets of the town and the approaches to the bridge, he ordered that the colonels, accompanied by several officers and with patrols, should go through the streets, sending those men of their regiments who were fit to their bivouac area, and all the wounded, sick, led horses, sutlers and carts to the other side of the bridge. General Saint-Cyr added that he would visit the town at daybreak and would suspend from duty any corps commander who had not carried out his instructions promptly. No excuse would be accepted. There was a rush to obey. The sick and wounded were carried to the left bank as well as everything which was not actually required for combat. That is to say all the impedimenta of the army. In this way the streets and the bridge were soon completely clear. The bridge was strengthened and the cavalry and guns brought back to the right bank and located in a suburb furthest from the enemy; and then, to improve his means of retreat, the prudent general had a second bridge made out of empty barrels and planks, which was for the sole use of the infantry. All these preparations having been completed before daylight, the army awaited its enemies with confidence. The latter, however, did not stir from their encampment on the open ground at the edge of the vast forest which surrounds Polotsk on the side opposite to the river.

General Saint-Cyr, who had expected to be attacked in the early morning, attributed the tranquillity which reigned in the Russian camp to the tremendous losses they had suffered the previous day. This may have been part of the reason, but the main cause of Wittgenstein's inactivity was that he expected the arrival, during the coming night, of a strong division of infantry and several squadrons of cavalry from St. Petersburg, and he had delayed his attack until he had received this powerful reinforcement so that he might the more easily defeat us on the day following.

Although the Polish nobles, the great landowners of the property round Polotsk, did not dare to support us openly, they did so in secret, and had no difficulty in providing us with spies. General Saint-Cyr, uneasy at what was going on in the Russian camp, arranged with one of these noblemen to have him send there one of his more enlightened vassals. The landowner sent to the Russian camp several cartloads of forage, and put amongst his carters his bailiff, dressed as a peasant. This man, who was highly intelligent, learned by chatting to Wittgenstein's soldiers that they were expecting a large body of troops. He even witnessed the arrival of some Cossacks and some cavalry, and was told that several battalions would arrive at the camp around midnight. Having gathered this information, the bailiff passed it to his master, who hurried to warn the commander of the French forces.

When he heard this news, Saint-Cyr determined to strike at Wittgenstein before the arrival of the expected reinforcements. But as he did not want to be involved in a long drawn-out affair, he warned his generals and corps commanders that he would not attack until six in the evening, so that, as night would put an end to the fighting, the Russians would be unable to exploit their success if things went their way. It is true that if we were victorious we would be unable to pursue the enemy in the dark, but Saint-Cyr had no intention of doing this, and for the moment wanted only to teach the Russians a lesson which would drive them away from Polotsk. As the French general aimed at taking the Russians by surprise, he ordered absolute calm to be maintained in the town and above all in the lines of outposts.

The day seemed very long. Everyone, even the General, in spite of his sang-froid, constantly looked at his watch. Having observed that, on the previous day, the absence of the French cavalry had allowed the Russians to drive our left wing almost into the Dvina, General Saint-Cyr, shortly before the attack, moved all his squadrons silently into a position behind some big buildings, on the other side of which lay the meadowland. It was on this level ground that the cavalry could manoeuvre to fall on the enemy right and give cover to the left wing of our infantry, of which the first two divisions were to attack the Russian camp while the third supported the cavalry and the remaining two formed the reserve and protected the town. All was ready when at last it was six o'clock, and the signal for the attack was given by the firing of a cannon, followed by a volley from all the French artillery which landed numerous projectiles on the enemy outposts and on the camp itself. At once our two first infantry divisions, led by the 23rd Light, fell on the Russian regiments positioned in the gardens, killing or capturing all whom they encountered and chasing the rest back to the camp, where they took many prisoners and captured several guns. This surprise attack, although carried out in broad daylight, was so successful that Wittgenstein was dining peacefully in a little country house near his camp when he was warned that French skirmishers were in the court-yard. He jumped out of a window and mounting a Cossack horse which happened to be there he galloped away to join his troops. Our skirmishers took some fine horses, documents, baggage wagons and wines belonging to the General also the silverware and some of the dinner laid on the table. An immense quantity of booty was seized in the camp by other units.

At the sound of this wholly unforeseen attack by the French, panic spread amongst our enemies, the majority of whom took to their heels without even picking up their weapons. The disorder was complete. No one was giving orders, even though the approach of our infantry was heralded by a fusillade of shots and the sound of the drums beating the charge. The scene seemed set for a resounding victory by the French troops, at whose head marched Saint-Cyr with his customary calm. However, in war an unexpected and often unimportant event can change a situation.

A large number of the enemy soldiers had reached in their flight the rear area of the camp, where was encamped the squadron of horse-guards which had arrived a few hours previously. This élite unit was made up of young men selected from the best of the nobility, and was led by a Major of proven courage, whose élan, it was said, was increased by generous draughts of liquor. When he saw what was happening, this officer leapt on his horse and followed by some hundred and twenty cuirassed riders, he rushed towards the French, whom he soon encountered. The first of our battalions which he attacked belonged to the 26th Light. They put up a vigourous resistance. The cavalry were repelled with casualties, and were rallying to prepare for a second charge when their Major, impatient at the time taken for the scattered horsemen to regain their ranks, abandoned the unsuccessful attack on the French battalion, and ordering his men to follow he led them at the gallop in open order through the camp, which was full of infantry, Portuguese, Swiss and even Bavarians, our allies, some of whom, dispersed by the victory itself, were trying to regroup while others were collecting the booty left by the Russians.

The cavalrymen killed or wounded many of these soldiers and threw the crowd into disarray. A disorderly withdrawal began which degenerated into a mass panic. Now, in a situation like this, soldiers can mistake for the enemy their own troops who are running to join them, so that, in a cloud of dust, it seems that they are being attacked by a large force, when in most cases it is only a handful of men. This is what happened here. The horse-guards, scattered widely over the plain and pressing on without a backward look, seemed to the fugitives to be a massive force of cavalry, and so the confusion grew until it enveloped the Swiss battalion in the middle of which General Saint-Cyr had taken refuge. He was so much jostled by the mob that his horse fell into a ditch.

The General, who was clad in a simple blue greatcoat, without any badges of rank, lay motionless on the ground as the cavalry drew near, and they thinking he was either dead or only a humble civilian employee, passed by and continued their pursuit of the fugitives. One does not know how matters would have ended had not the gallant and quick-witted General Berckheim, at the head of the 4th Cuirassiers, charged down upon the Russian cavalry, who in spite of bravely defending themselves, were almost all killed or made prisoner. Their valiant Major was among the dead. The charge carried out by this handful of men could have had a dramatic result if it had been followed up, and this fine feat of arms goes to show once more that it is unexpected attacks by cavalry that have the best chance of success.

General Saint-Cyr, having been picked up by our Cuirassiers, ordered all the infantry divisions to advance immediately and attack the Russians before they could recover from their confusion. In this they were successful and the enemy were decisively beaten, losing many men and a number of guns.

While this infantry battle was taking place before Polotsk, another action was under way on their left, in the open plain which bordered the Dvina. As soon as the cannon shot gave the signal to engage, our cavalry regiments, led by Castex's brigade, advanced rapidly towards the enemy who, for their part, advanced towards us.

A major encounter seemed imminent, and the good General Castex said that although in spite of my recent injury, I had been able to command the regiment during the fighting round Sivotschina and Svolna, where it had been solely a matter of facing the fire of the infantry and the guns, it would not be the same today when in action against cavalry. During a charge I would be unable to defend myself since, with my one arm, I could not hold my horse's bridle and at the same time use my sabre. He therefore urged me to remain behind on this occasion, with the reserve division of infantry. I did not think that I should accept this well-meaning advice, and I expressed so vehemently my wish not to be removed from the regiment that the General gave way, but he arranged for me to have behind me six of the best cavalrymen, led by Sergeant Prud'homme, while at my side were four warrant officers, a trumpeter and my orderly Fousse, one of the finest soldiers in the regiment. Surrounded in this way, and placed in front of the centre of a squadron, I was sufficiently protected; besides, in an emergency, I would have dropped the reins to wield my sabre, which hung by its sword-knot from my right wrist.

The meadow was large enough to hold two regiments in battle order, so the 23rd and the 24th advanced in line. General Corbineau's brigade, consisting of three regiments was in the second line and the Cuirassiers followed, in reserve. The 24th, which was on my left, faced a body of Russian dragoons, while I was opposed to the Cossacks of the Guard, recognisable by the red colour of their jackets and the fine quality of their horses which although they had arrived only a few hours ago did not appear in the least tired. We moved forward at the gallop, and when we were at a suitable distance from the enemy, General Castex ordered the charge and his whole brigade fell in one line on the Russians. By the violence of this attack, the 24th overwhelmed the dragoons who opposed them, but my regiment experienced more resistance from the Cossacks, a chosen band of men of superior stature, each armed with a 14 foot lance which he well knew how to use. Some of my Chasseurs were killed and many wounded, but once my gallant troopers had broken through this line bristling with steel they had the advantage, for the long lances are ineffective against cavalry when those carrying them are disorganised and closely engaged by adversaries who are armed with sabres which they can use with ease, while the lancers have great difficulty in presenting the point of their weapons. Thus the Cossacks were forced to turn their backs, whereupon my men slaughtered many of them and captured a large number of splendid horses.

We were about to follow up this success when our attention was drawn to a great tumult on our right, where we saw the plain covered with fugitives, for this was the moment when the Russian Chevalier-Gardes made their desperate attack. General Castex, thinking it would be unwise to advance any further when our centre appeared to be retreating in disorder, called for the rally to be sounded and the brigade came to a halt.

We had, however, scarcely re-formed our ranks when the Cossacks, emboldened by what was going on in the centre and burning to avenge their previous defeat, charged back on the attack and hurled themselves furiously on my squadrons, while the Grodno Hussars attacked the 24th. The Russians, driven back at every point by Castex's brigade, brought up successively their second and third line, whereupon Corbineau came to our assistance with the 7th and 20th Chasseurs and the 8th Lancers, and there ensued a great cavalry battle, the outcome of which hung in the balance. Both our own and the Russian Cuirassiers were advancing to join in when Wittgenstein, seeing his infantry beaten and hard pressed by ours, sent word to his cavalry to retire. They, however, were too hotly engaged for this command to be easily executed. In the event, Generals Castex and Corbineau, knowing that they would be supported by the Cuirassiers who were close behind them, committed in turn both their brigades against the Russians who were thrown into the greatest disorder and suffered heavy casualties.

On arriving at the other side of the wood where our victorious infantry and cavalry divisions were regrouping, General Saint-Cyr, seeing that night was approaching, called off the pursuit, and the troops returned to their bivouacs at Polotsk, which they had quitted a few hours earlier. During the fighting my wound had given me much pain, particularly when I had to gallop my horse. My inability to defend myself often put me in a difficult situation in which I might not have survived had I not been surrounded by a group of stalwarts who never let me out of their sight.

On one occasion, amongst others, I was pushed by the mob of combatants into a group of Cossacks, where to save myself I had to let go of the bridle and take up my sabre. I had, however, no need to use it, for seeing their commanding officer in danger all ranks of my escort furiously attacked the Cossacks who were now surrounding me, laid several of them in the dust and put the rest to flight. My orderly Fousse, the finest of Chasseurs, killed three of them and Warrent-Officer Joly two. So I came back safe and sound from this action, in which I had been determined to take part in order to encourage the regiment, and to show them afresh that as long as I could mount a horse it would be my honour to lead them when danger threatened. Both the officers and men of the regiment appreciated this, and the affection with which I was already regarded by them was increased, as you will see later, when I speak of the misfortunes of the great retreat.

Combat between cavalry units is infinitely less murderous than that involving the infantry, also the Russians are as a rule maladroit in the handling of their weapons, and their incompetent leaders do not always know how to employ their cavalry to best advantage. So that although my regiment was fighting the Cossacks of the Guard, considered one of the finest units in the Russian army, we did not suffer a great many casualties. I had eight or nine men killed and some thirty wounded; but amongst those last was Major Fontaine. This very fine officer was in the thick of the fighting when his horse was killed. His feet were entangled in the stirrups and he was trying to free himself with the help of some Chasseurs who had gone to help him when a Cossack officer, bursting through the group at the gallop, leaned dexterously from his saddle and dealt Fontaine a terrible sabre slash which blinded his left eye, damaged the other and split open his nose. However, as the Russian officer, proud of this exploit, was leaving the scene, one of our Chasseurs shot him in the back at six paces, so avenging his squadron commander. As soon as possible M. Fontaine's injury was dressed and he was taken to Polotsk to the Jesuit monastery, where I visited him that same evening. I admired the resignation with which this courageous soldier bore the pain and disability of becoming almost completely blind, since which time he has not been able to continue in active service. This was a great loss for the 23rd, in which he had been since its creation, liked and respected by all; I was much moved by his misfortune.

I was now the only senior officer in the regiment and I had to see to all the requirements of the service, which was a major task.

Anyone but Saint-Cyr, after such a hard-fought action would

have reviewed his troops to congratulate them on their success and enquire into their needs. Scarcely, however, had the last shot been fired, when Saint-Cyr shut himself up in the Jesuit monastery and spent all his days and part of the night playing his violin...a ruling passion from which only marching to attack the enemy could distract him. Generals Lorencez and Wrède, given the task of deploying the troops, sent two divisions of infantry and the Cuirassiers to the left bank of the Dvina. The third French division and the Bavarians stayed in Polotsk, where they were employed to build the fortifications of a vast entrenched camp, before acting as a support to the troops which from this important point were covering the left and rear of the "Grande Armee" on its march to Smolensk and on to Moscow. The light cavalry brigades of Castex and Corbineau were positioned two leagues in front of this camp, on the left bank of the Polota, a little river which joins the Dvina at Polotsk. My regiment went into bivouac near a village called Louchonski. The colonel of the 24th set up his a quarter of a league to the rear, covered by the 23rd. We stayed there for two months, during the first of which we did not go very far. When he heard of the victory won at Polotsk by Saint-Cyr, the Emperor sent him the baton o Imperial Marshalf. Instead of using the occasion to visit his troops, the new Marshal retired into even deeper seclusion, if that were possible. No one could approach the head of the army, which earned him the nick-name amongst the soldiers of the "Owl". More than this, although the huge monastery had more than a hundred rooms which would have been most useful for the wounded, he lived there alone, and considered it a great concession that he allowed senior officers who were wounded to be received in the outhouses. They were allowed to remain there for forty-eight hours, after which their comrades had to take them to the town. The cellars and granaries of the monastery were bursting with provisions amassed by the Jesuits; wine, beer oil, flour, etc. All were there in abundance; but the Marshal had taken charge of the keys of the store-rooms and nothing came from them, even for the hospitals. It was with the greatest difficulty that I obtained two bottles of wine for the injured Fontaine. The extraordinary thing was that the Marshal used hardly any of these provisions for himself, for he was a man of extreme sobriety, if also highly eccentric. The army complained loudly about his behaviour, and those same provisions which he refused to distribute to his troops were, two months later, consumed by flames and the Russians, when the French were forced to abandon the burning monastery and town.

Chapter 11
The Battle of Borodino

While all this was going on at Polotsk and on the banks of the Drissa, the Emperor remained at Witepsk, from where he exercised overall control of the operations of the numerous units of the army. There are those who have reproached Napoleon with wasting too much time, first at Wilna, where he stayed for nineteen days, and then at Witepsk where he stayed for seventeen. They claim that these thirty-six days could have been better employed, particularly in a country where the summer is very short, and the rigours of winter begin to be felt about the end of September. This claim has some justice up to a point, but it should be remembered, firstly that the Emperor hoped that the Russians would request some compromise and, in the second place that it was necessary to concentrate once more all the units which had been scattered in the pursuit of Bagration. In addition it was essential to give some rest to the troops who, as well as their regular marches had to scour the countryside each evening, far from their bivouacs, in a search for food; because the Russians having burned all the stores as they retreated, it was impossible to make any daily distribution of rations. There was, however, for a long time a happy exception to this state of affairs, in the case of Davout's Corps. Davout was as good an administrator as he was a fighting soldier, and well before the crossing of the Nieman he had organised an immense convoy of little carts which followed his army. These carts carried biscuits, salted meat and vegetables and were drawn by oxen, a number of which could be slaughtered daily to provide food. This arrangement contributed greatly to keeping his men from straying from their ranks.

The Emperor left Witepsk on the 13th August, and moving further and further away from 2nd and 6th Corps, which he left at Polotsk under the command of Saint-Cyr, he went to Krasnoe, where a part of the Grande Armée faced the enemy. It was hoped that there would be a battle, but all that took place was a minor action against the Russian rear-guard, which was defeated and promptly withdrew. On the 15th of August, his birthday, the Emperor reviewed his troops, who welcomed him with enthusiasm. On the 16th the army reached Smolensk, a fortified town which the Russians call the holy of holies because they consider it to be the key to Moscow and the palladium of their empire. Ancient prophecies foretold disaster to Russia the day Smolensk was taken. This superstition, carefully nurtured by the government, dates from the time when Smolensk, situated on the Dnieper, was the furthest Muscovite frontier, from where they issued to make enormous conquests.

Murat and Ney, who were the first two to arrive before Smolensk, both thought, for some unknown reason, that the Russians had abandoned the place. The reports given to the Emperor having convinced him that this was the case, he ordered that the advance-guard should be sent into the town. The impatient Ney was waiting only for this command, he advanced toward the town gate escorted by a small body of Hussars, but suddenly a regiment of Cossacks, hidden by a fold in the ground covered by scrub, fell on our riders, drew them off and surrounded Marshal Ney, who was so hard pressed that a pistol shot fired at point blank range tore the collar of his coat. Fortunately the Domanget brigade hurried to the spot and freed the Marshal. The arrival of General Razout's infantry enabled Ney to get close enough to the town to convince himself that the Russians intended to defend it.

Seeing the ramparts armed with a great number of cannon, the artillery general, Éblé, a highly competent officer, advised the Emperor to by-pass the place by sending the Polish Corps commanded by Prince Poniatowski to cross the Dnieper two leagues further upstream; but Napoleon, accepting the advice of Ney, who assured him that Smolensk would be easily captured, gave the order to attack. Three army Corps, those of Davout, Ney and Poniatowski, launched an assault on the town from different directions. A murderous fire was poured down on them from the ramparts, and one even more deadly came from the batteries which the Russians had established on the opposite bank of the river. A most bloody struggle ensued; bullets, grape-shot and bombs decimated our troops, without the artillery being able to breach the walls. At last, as night was approaching, the enemy, who had bravely disputed every foot of ground, were driven back into the town itself, which they now prepared to abandon. Before they did so, however, they set all of it on fire. The Emperor thus saw an end to his hopes of capturing a town which was rightly supposed to be full of supplies. It was not until dawn the next day that the French entered the place, the streets of which were strewn with the dead bodies of Russians and smoking debris. The taking of Smolensk had cost us 12,000 men killed or wounded, an enormous loss which could have been avoided by crossing the Dnieper upstream, as had been proposed by General Éblé; for, seeing himself at risk of being cut off, General Barclay de Tolly, the enemy commander, would have evacuated the place and retired towards Moscow.

The Russians, after burning the bridge, halted for a short time on the heights of the right bank and then resumed their retreat on the road to Moscow. Marshal Ney followed them with his army corps, reinforced by Gudin's division which was detached from Davout's corps.

Not far from Smolensk, Marshal Ney caught up with the Russians as they passed, with all their baggage, through a narrow defile. A major engagement took place which could have been disasterous for the enemy if General Junot, who commanded 8th Corps and who had been slow in crossing the Dnieper two leagues above Smolensk, and who had then halted for forty-eight hours, had hastened to the sound of Ney's guns, which were no more than a league away. Although informed of the situation by Ney, Junot did not budge. He was then ordered, in the name of the Emperor to come to the assistance of Ney, but still he did not move.

Ney, facing greatly superior numbers, having engaged successively all the troops of his corps, ordered Gudin's division to take some strong positions held by the Russians. This order was executed with the greatest alacrity, but in the first wave the brave general fell mortally wounded. However, retaining his usual calm, and wishing to assure the success of the troops which he had so often led to victory, he appointed General Gérard to take over the command, although he was the most junior brigade commander in the division.

Gérard, at the head of the division attacked the enemy, and by ten in the evening, after losing 1800 men and killing some six thousand, he was master of the field of battle, from which the Russians made a hasty departure.

The next day the Emperor came to visit the troops who had fought so bravely; he rewarded them generously and promoted Gérard to the rank of divisional general. Gudin died a few hours later.

If Junot had taken part in the action, he could have trapped the Russians in a narrow defile when, caught between two fires, they would have been forced to surrender, and thus brought the war to an end. One regretted the departure of King Jérôme, whom Junot had replaced, for although a mediocre general, he would probably have gone to help Ney. We expected to see Junot severely punished, but he was one of Napoleon's earliest adherents and had supported him in all his campaigns, from the siege of Toulon in '93 to the present. The Emperor was fond of him and he forgave him. This was a pity, for it was becoming necessary to make an example.

When the Russian people heard of the fall of Smolensk, there was a general outcry against Barclay de Tolly. He was a German; the nation accused him of not putting enough effort into the war, and for the defence of ancient Muscovy they demanded a Muscovite general. Compelled to give way, Alexander handed the command of all the Russian armies to General Koutousoff, an elderly man of little ability, renowned only for his defeat at Austerlitz, but having the great merit, in the circumstances, of being an out and out Russian, which gave him a considerable influence in the eyes of the troops and the populace at large.

The French advance-guard, driving the enemy before it, had already passed Dorogobouje when, on the 24th of August, the Emperor decided to leave Smolensk. The heat was stifling; we marched on loose sand; there was insufficient food for such a large body of men and horses, for the Russians left nothing behind them but burning farms and villages. When the army entered Vyazma, this pretty town was in flames, and it was the same at Gzhatzk. The nearer we got to Moscow the fewer resources the countryside had to offer. Several men died and many horses. A few days later, the intolerable heat was succeeded by a cold rain which lasted until the 4th of September; autumn was approaching. The army was no more than six leagues from Mojaisk, the last town we had to take before reaching Moscow, when it was noticed that the strength of the enemy rear-guard had been considerably increased; an indication that a major battle was at last in prospect.

On the 5th, our advance-guard was briefly held up by a large Russian column, well entrenched on a small hill, garnished with a dozen guns. The 57th line regiment, which in the Italian campaign the Emperor had named the "Terrible", worthily upheld its reputation in capturing the redout and the enemy guns. We were already on the terrain upon which, forty-eight hours later, would be fought the battle which the Russians call Borodino and the French Moscow.

On the 6th, the Emperor announced in an order of the day that there would be a battle on the day following. The army welcomed this announcement with pleasure, in the hope that it would mean an end to their privations, for there had been no supply of rations for a month, and everyone had lived from hand to mouth. On both sides the evening was employed in taking up positions of readiness.

On the Russian side, Bagration, commanding 62,000 men was on the left wing; in the centre was the Hetman Platov with his Cossacks and 30,000 infantry in reserve; the right was made up of 70,000 men under the command of Barclay de Tolly, who was now the second in command, while the elderly General Koutousoff was the overall commander of all these troops, amounting to 162,000 men. The Emperor Napoleon had no more than 140,000, who were disposed as follows: Prince Eugène commanded the left wing, Marshal Davout the right, Marshal Ney the centre, King Murat the cavalry, while the Imperial Guard was in reserve.

The battle took place on the 7th of September; the weather was overcast and a cold wind raised clouds of dust. The Emperor, who was suffering from severe migraine, went down into a sort of ravine, where he spent the greater part of the day walking on foot. From this spot he could see only part of the battlefield, and to see its entirety he had to climb a nearby hillock, which he did only twice during the action. The Emperor has been blamed for his lack of activity, but it should be borne in mind that in the central position which he occupied with his reserves, he was able to receive frequent reports of events occurring at all points of the line, whereas if he had been on one wing or the other, the aides-de-camp, hurrying with urgent information over such broken ground, might not have been able to see him or known where to look for him. Also it must not be forgotten that the Emperor was ill and a strong and glacial wind prevented him from remaining on horseback.

I took no part in the battle of Moscow, so I shall refrain from going into any detail about the various manoeuvres carried out during this memorable action. I shall say only that after almost unheard of efforts the French succeeded in overcoming the most obstinate resistance of the Russians, and that the battle was one of the most bloody fought during the century. The two armies suffered casualties to a total of 50,000 dead or wounded. The French had 49 generals killed or wounded and 20,000 men put out of action. The Russian losses were a third greater. General Bagration, the best of their officers was killed, and by a bizarre turn of fate he happened to be the owner of the land on which the battle was fought. Twelve thousand horses were left on the field. The French took few prisoners, an indication of the courage and determination of the Russian resistance.

During the action there were several interesting episodes. When the Russian left had been twice driven back by the supreme efforts of Murat, Davout and Ney and had yet rallied for the third time and returned to the charge, Murat asked General Belliard to beg the Emperor to send part of his guard to secure a victory, failing which it would be necessary to fight another battle to beat the Russians. Napoleon was inclined to comply with this request, but Marshal Bessières, commandant of the Guard said to him "I shall permit myself to remind your majesty that you are at this moment some seven hundred leagues from France." Whether it was this observation or whether the Emperor thought that the battle had not reached the stage when he should commit his reserve, he refused the request. Two other demands of this kind met the same fate.

There was another remarkable incident which occurred in this battle so full of gallant deeds. The enemy front was covered by some high ground on which were redouts and redans and in particular, a crenelated fort armed with 80 guns. The French, after considerable losses had gained control of these field works but had not been able to retain the fort, and to regain it would be a very difficult task even for infantry. General Montbrun, who commanded the 2nd Cavalry Corps, had noticed, with the help of his field-glass, that the gate of the fort was not closed and that platoons of Russian soldiers were going through it. He also noticed that if one went round the side of the high ground, one could avoid the ramparts, ravines and rocks and lead a cavalry unit to the gate up a gentle slope suited to horses. General Montbrun proposed to get into the fort with his cavalry from the rear, while the infantry attacked the front. This hazardous operation having been approved by Murat and the Emperor, Montbrun was entrusted with its execution; but while the intrepid general was finalising his plan, he was killed by a cannon-ball. This was a great loss for the army, but it did not put an end to the project he had conceived, and the Emperor sent General Coulincourt to replace him.

One now saw something unheard of in the annals of war. A huge fort defended by numerous guns and several battalions of infantry attacked and taken by a column of cavalry. Coulincourt pressing ahead with a division of Cuirassiers, headed by their 5th regiment commanded by Colonel Christophe, broke through all those defending the approach to the fort, reached the gate, entered the interior and fell dead with a bullet through his head. Colonel Christophe and his troopers avenged their general by putting part of the garrison to the sword. The fort remained in their hands, which helped to assure a French victory.

Today, when the thirst for promotion has become insatiable, one would be astonished if, after such a feat, a colonel was not promoted; but during the Empire ambition was more modest. Christophe did not become a general until some years later, and never showed any discontent with this delay.

The Poles, usually so courageous, particularly those from the Grand Duchy of Warsaw commanded by Prince Poniatovski, fought so badly that the Emperor sent his major general to upbraid them. In this battle of Moscow, General Rapp was wounded for the twenty-first time.

Although the Russians had been defeated and forced to leave the field of battle, their generalissimo, Koutousoff, had the impudence to write to the Emperor Alexander claiming that he had just won a great victory over the French. This falsehood, which arrived in St.Petersburg on Alexander's birthday, gave rise to much rejoicing. A Te Deum was sung and Koutousoff was promoted to field-marshal. However it was not long before the truth was known and the joy turned to grief; but Koutousoff was now a field-marshal, which was what he wanted. Anyone but the timid Alexander would have severely punished the new field-marshal for this outrageous lie; but Koutousoff was needed, and so he remained head of the army.

Chapter 12
The French Enter Moscow

The Russians, retreating towards Moscow, were contacted on the morning of the eighth, when there was a sharp cavalry engagement in which General Belliard was wounded. Napoleon spent three days at Mojaisk, partly to draw up the orders necessary in the circumstances and partly to reply to the back-log of despatches. One of these, which had arrived on the eve of the battle, had affected him greatly and had contributed to making him ill, for it announced that the so-called army of Portugal, commanded by Marshal Marmont, had suffered a severe defeat at Arpiles, near Salamanca, in Spain.

Marmont was one of Napoleon's mistakes. He had been one of Napoleon's companions at the college of Brienne and later in the artillery, and Napoleon took an interest in him. Misled by some success achieved by Marmont at school, the Emperor had a belief in the Marshal's military talents which his performance in the field never justified. In 1811, Marmont had replaced Masséna as commander of the army of Portugal, proclaiming that he would defeat Wellington, but the contrary proved to be the case. Marmont, defeated, wounded, with his army in disarray and obliged to abandon several provinces, would have suffered even worse reverses if General Clausel had not come to his aid.

When he learned of this disaster, the Emperor must have reflected deeply on the present operation, for while he was about to enter Moscow at the head of his largest army, a thousand leagues away another army had just been defeated. By invading Russia was he about to lose Spain? Major Fabvier, who brought this despatch, volunteered to join in the battle for Moscow and was wounded in the assault on the great redout. It was a long way to come to be hit by a bullet.

On the 12th of September Napoleon left Mojaisk, and on the 15th he entered Moscow. This enormous city was deserted.

General Rostopschine, its governor, had forced all the inhabitants to leave. This Rostopschine whom some have described as a
hero, was a barbarian, who would shrink from nothing to achieve
his aims. He had allowed the populace to strangle a number of
foreign merchants, mainly the French, who were living in Moscow, on the sole grounds that they were suspected of hoping
for the arrival of Napoleon's troops. Some days before the battle of Moscow, the Cossacks having captured about a hundred
sick Frenchmen, Koutousoff sent them by a roundabout road to
the governor of Moscow, who, regardless of their condition, left
them for forty-eight hours without food and then paraded them
triumphantly through the streets, where a number of these unfortunates collapsed and died of starvation. As this was happening,
policemen read to the populace a proclamation by Rostopschine
in which, to encourage them to take up arms, he declared that
all the French were in a similar feeble state and would be easily
overcome. When this disgusting performance was over, the majority of the soldiers still alive were killed by the mob, without
Rostopschine doing anything to protect them.

The defeated Russian troops had only passed through Moscow, and had gone to re-group some thirty leagues from there,
around Kalouga. Murat followed them with all his cavalry and
several infantry corps. The Imperial Guard stayed in the town and
Napoleon took up residence in the Kremlin, the ancient fortified
palace of the Czars. Everything seemed peaceful, when, during
the night 15th-16th September, some French and German merchants who had escaped the governor's attentions came to warn
Napoleon's staff that the city was to be set on fire. This information was confirmed by a Russian policeman, who refused to carry
out the orders of his superiors. He stated that before leaving Moscow, Rostopschine had thrown open all the prisons and released
the prisoners and convicts, to whom he had given torches said to
have been supplied by the British, and that these persons were lying hidden in the abandoned houses waiting for the signal. When
the Emperor heard of this he instituted the strictest precautionary
measures. Patrols went about the streets and killed a number of
those caught setting fires alight, but it was too late; fire broke out
in various parts of the city and spread rapidly owing to the fact

that Rostopschine had taken away all the fire-fighting equipment. It was not long before the whole of Moscow was ablaze. The Emperor left the Kremlin and went to the château of Peterskoe. He did not return until three days later, when the fire was beginning to subside for lack of fuel. I shall not go into any details about the fire itself, as there are several eye-witness accounts, but later I shall examine the consequences of this catastrophic conflagration.

Napoleon, who did not understand the position in which Alexander found himself, hoped always for some accommodation and eventually, tired of waiting, he decided to write to him personally. In the meantime the Russian army was being reorganised in the area of Kalouga, from where agents were sent to direct stray soldiers back to their units. It was estimated that there were about 15,000 of them concealed in the suburbs and able to wander about our bivouacs without being challenged. They sat round the fires with our men and ate with them, yet no one thought of making them prisoners. This was a great mistake, for they gradually returned to the Russian army, while our strength diminished daily owing to sickness and the increasing cold. We lost an enormous number of horses, which was thought due to the extraordinary efforts demanded by Murat from the cavalry, of which he was the commander. Murat, recalling the brilliant successes obtained against the Prussians in 1806 and 1807 by pursuing them closely, thought that the cavalry should be equal to any demands and should march twelve to fifteen leagues a day without worrying about the fatigue of the horses, the essential being to reach the enemy with at least some of the columns. However the climate, the shortage of rations and fodder, the long duration of the campaign and above all the tenacious resistance of the Russians had greatly changed the situation, so that by the time we reached Moscow, half our cavalrymen had no horses, and Murat managed to finish off the rest at Kalouga. Prince Murat was proud of his tall stature and his bravery; and being always decked out in strange but brilliant uniforms he had attracted the notice of the enemy, with whom he was pleased to parley, even exchanging gifts with the Cossack officers. Koutousoff took advantage of these meetings to encourage in the French the false hopes of a peace, hopes which Murat passed on to the Emperor.

One day however, this enemy who claimed to be so weakened, arose, slipped into our cantonments and captured some supplies, a squadron of dragoons and a battalion of troops. After this Napoleon forbade, under pain of death, any communication with the Russians which he had not authorised.

The Emperor never entirely lost hope of concluding a peace. On the 4th of October he sent General Lauriston, his aide-de-camp, to General Koutousoff's headquarters. The cunning Russian showed General Lauriston a letter which he had addressed to the Emperor Alexander, urging him to agree to the French proposals, seeing that, as he alleged, the Russian army was in no state to continue the war. The officer carrying this despatch had hardly left for St. Petersburg, armed with a pass from Lauriston which would preserve him from attack by any of our men who were in the area between the two armies, when Koutousoff sent off a second aide-de-camp to his Emperor. This officer, having no French laissez-passer, was stopped by one of our patrols, taken prisoner and his despatches sent to Napoleon. The contents were the exact opposite to what had been shown to Lauriston. After imploring his sovereign not to treat with the French, he informed him that Admiral Tchitchakoff's army, freed from its duties on the frontier by the peace with Turkey, was moving towards Minsk in order to cut the French line of retreat. He also told Alexander of the discussions he had conducted freely with Murat, with the aim of encouraging the false sense of security entertained by the French in remaining in Moscow so late in the year.

When he saw this letter, Napoleon, realising that he had been tricked, fell into a furious rage, and is said to have contemplated marching on St.Petersburg; but beyond the diminished strength of the army and the rigours of the winter, which militated against such an undertaking, there were pressing reasons for the Emperor to get closer to Germany, in order to watch over that country and to see what was going on in France, where there had been a conspiracy whose leaders had been, for one day, in control of the capital. A fanatic, General Malet, had tossed a spark into Paris which could have started a fire, which, had he not encountered a man as far-seeing and energetic as Adjutant-major Laborde, might have put an end to the imperial government.

This was not heartening, and one can imagine the anxiety of Napoleon when he learned of the danger which had threatened his family and his government.

Chapter 13

Retreat!

In Moscow, Napoleon's position grew worse daily. The cold was already bitter and only the French-born soldiers maintained their morale, but they composed no more than half the force which Napoleon had led into Russia. The remainder was made up of Germans, Swiss, Croats, Lombards, Romanians, Piedmontais, Spaniards and Portuguese. All these foreigners, who stayed loyal as long as the army was successful, now began to complain and led astray by the leaflets in various languages which the Russians spread widely through our camps, they deserted in droves to the enemy, who promised to repatriate them.

Added to this, the two wings of the Grande Armée, which consisted entirely of Austrians and Prussians, were now no longer in line with the centre as they had been at the beginning of the campaign, but were in our rear, ready to bar our way on the first command of their sovereigns, ancient and irreconcilable enemies of France. The position was critical, and although it would greatly hurt Napoleon's pride to display to the whole world that he had failed in his objective of imposing a peace on Alexander, the word "retreat" was at last uttered, but neither the Emperor nor the marshals nor anyone else thought of abandoning Russia and recrossing the Nieman; the idea was to go into winter quarters in the least unpleasant of the Polish provinces.

The evacuation of Moscow was agreed on in principle, but before taking this step, Napoleon, in a last endeavour to obtain a settlement, sent an emissary to Marshal Koutousoff, who did not make any response.

During these delays our army was melting away, day by day, and in blind overconfidence our outposts remained at risk in the province of Kalouga in untactical positions, when suddenly a wholly unforeseen event occurred which opened the eyes of the most incredulous and destroyed any illusions which the Emperor still had of achieving peace.

General Sébastiani, whom we saw allowing himself to be surprised at Drouia, had replaced General Montbrun as commander of the 2nd Cavalry Corps, and although close to the enemy, he spent his days in his slippers, reading Italian poetry and carrying out no reconnaissance. Taking advantage of this negligence, Koutousoff attacked Sébastiani on the 18th of October, surrounded him and overwhelmed him by numbers, forcing him to abandon part of his artillery. Sébastiani's three divisions of cavalry, separated from the rest of Murat's troops were able to rejoin them only after fighting their way through several enemy battalions who stood in their way. In the course of this savage combat, Sébastiani displayed his valour, for he was a brave man, if a noticeably mediocre general. Something which will be demonstrated anew when we come to the campaign of 1813.

At the same time as he surprised Sébastiani, Koutousoff ordered an attack on Murat's lines, in which the Prince was slightly wounded. Having learned of this unsatisfactory affair, and on the same day been told of the arrival in the enemy camp of a reinforcement of ten thousand cavalry from the Russian army in Wallachia which the Austrians, our allies, had allowed to pass, the Emperor gave the order for the departure to begin on the following day.

In the morning of the 19th of October, the Emperor left Moscow, which he had entered on the 15th of September. His Majesty, the old guard and the bulk of the army took the road to Kalouga; Marshal Mortier and two divisions of the Young Guard remained behind for twenty-four hours to complete the destruction of the city and blow up the Kremlin, after which they brought up the rear of the march.

The army trailed behind it more than forty thousand carriages, which caused an obstruction whenever the road narrowed. When this was remarked on to the Emperor, he replied that each of these coaches could carry two wounded men and food for several, and that their number would gradually diminish. The employment of this philanthropic system could, I think, be objected to, on the grounds that the need to speed the march of a retreating army seems to me to outweigh all other considerations.

During the French occupation of Moscow, Murat and the cavalry corps had been stationed in part of the fertile province of

Kalouga, but without seizing the town of that name. The Emperor wished to avoid passing through the area of the battle of Moscow (Borodino) and down the road to Mojaisk, which had been stripped of resources by the army on its approach to Moscow; and for this reason he took the road to Kalouga, from where he counted on getting to Smolensk through fertile and, as it were, unspoiled country, but at the end of several day's march, the army, which after joining with Murat's force amounted still to more than 100,000 men, found itself confronting the Russian army which occupied the little town of Malo-Iaroslawetz. The enemy was in an exceedingly strong position, nevertheless the Emperor sent into the attack Prince Eugène, at the head of the Italian Corps and the French divisions of Morand and Gerard. Nothing could stand in the way of these men and they took the town after a long and murderous fight which cost us 4000 killed or wounded. Among the dead was General Delzons, a very fine officer.

The next day, the 24th of October, the Emperor, surprised at the degree of resistance he had encountered, and knowing that the whole Russian army barred his way, halted the march and spent three days considering what course he should follow.

On one occasion, during a reconnaissance of the enemy line, the Emperor nearly fell into their hands. There was a very thick fog, and suddenly shouts of "Hourra! Hourra!" were heard. It was a group of Cossacks who were emerging from a wood bordering the road, which they had been going through not twenty paces from the Emperor, knocking down and spearing anyone that they came across: but General Rapp rushed forward with the two squadrons of Chasseurs and mounted Grenadiers which went everywhere with the Emperor who, wielding their sabres, put the enemies to flight. It was during this encounter that M. Le Couteulx, my former companion on the staff of Marshal Lannes, and now an aide-de-camp to Prince Berthier, having armed himself with the lance belonging to a Cossack whom he had killed, was unwise enough to come back brandishing this weapon, and, furthermore, dressed in a pelisse and a fur hat which concealed the French uniform. A mounted Grenadier of the Guard mistook him for a Cossack officer, and seeing him heading towards the Emperor, went after him and slashed him across the body with his heavy sabre. In spite of this serious wound, M. Le Couteulx, placed in one of the Emperor's carriages, survived the cold and the exhaustion of the retreat, and managed to reach France.

The reconnaissance carried out by the Emperor had convinced him that it would be impossible to continue his march towards Kalouga without fighting a sanguinary battle against the large force commanded by Koutousoff. He decided, therefore, to reach Smolensk by taking the road leading through Mojaisk. The army then left the fertile countryside to take once more the now devastated route along which, marking their passage with fires and dead bodies, they had travelled in September. This movement by the Emperor left him, after ten weary days, no more than twelve leagues from Moscow, and caused the troops to feel increasing anxiety about the future. The weather turned much worse; Marshal Mortier rejoined the Emperor after having blown up the Kremlin.

The army saw once more Mojaisk and the battlefield of Borodino. The ground, furrowed by cannon-balls, was covered with the debris of helmets, cuirasses, wheels, weapons, fragments of uniform and thirty thousand bodies, partly eaten by wolves. The Emperor and the troops passed by quickly, casting a sad look at this immense graveyard.

After they had reached Vyazma the snow began to fall and a bitter wind to blow, which slowed their progress. Many of the vehicles were abandoned, and some thousands of men and horses perished of cold by the roadside. The flesh of the horses provided some nourishment for the men and also for the officers. The command of the rearguard passed successively from Davout to Prince Eugène and finally to Marshal Ney, who kept this unpleasant job for the rest of the campaign.

Smolensk was reached on the 1st of November. The Emperor had arranged for a great quantity of food clothing and footwear to be collected there, but those in charge of these supplies did not realise the state of disorganisation into which the army had fallen, and insisted on the paperwork and formalities of a normal distribution. This delay so exasperated the men, who were dying of cold and hunger, that they broke into the stores and took forcibly, whatever they could. With the result that some had too much, some enough and some nothing.

As long as the troops had maintained a proper order of march, the mixture of nationalities had given rise to no more than minor inconveniences, but once fatigue and privation had broken the ranks, discipline was lost. There was no way in which it could be maintained in a vast body of isolated individuals, lacking every necessity, walking on their own, without understanding why; for in this disorderly mass there ruled a veritable babel of tongues. A few regiments, mainly those in the Guard, held together. Almost all the troopers of the cavalry, having lost their horses, were formed into infantry battalions, and those of their officers who still were mounted were made into special squadrons, commanded by Generals Latour-Mauberg, Grouchy and Sébastiani, who acted as ordinary captains, while brigade commanders and colonels filled the post of sergeant and corporal. This resort alone, shows to what extremity the army was reduced.

In this critical position, the Emperor had counted on a strong division of troops of all arms, which General Baraguey d'Hilliers was supposed to bring to Smolensk; but, as we neared the town, we heard the General had laid down his arms before a Russian column, with the provision that he alone would not be made prisoner and would be allowed to rejoin the French army in order to explain his actions. The Emperor, however, refused to see Baraguey d'Hilliers and ordered him to return to France and to consider himself under arrest until he was brought before a court-martial. Baraguey d'Hilliers avoided court-martial by dying in Berlin, it was said, of despair.

This General was another of Napoleon's mistakes. He had been impressed by him at the time of the encampments at Boulogne when he had promised that he could train dragoons to serve either as cavalry or infantry. However, when this system was tried out in 1805, during the Austrian campaign, the Dragoons, now on foot and commanded by Baraguey d'Hilliers in person, were defeated at Wertingen before the eyes of the Emperor, and when placed once more on horseback, they once more suffered the same fate. It was several years before the unit recovered from the effects of this experiment. The originator of the system, having fallen from favour and hoping to re-establish himself by asking to come to Russia, had completed his downfall by capitulating without a struggle, and violating a decree stating that a commander forced to surrender should accompany his men into captivity, and forbidding him from negotiating terms favourable only to himself.

After spending several days at Smolensk, to allow stragglers to catch up with him, the Emperor went to Krasnoe, from where he despatched an officer to 2nd Corps, which was still by the Dvina and was now his only hope of safety.

The regiments of this corps, although they had not suffered the hardship and privation of those who had gone to Moscow, had however been more often in action against the enemy. Napoleon wishing to reward them by appointments to vacant positions, had brought to him for his approval a number of proposals for promotions, several of which related to me. One of these recommended me for the rank only of lieutenant-colonel and it was this that was put before the Emperor for his signature. I have it from General Grundler who, having been detailed to carry the despatch, found himself in the Emperor's office during the signing, that the Emperor scratched out with his own hand the words Lieutenant-colonel and wrote in the word Colonel, saying "I am paying off an old debt." So, on the 15th of November, I at last became Colonel of the 23rd Chasseurs, although I did not know it until some time later.

The painful retreat was resumed. The enemy, whose strength increased continually, cut off the corps of Prince Eugène, Davout and Ney from the rest of the army. The first two managed to fight their way through to join the Emperor, who was very distressed at the absence of Ney, of whom he had had no news for several days.

On the 19th of November Napoleon reached Orscha. It was now a month since he had left Moscow and there was still a hundred and twenty leagues to cover before reaching the Nieman. The cold was intense.

While the Emperor worried unhappily about the fate of his rear-guard and the gallant Marshal Ney, the latter was engaged in one of the finest feats of arms recorded in history. Leaving Smolensk on the morning of the 17th, after blowing up the ramparts, the Marshal had hardly begun his march when he was assailed by a myriad of the enemy, who attacked both flanks and the front and rear of his column.

Driving them off continually, Ney marched, surrounded by

them for three days, to halt eventually before the dangerous pass of the Krasnoe ravine, beyond which could be seen a great mass of Russian troops and an array of guns which opened a lively and sustained fire.

Without being cast down by this unforeseen obstacle the Marshal took the bold decision to force a passage, and ordered the 48th of line, commanded by Colonel Pelet, to attack with the bayonet. At Ney's command, the French soldiers, although tired, hungry and numb with cold, rushed the Russian batteries and captured them. They were regained by the enemy and captured once more by our men but in the end they had to yield to the superiority in numbers. The 48th, shattered by grape-shot, was largely destroyed. Of the six hundred and fifty men who entered the ravine only about a hundred emerged. Colonel Pelet, gravely wounded was among them.

Night fell, and for the rearguard, all hope of rejoining the Emperor and the rest of the army seemed to be lost; but Ney had confidence in his men, and above all in himself. He ordered lines of fires to be lit, in order to keep the enemy in their camp, in the expectation of a renewed attack the next day, but he had decided to put the Dnieper between himself and the Russians and to entrust his fate and that of his troops to the strength of the ice covering the river. It was while he was trying to decide which was the shortest route to the river that a Russian colonel from Krasnoe arrived, as an envoy, and demanded that Ney should surrender. Ney was indignant, and as the officer was carrying no written instructions, he replied that he did not regard him as an envoy but as a spy who would be executed if he did not guide them to the nearest spot on the bank of the Dnieper. The Russian Colonel was forced to obey.

Ney immediately gave the order to quit the camp in silence, leaving behind the guns, wagons, baggage and those wounded unable to march with him; and helped by the darkness, he reached, after four hours, the banks of the Dnieper. The river was frozen over, but the ice was not everywhere thick enough to bear the weight of a number of men, so the Marshal sent his troops across one by one. Once over the river the troops thought they had reached safety, but dawn revealed an encampment of Cossacks. This was commanded by Hetman Platov who, as was his custom, had spent the evening drinking and was still asleep.

Discipline is so rigid in the Russian army that no one dared wake him nor take up arms without his orders, so the remains of Ney's Corps were able to pass within a league of the camp without being attacked. The Cossacks did not appear until the next day.

Under constant attack, the Marshal marched for three days along the winding bank of the Dnieper, which would lead him to Orscha, and on the 20th he at last saw this town where he hoped to find the Emperor and the army. He was, however, still separated from Orscha by a large area of open ground in which were many enemy troops, while the Cossacks were preparing to attack him from the rear. Taking up a good defensive position, he sent of a succession of officers to find out if the French were still in Orscha, failing which resistance would no longer be possible. One of these officers reached Orscha where the general headquarters still was. The Emperor was delighted to hear of the return of Marshal Ney, and to rescue him from his dangerous position he sent Prince Eugène and Marshal Mortier who drove off the enemy and brought back Ney and what remained of his unit.

The next day the Emperor continued the retreat. He was joined by troops under the command of Marshal Victor who had recently arrived from Germany, and he made contact with 2nd Corps, where Saint-Cyr had just returned the command to Marshal Oudinot.

Chapter 14
With the 2nd Corps

As it is important to understand the events which led to the re-union of 2nd Corps with the army from which it had been separated since the start of the campaign, I must describe briefly what happened after the month of August, when, having defeated the Russians at Polotsk, Saint-Cyr set up near there an immense entrenched camp, protected by a part of his force, the remainder of which he spread out on both banks of the Dvina. The light cavalry provided cover for these cantonments and so, as I have already said, Castex's brigade, to which my regiment belonged, was stationed at Louchonski, on a little river named the Polota, from where we could keep an eye on the main roads leading from Sebej and Newel.

Wittgenstein's army, after its defeat, had retired beyond those towns, so that there was between the French and the Russians a space of more than twenty-five leagues of no-mans-land, into which both sides sent reconnaissance parties of cavalry, giving rise to unimportant skirmishes. For the rest, as the area round Polotsk was well supplied with forage and standing crops of grain, and as it seemed plain that we were in for a long stay, the French soldiers started to reap and thresh the corn, and grind it in the small hand-mills which are to be found in every peasant dwelling.

This process seemed to me to be too slow, so we repaired, with much difficulty, two water-mills, which stood by the Polota near Louchonski, and from that time on, a supply of bread for my regiment was assured. As for meat, the neighbouring woods were full of abandoned cattle; but as it was necessary to track them down every day, I had the idea of doing what I had seen done in Portugal, and that was to form a regimental herd. In a short time I had rounded up 7 or 8 hundred beasts which I put in the charge of some unmounted Chasseurs, to whom I gave local ponies, too small for military use. This herd, which I increased by frequent searches, lasted for several months and allowed me to make regular distributions of meat to the regiment, which maintained the men's health and earned me their gratitude for the care I took of them. I extended my care to the horses, for which we made big shelters, thatched with straw, and placed behind the men's huts, so that our bivouac was almost as comfortable as a regular camp in peacetime. The other unit commanders did the same sort of thing, but none of them had a regimental herd: their men lived from day to day.

While the French, Swiss, Croat and Portuguese regiments worked unceasingly to improve their conditions, the Bavarians alone made no effort to escape from want and sickness. It was in vain that General the Comte de Wrède tried to rouse them by pointing out how the French soldiers were building huts, reaping and threshing grain, milling it into flour, making ovens and baking bread, the wretched Bavarians, totally demoralised since they no longer were issued with regular rations, admired the work done by our men without attempting to imitate them. So they were dying like flies and there would have been none left if Marshal Saint-Cyr, shaking off for a moment his habitual indifference, had not persuaded the colonels of the other divisions to provide a daily supply of bread for the Bavarians. The light cavalry, stationed out in the country and near the woods, sent them some cattle.

However, these Germans, so feeble when it came to work, were brave enough in action against the enemy, but the moment the danger was over they relapsed into complete apathy. Nostalgia or home-sickness took them; they dragged themselves to Polotsk, and entering the hospitals established by their commanders, they asked for somewhere to die, and laying themselves on the straw, they never rose again. A great many died in this way and General de Wrède had to take into his wagon the flags of a number of regiments who had not sufficient men to defend them. And yet it was only September, the cold weather had not begun and on the contrary it was very mild. The other troops were in good heart and awaited cheerfully the outcome of events.

The men of my regiment were noted everywhere for their good health, which I attribute firstly to the quantity of bread and meat which I was able to give them and secondly to the liquor which I was able to obtain by an arrangement with the Jesuits of Polotsk. These good Fathers, all of them French, had a big farm at Louchonski, where there was a distillery for making grain spirit, but on the approach of war all the workers had fled back to the monastery, taking with them the stills and utensils, so that production had stopped, thus depriving the monastery of part of its revenue. The arrival of so many soldiers in the region had made alcoholic drinks so scarce and expensive that the owners of the canteens were undertaking a journey of several days to Wilna to obtain supplies. It occurred to me that I might be able to reach an agreement with the Jesuits whereby I would protect their distillery and have my men reap and thresh the necessary grain, in return for which my regiment would receive a daily share of the resulting product. My proposition was accepted by the monks, who benefitted greatly by being able to sell alcohol in the camps, while I had the advantage of being able to distribute a daily ration to my men who, since crossing the Nieman, had drunk nothing but water.

At first glance these details may seem pointless, but I am happy to recall them because the care I took of my men saved many of their lives and maintained the strength of the 23rd far above that of the other cavalry regiments in the corps, which earned me a token of his satisfaction from the Emperor which I shall refer to later.

Among the measures which I took are two which protected the lives of many of my troopers. The first of these was to insist that from the 15th of September they should each equip themselves with a sheepskin coat, many of which were to be found in abandoned peasant dwellings. Soldiers are like great children, for whom one must care sometimes against their will. Mine complained that these heavy pelisses were useless and overburdened their horses, but come October they were happy to put them on under their capes, and when it grew really cold they thanked me for having made them keep them.

The second step which I took was to send to the rear all those troopers who were without a mount, either because of enemy fire or because their horse had died for some other reason. A standing order required that these men should be sent to Lepel in Lithuania, to await horses which were to be sent from Warsaw. I was preparing to do this when I learned that Lepel was crammed with dismounted troopers, who were short of all supplies and had nothing to do because not a single remount had arrived there. So I took it on myself to send my dismounted men directly to Warsaw under the command of Captain Poitevin, who had been wounded. I knew that this was in breach of the regulations, but in a huge army, so far from its base and under such abnormal conditions, it was not possible for the general staff to attend to all the needs of the troops. Occasions therefore arose when a unit commander had to use his own judgement. General Castex, who could not give me official authorisation, having told me that he would close his eyes to what I was doing, I continued in this manner for as long as it was possible, so that in the end I had sent 250 men to Warsaw. After the campaign I found them once more on the Vistula, all in new uniforms, well equipped and well mounted and a welcome reinforcement for the regiment. The dismounted men from other regiments, amounting to some 9000, who had been sent to Lepel, caught unaware by the great retreat from Moscow, were almost all taken prisoner or died of cold on the roads. Yet it would have been so easy to have sent them during the summer and autumn to the remount depot at Warsaw, where there were plenty of horses but a shortage of riders.

I remained for a whole month resting at Louchonski, which helped to heal the wound I had received at Jakoubowo. We were very comfortable in our camp from the material point of view, but very worried about the events at Moscow, and it was only on rare occasions that we had news from France. At last I had a letter in which my dearest Angelique told me she had given birth to a boy. My joy at this was mixed with sadness, for I was a long way from my family, and although I could not foresee all the dangers to which I would soon be exposed, I could not pretend that there were not many obstacles to be overcome before our reunion.

About the middle of September, Marshal Saint-Cyr sent me on a rather delicate mission. It had two objectives: first to find out what the enemy were up to in the region round Newel and then to return via Lake Ozerichtchi in order to get in touch with Count Lubenski, one of the few Poles who were willing to do anything to shake off the Russian yoke. The Emperor who, although unwilling to proclaim the re-establishment of the former Poland, wanted to organise the areas already conquered into departments, had received many refusals from the noblemen to whom he had proposed to confide the administration; but having been assured of Count Lubenski's patriotism, His Majesty had nominated him Prefect of Witepsk. As this nobleman lived in an isolated spot outside the area under French control, it was difficult to inform him of his nomination and to ensure his safe arrival. Napoleon had therefore ordered that a body of light cavalry should be sent to the Count.

Detailed to undertake this mission, with three hundred men of my regiment, I picked the boldest and best-mounted men and having provided them with bread, cooked meat and vodka, as well as other necessities, I left the camp on the 14th of September, taking with me Lorentz to act as interpreter.

The life of a partisan is perilous and very tiring. One avoids the main roads and hides by day in the forest without daring to make a fire. One takes from a hamlet food and fodder to be eaten several leagues away to confuse enemy spies; one marches all night, sometimes arriving at different point from that intended, and one is constantly on the look-out. Such was the life I led when I found myself with no more than three hundred men, in a huge area which I did not know, out of touch with the French army and approaching that of the Russians, a numerous detachment of whom I might encounter at any time. It was a difficult situation, but I had confidence in myself and in the men who followed me, so I went forward resolutely, skirting by two or three leagues the road which runs from Polotsk to Newel.

Nothing much of interest happened to us. It is sufficient to say that thanks to the information given to us by the peasants, who hated the Russians, we made a tour round Newel, avoiding all the enemy positions, and after eight days, or rather eight nights, of marching we came to the shore of Lake Ozerichtchi, where there is the magnificent château which at that time belonged to Count Lubenski. I shall never forget the scene which greeted us on our arrival before this ancient and vast manor. It was a splendid autumn evening. The family of the Count had gathered to celebrate his birthday and to rejoice in the capture of Moscow by Napoleon, when some servants ran to announce that the château was surrounded by soldiers on horseback, who had posted sentries and guards and were now entering the courtyards. It was thought that these were the Russian police who had come to arrest the Count, and he, a man of great courage, was waiting calmly to be taken to the prison of St.Petersburg, when his son, who out of curiosity had opened a window, came to say that the troopers were speaking French.

On hearing this, the Count and his family followed by a crowd of servants rushed out of the château and gathered on an immense peristyle. When I mounted the steps, he advanced towards me with arms outstretched to embrace me, and declaimed in theatrical tones a most fulsome welcome. Not only did the Count embrace me, but his wife and daughters did the same, then the almoner, the tutors and governesses came to kiss my hand, and the domestic staff touched my knee with their lips. I was greatly astonished at these various honours, and accepted them with all the gravity I could muster. I had thought the whole performance was over when, at a word from the Count, they all knelt down and commenced to pray.

When we re-entered the château, I handed the Count his appointment as Prefect of Witepsk, adorned with the signature of the French Emperor, and asked him if he accepted it. "Yes". He cried, "and I am ready to go with you." The Countess was equally enthusiastic, and it was agreed that the Count with his eldest son and two servants would leave with me. I gave them an hour to get ready, which time was employed in giving my men a good supper, which they had to eat on horseback because of my fear of a surprise attack. Having said our farewells, we left to go and sleep in a forest four leagues from there, where we stayed hidden all the next day. At night we continued our march, but to put off our trail any of the enemy who might have been warned of our presence in the area, I took a different route to that by which I had come, and going by paths and at times across country, after five days I reached Polotsk. It was as well that I had taken a different route, because I learned later from some merchants who lived in Newel that the Russians had sent a regiment of Dragoons and 600 Cossacks to wait for me at the source of the Drissa, near a village I had passed on my way in.

After reporting to Marshal Saint-Cyr and presenting to him Count Lubenski, I went back to the camp at Louchonski, where I rejoined General Castex and the rest of my unit. My expedition had lasted for thirteen days, during which time we had suffered fatigue and privation; but I was bringing my men back in good shape. We had not been obliged to fight since any small bands of the enemy we did encounter fled when they saw us.

The journey which Count Lubenski had taken with us had allowed me to assess his character. He was a well educated man, capable and patriotic, but one whose enthusiasm was inclined to cloud his judgement when it came to considering how best to re-build Poland. Nevertheless, if all his compatriots had shown his vigour, and had taken up arms on the arrival of the French, Poland might have regained its freedom in 1812; but, with few exceptions, they remained profoundly apathetic.

After leaving Polotsk, the Count went to take up his post as prefect. He did not keep the position for long, for a month had hardly passed before the French army, having left Moscow passed through Witepsk on its retreat. Compelled by this disaster to abandon his prefecture and to shelter from the vengeance of the Russians, he took refuge in Galicia in Austrian Poland, where he had large landholdings. He lived there peacefully until 1830 when he returned to Russian Poland to take up arms against the Czar. I do not know what happened to him after this uprising, but I have been told by some of his countrymen that he went back to Galicia. He was a good patriot and a fine man.

A few days after our return to Louchonski, I was greatly surprised by the arrival of a detachment of thirty troopers belonging to my regiment. They had come from Mons and had in consequence travelled through Belgium, the Rhenish provinces, all of Germany and part of Prussia and Poland, and had come more than 400 leagues under the command of a simple N.C.O. However not a man had fallen out and not a horse was injured. That shows the sort of stuff of which the troopers of the 23rd were made.

Chapter 15
Retreat from Polotsk

On about the 12th of October, 2nd Corps which, since the 18th of August had been living in peace and plenty in and around Polotsk, had to prepare itself to run once more the dangers of war. We learned that Admiral Tchitchakoff, commander-in-chief of the Russian army in Walachia, having made peace with the Turks through the intervention of the English, was heading for Moghilew with the intention of getting in the rear of Napoleon who, still nursing the hope of concluding a treaty with Alexander, had not yet left Moscow. One might be astonished that Prince Schwartzenberg, who with thirty thousand Austrians, our allies, was supposed to be watching over the Russian forces in Walachia, had allowed them to pass, but that is what happened. Not only had the Austrians failed to block the road taken by the Russians, which they could have done, but instead of following behind them, they had stayed comfortably in their cantonments.

Napoleon had trusted too much in the good faith of the generals and ministers of his father-in-law, the Emperor of Austria, in giving them the responsibility of covering the right flank of the Grande Armée. Whatever excuses are offered, there can be, in my opinion, no escaping the fact that this was flagrant treachery on their part, and history will condemn them for it.

While on our right the Austrians were allowing passage to the Russian troops coming from Turkey, the Prussians who had so unwisely been placed on our left wing, were preparing to do a deal with the enemy, and that almost openly, without concealment from Marshal Macdonald, whom the Emperor had put at their head to ensure their fidelity. As soon as these foreigners learned that the occupation of Moscow had not led to a peace, they foresaw the disasters which would befall the French army, and all their enmity towards us was rekindled. They did not break out in open revolt, but Marshal Macdonald's orders were obeyed with reluctance, and the Prussians encamped near Riga could at any moment join Wittgenstein's Russians to crush 2nd Corps camped round Polotsk.

Plainly, Marshal Saint-Cyr's position was becoming difficult. He, however, did not seem perturbed, and as impassive as ever, he issued calmly and clearly the orders for an obstinate defence. All the infantry was concentrated in the town and the entrenched camp. Several bridges were added to those already uniting the two banks of the Dvina. The sick and the non-combatants were sent to Old Polotsk and Ekimania, which were fortified posts on the left bank. The Marshal did not consider he had enough troops to dispute the open ground with Wittgenstein, who had received powerful reinforcements from St. Petersburg, so he did not keep more than five squadrons with him, of which he took one from each regiment of light cavalry. The rest went over to the other bank.

On the 16th of October the enemy scouts appeared before Polotsk, the aspect of which had greatly changed, partly because of the huge, newly established, entrenched camp and partly because of the numerous fortifications which covered the open country. The biggest and strongest of these was a redoubt called the Bavarian. The unhappy remnant of General de Wrède's force asked if they might defend this redoubt, which they did with much courage.

The fighting began on the 17th and went on all day without Marshal Saint-Cyr being forced out of his position. This angered General Wittgenstein, who attributed the hold-up to his officers not having distinguished between the stronger and weaker of our defence works, and wishing to inspect them himself, he boldly approached them. This devotion to duty nearly cost him his life, for Major Curély, one of the finest officers in the army, having spotted the General, dashed forward leading a squadron of the 20th Chasseurs, who sabred some of the escort while he, forcing his way to General Wittgenstein, put the point of his sword to his throat and forced him to surrender.

Having effected the capture of the enemy commander, Major Curély should have retired swiftly, between two redoubts, and taken his prisoner into the entrenched camp; but the Major was too keen, and seeing that the General's escort was about to attempt his rescue, he thought it would be more creditable if he could keep his prisoner in spite of all their efforts. Wittgenstein then found himself in the middle of a group fighting for the possession of his person. In the course of the struggle Curély's horse was killed, several of our Chasseurs dismounted in order to pick up their leader, and in the confusion this created Wittgenstein made off at the gallop, calling for his men to follow.

When this event became generally known throughout the army, it gave rise to much debate. Some maintained that Major Curély should have killed Wittgenstein as soon as his escort returned to fight for his rescue, others thought that having accepted his surrender, Curély was not entitled to do so. Others again, thought that, having once surrendered, Wittgenstein should not have tried to escape. Whatever the rights or wrongs of these arguments may be, when Curély was presented to the Emperor during the crossing of the Beresina, where General Wittgenstein caused us many losses, Napoleon said to him, "This would probably not have happened if you had used your right to kill Wittgenstein at Polotsk, when the Russians were trying to take him from you." In spite of this reproach, merited or not, Curély became a colonel shortly after, and a general in 1814.

To return now to Polotsk where the enemy, repelled on the 17th, returned to the attack on the 18th in so much greater numbers that, after suffering very heavy losses, Wittgenstein's men captured the entrenched camp. Saint-Cyr, at the head of Legrand's and Maison's divisions drove them out at bayonet point. Seven times the Russians returned to the attack, and seven times the French and the Croats drove them off, to remain finally in control of all their positions.

Although now wounded, Saint-Cyr continued to direct his troops. His efforts were crowned with success, for the enemy left the field and retired into the nearby forest. 50,000 Russians had been defeated by 15,000 of our men. There was rejoicing in the French camp, but on the morning of the 19th we heard that General Steinghel with 14,000 Russians had just crossed the Dvina above Disna and was moving up the left bank to get behind Polotsk, seize the bridges and trap Saint-Cyr's force between his own and Wittgenstein's. Indeed it was not long before Steinghel's advance-guard appeared, heading for Ekimania, where there were the division of Cuirassiers and the regiments of Light Cavalry from each of which the Marshal had retained only one squadron at Polotsk.

At once we were all on horseback and we drove off the enemy who would in the end have gained the upper hand, for they were being strongly reinforced, while we had no infantry support until Saint-Cyr sent us three regiments taken from the divisions who were protecting Polotsk. However at this point Steinghel, who had only to make a little effort to reach the bridges, stopped short, while on the other side of the river Wittgenstein did the same. It seemed that the two Russian generals, after combining to draw up an excellent plan of attack, were unwilling to put it into operation. Each one leaving it to the other to overcome the French.

The French position was now highly critical, for on the right bank they were pressed back by an army three time their strength towards a town built entirely of wood and a sizeable river, with no means of retreat except the bridges which were threatened by Steinghel's troops on the left bank.

All the generals urged Saint-Cyr to order the evacuation of Polotsk, but he wanted to wait for nightfall, because he felt sure that the 50,000 Russians who faced him were waiting only for his first backward move to throw themselves on his weakened army and create a state of disorder in the ranks. So he stayed where he was and took advantage of the extraordinary inactivity of the enemy generals to wait for the onset of the dark, which was hastened, luckily, by a thick fog which prevented the three armies from seeing one another. The Marshal seized this favourable opportunity to effect his withdrawal.

The large number of guns and some cavalry squadrons who had remained on the right bank, had already crossed the bridges in silence, and the infantry were about to follow, their movement invisible to the enemy, when the men of Legrand's division, unwilling to leave their huts for the benefit of the Russians, set them on fire. The two other divisions, believing that this was an agreed signal, did the same and in an instant the whole line was aflame. This great conflagration having alerted the Russians to our retreat, all their guns opened up. Their mortars set fire to the suburbs and the town itself, toward which their columns charged. However, the French, mainly Maison's division, disputed every foot of ground, for the fires lit the place as if it were day.

Polotsk was burned to the ground. The losses on both sides were considerable. Nevertheless our retreat was carried out in an orderly fashion. We took with us those of our wounded whom it was possible to carry; the rest, together with a great many Russians, perished in the flames.

It seemed that there was a complete lack of co-operation between the leaders of the two enemy armies, for during this night of fighting Steinghel stayed peacefully in his camp, and made no more effort to support Wittgenstein than the latter had made to support him on the previous day. It was only when Saint-Cyr, after evacuating the place, had put himself beyond the reach of Wittgenstein by burning the bridges, that Steinghel, on the morning of the 20th, deployed his troops to attack us; but the French force was now united on the left bank, and Saint-Cyr mounted an assault against Steinghel, who was overcome with the loss of more than 2000 men killed or captured.

In the course of these fierce engagements, over four days and a night, the Russians had six generals and 10,000 men killed or wounded, while the losses of the French and their allies did not amount to more than 5,000, a huge difference which can be attributed to the superior firepower of our troops, particularly the artillery. The advantage which we had in respect of numbers was in part compensated for by the fact that the wounds which Marshal Saint-Cyr had suffered would deprive the army of a leader in whom it had entire confidence. It was necessary to replace him. The Comte de Wrède claimed that his position as commander in chief of the Bavarian Corps entitled him to command the French divisional generals, but they refused to obey a foreigner, so Saint-Cyr, although in much pain, agreed to remain in control of the two army corps and ordered a retreat towards Oula, in order to reach Smoliany and thus protect on one side the road from Orscha to Borisoff, by which the Emperor was returning from Moscow.

This retreat was so well organised that Wittgenstein and Steinghel who, after repairing the bridges across the Dvina, were following our trail with 50,000 men, did not dare to attack us, although we had no more than 12,000 combatants; and they advanced only fifteen leagues in eight days. As for the Comte de Wrède, his injured pride led him to refuse to accept instructions, so he marched off on his own with the thousand Bavarians which he had left and a brigade of French cavalry which he had acquired by subterfuge, having told General Corbineau that he had received orders to take it, which was not the case. His presumption was soon punished: he was attacked and defeated by a Russian division. He then retired without authorisation to Wilna, from where he reached the Nieman. The Corbineau brigade refused to go with him and returned to join the French army, for whom its return was a piece of good fortune, as you will see when we come to the crossing of the Beresena.

Ordered by the Emperor, Marshal Victor, Duc de Bellune, at the head of the 9th Army Corps consisting of 25,000 men, half of whom came from the Confederation of the Rhine, hurried from Smolensk to join Saint-Cyr for the purpose of driving Wittgenstein back across the Dvina. This project would have certainly been carried out if Saint-Cyr had been in overall command; but Victor was the more senior of the two marshals and Saint-Cyr was unwilling to serve under his orders, so the evening before their union which took place at Smoliany on the 31st of October, he declared that he could no longer continue the campaign and handing over the command to General Legrand, he set off to return to France. The departure of Saint-Cyr was regretted by the troops who, although they disliked him personally, gave him credit for his courage and his outstanding military talent. Saint-Cyr could have been a first class army commander if he had been less egoistic and if he had taken the trouble to gain the affection of officers and men by caring for their welfare. No man, however, is perfect.

Marshal Victor had no sooner gathered 9th and 2nd Corps under his command than chance offered him the opportunity of achieving a major victory. Wittgenstein, who was unaware of this union, relying on his superiority in numbers, had decided to attack us at a place where his line of retreat would be through some narrow defiles. It would only have required a combined effort from the two corps to destroy him, for our troops were now as numerous as his, were inspired by a better spirit and were keen for action; but Victor, doubtful perhaps of success on terrain which he was seeing for the first time, retreated during the night, and having reached Sienno he put the two units into cantonment in the district. The Russians also withdrew leaving only some Cossacks to keep an eye on us. This state of affairs which lasted for the first fortnight of November did the troops much good, for they lived well as the country offered many resources.

One day, Marshal Victor having been told that there was a considerable enemy force in the area of a certain village, ordered General Castex to send one of his units to reconnoitre the place. It was for me to go. We left at dusk and reached the village without any difficulty. It was situated in a hollow, in the middle of a huge dried marshland and was entirely peaceful, the inhabitants whom I interrogated with the aid of Lorentz said that they had not seen a Russian soldier in the past month, so I prepared to return to my base. However our return was not as trouble-free as our journey there had been.

Although there was no mist, the night was extremely dark and I was afraid of leading the regiment astray on the many embankments of the marsh, which I had to cross once more; so I took as a guide one of the villagers who seemed to me to be the least stupid. My column had been going along in good order for half an hour, when suddenly I saw camp fires on the slopes overlooking the marsh. I halted the column and sent two sous-officiers to have a look. They reported that there was a large force barring our advance and another in our rear. I could now see fires between me and the village which I had just left and it appeared that I had landed, without knowing it, in the middle of an army corps which was making ready to bivouac for the night. The number of fires grew, and I estimated that there was a force of about 50,000 men present and I was in the middle of it, with 700 troopers. The odds were too great, and there seemed only one thing to do, and that was to gallop along the main embankment, on which we were, and taking the enemy by surprise, cut a path for ourselves with our sabres. Once free from the light of the fires, the darkness would prevent the enemy from following us. I made sure that all my troops knew what I proposed to do, and I have to admit that I was very uneasy, for the enemy infantry could take up their arms at the first cry of warning, and cause us many casualties.

I was in this state of anxiety when the peasant who was our guide burst into loud laughter, seconded by Lorentz. I asked them what they were about, but they did not know enough French to explain fully. Eventually, however, we understood that these were not camp fires but marsh fires, or will-of-the-wisp; something none of us had ever seen before; and so, relieved of one of the nastiest frights I have ever had, I returned to my camp.

Chapter 16
Colonel Marbot, 23rd Chasseurs á Cheval

After several days I was given a new mission, in which we would face not marsh fires but the muskets of the Russian dragoons. It happened that General Castex had gone to visit Marshal Victor, and the 24th was out on patrol, so that my regiment was alone in the camp when there arrived two peasants, one of whom I recognised as Captain Bourgoing, Oudinot's aide-de-camp.

The Marshal, who had gone to Wilna after he had been wounded at Polotsk on the 18th of August, having heard that Saint-Cyr had been wounded in his turn on the 18th of October, and had left the army, decided to rejoin 2nd Corps and take up its command.

Oudinot knew that his troops were somewhere in the region of Sienno and was heading for that town when, on arriving at Rasna, he was warned by a Polish priest that a body of Russian Dragoons and some Cossacks was roaming the area. The Marshal knew that there was a French cavalry unit at Zapolé, so he wrote to the commander of this unit to request a strong escort, and sent the letter by Captain Bourgoing, who for additional safety disguised himself as a peasant. It was as well that he did so, for he had scarcely covered a league when he encountered a large detachment of enemy cavalry who, thinking that he was a local inhabitant, took no notice of him. Soon after this, Captain Bourgoing heard the sound of gunfire, and increased his pace towards Zapolé.

As soon as I heard of the serious position in which the Marshal found himself, I left with my regiment at the trot to bring him help. It was a good thing that we arrived when we did, for although the Marshal, joined by his aides-de-camp and some dozen French soldiers, was barricaded in a stone house, he was on the point of being captured by the Dragoons when we arrived. When they saw us, the enemy mounted their horses and fled. My troopers went after them and managed to kill about twenty of them and take some prisoners. I had two men wounded. The marshal, glad to have escaped from the Russians, expressed his thanks, and I escorted him back to the French cantonments where he was out of danger.

At this period in time, it seemed that none of the marshals was prepared to recognise the right of seniority amongst themselves, for not one of them was willing to serve under the orders of his comrade, no matter how serious the situation. So as soon as Oudinot took command of the 2nd Corps, Victor, rather than remaining under his authority to join in combating Wittgenstein, took himself off with his 25,000 men to Kokhanov. Marshal Oudinot, left on his own, marched his men for several days round various parts of the province before setting up his headquarters at Tschereia, with his advance-guard at Loucoulm. It was here, during a minor action involving Castex's brigade that I received my promotion to colonel. If you recall that I had suffered, in the rank of major, a wound at Znaim in Moravia, two at Miranda de Corvo in Portugal, one at Jakoubowo, that I had fought in four campaigns in the same rank and that finally I had been in command of a regiment since the French entry into Russia, you may think that I had earned my new epaulets. I was grateful to the Emperor when I learned that he intended to keep me with the 23rd Chasseurs for whom I had great affection, and where I was liked and valued. In fact this decision was welcomed by all ranks, and the troops whom I had so often led into battle came, both officers and men, to tell me of their satisfaction at my remaining their commander. The good General Castex, who had always treated me as a brother, welcomed me in front of the regiment, and even the Colonel of the 24th, with whom I had few dealings, came to congratulate me with all his officers, whose respect I had acquired.

However, the situation of the French army grew worse by the day. General Schwartzenberg, the Austrian commander-in-chief whom Napoleon had placed on the right wing of his army, had, by an act of low treachery, allowed the troops belonging to Admiral Tchitchakoff to pass, and they had seized control of Minsk, from where they threatened our rear. The Emperor must now have much regretted that he had given the command of Lithuania to the Dutchman Hogendorf, his aide-de-camp who, having never been in action did not know what to do to save Minsk, where he could have easily have combined the 30,000 men of the Durette, Loison and Dombrowski divisions which had been placed at his disposal. The fall of Minsk, although a serious matter, was one to which the Emperor attached little importance, for he relied on crossing the Beresina at Borisoff, where there was a bridge, protected by a fort in good condition and manned by a Polish regiment. The Emperor was so confident about this that, in order to speed the march of his army he burned all his bridging equipment at Orscha. This was a disastrous mistake, for these pontoons would have assured us a quick crossing of the Beresina which, in the event, we had to effect at the cost of so much blood.

Despite his confidence in relation to the crossing, Napoleon, when he heard of the Russian occupation of Minsk, ordered Oudinot to proceed by forced marches to Borisoff; but we arrived there too late, because General Bronikovski who was in command of the fort, seeing himself surrounded by a numerous enemy, thought it would be a praiseworthy act to save his garrison. So instead of putting up a determined resistance, which would have given Oudinot the time to come to his help, he abandoned the fort, crossed the bridge to the left bank with all his men, and set out for Orscha to join Oudinot's corps, which he met on the road. The Marshal gave him a very rough reception and ordered him to return with us to Borisoff.

Not only were the town, the bridge across the Beresina and the fort which dominates it in the hands of Tchitchakoff, but the Admiral, carried away by this success and anxious to challenge the French, had marched from the town with the bulk of his army, the vanguard of which, consisting of a strong cavalry division, was led by General Lambert, the most competent of his lieutenants.

As the country was open Oudinot put ahead of his infantry the division of Cuirassiers, and ahead of them Castex's brigade of light cavalry.

It was about three leagues from Borisoff that the Russian advance-guard, going in the opposite direction to us, came up against our Cuirassiers, who having done little fighting during the campaign, had asked to be in the front line. At the sight of this fine regiment, still strong in numbers and well mounted, with their cuirasses gleaming in the sunlight, the Russian cavalry pulled up short; then, gathering their courage, they moved forward again, at which point our Cuirassiers, in a furious charge, overran them, killing or capturing about a thousand. Tchitchakoff, who had been assured that Napoleon's army was no more than a disorganised mass of men without arms, had not expected this display of vitality, and he beat a hurried retreat towards Berisoff.

It is well known that after putting in a charge, the big horses of the heavy cavalry, and above all those of the Cuirassiers, cannot continue to gallop for very long. So it was the 23rd and the 24th Chasseurs who took up the pursuit of the enemy, while the Cuirassiers followed in the second line, at a slower pace.

Tchitchakoff had not only made a mistake in attacking Oudinot but he had also brought with him all the baggage of his army, which filled more than fifteen hundred vehicles, so that the rapid retreat of the Russians caused such confusion that the two regiments of Castex's brigade often found themselves hindered by the carts which had been abandoned by the enemy. This confusion became even worse when we entered the town, where the streets were cluttered with baggage and draught horses, through which obstructions Russian soldiers, who had thrown away their arms, wove their way as they sought to rejoin their units. We managed to reach the centre of the town, but only after losing precious time, which allowed the Russians to cross the river.

Our orders were to reach the bridge and try to cross it at the same time as the fleeing Russians; but to do this one had to know where the bridge was, and none of us knew the town. My troopers brought me a Jew whom I questioned in German, but he either did not know, or pretended not to know the language, and I could get no information from him. I would have given a great deal to have had with me my Polish servant Lorentz to act as interpreter, but the coward had remained behind as soon as there was any fighting. So we had to comb the town until we eventually came to the Beresina. The river was not yet sufficiently frozen to permit one to cross on the ice, so it was necessary to use the bridge, but to take the bridge would require infantry, and our infantry was still three leagues from Borisoff. To take their place, Marshal Oudinot, who had arrived on the scene, ordered General Castex to dismount three quarters of the troopers of the two regiments, who armed with muskets could attack the bridge on foot. We left the horses in the nearby streets guarded by one or two men, and headed for the river behind General Castex who, on this perilous enterprise, wished to be at the head of his brigade.

The defeat suffered by the advance-guard had produced consternation in Tchitchakoff's army, the utmost disorder ruled on the side of the river which it occupied, where we could see a mass of fugitives disappearing into the distance; so although it had at first seemed to me that it would be extremely difficult for dismounted troopers, without bayonets, to force a passage over the bridge, and keep possession of it, I began to hope for a successful outcome, for the opposition was no more than a few musket shots. I therefore ordered that as soon as the first platoon reached the right bank it should occupy houses adjoining the bridge so that being in control of both ends we could defend it until the arrival of our infantry. Suddenly, however, the cannons of the fort thundered into action, covering the bridge with a hail of grape-shot, which forced our little group to fall back. A body of Russian sappers used this breathing space to set fire to the bridge, but as their presence prevented the gunners from firing, we took the opportunity to attack them, killing or throwing into the river the greater part of them. Our Chasseurs had already extinguished the fire when they were charged by a battalion of Russian Grenadiers, and driven at bayonet point off the bridge, which was soon set alight in many places and became a huge bonfire whose intense heat made both sides move away.

The French had now to give up hope of crossing the Beresina at this point, and their line of retreat was cut. This was for us a fatal calamity, and contributed largely to changing the face of Europe, by shaking the Emperor on his throne. Marshal Oudinot, once he saw that it was impossible to force a passage over the river at Borisoff, considered that it would be dangerous to have the town choked by the rest of his troops, so he ordered them to halt and set up camp while they were still some distance away. Castex's brigade stayed on its own in Borisoff and was forbidden to communicate with the other units, from which it was hoped to conceal for as long as possible the disastrous news of the burning of the bridge, which they did not hear about until forty-eight hours later.

Under the conventions of war, the enemy's baggage belongs to the captors. General Castex therefore authorised the troopers of my regiment and those of the 24th to help themselves to the booty contained in the 1500 wagons and carts abandoned by the Russians in their flight to the other side of the bridge. The quantity of goods was immense, but as it was a hundred times more than the brigade could carry, I called together all the men of my regiment and told them that as we were to make a long retreat, during which I would probably be unable to make the distributions of rations which I had done during all the campaign, I would advise them to provide themselves mainly with foodstuff, and think also about protection from the cold, I reminded them that an overloaded horse will not last for long, and that they should not weigh theirs down with articles of no use in war. "What is more", I told them, "I shall hold an inspection, and anything which is not food, clothing, or footwear will be rejected without exception". General Castex, to avoid all argument, had planted markers which divided the mass of vehicles into two parts, so that each regiment had its own area.

Oudinot's forces surrounded the town on three sides, the fourth was bounded by the Beresina, and there were a number of observation posts, so that our soldiers could examine the contents of the Russian carts in safety. It appeared that the officers of Tchitchakoff's army treated themselves well, for there was a profusion of hams, pastries, sausages, dried fish, smoked meat and wines of all sorts, plus an immense quantity of ships biscuits, rice, cheese, etc. Our men also took furs and strong footwear, which saved the lives of many of them. The Russian drivers had fled without taking their horses, almost all of which were of good quality. We took the best to replace those of which the troopers complained, and officers used some as pack-horses to carry the foodstuff which they had acquired.

The brigade spent another day in Borisoff, and as in spite of the precautions which had been taken, the news of the destruction of the bridge had spread throughout 2nd Corps, Marshal Oudinot, in order to allow all his troops to take advantage of the goods contained in the enemy vehicles, arranged that successive detachments from all the regiments might enter the town to take their share of the plunder. Notwithstanding the quantity of goods of all kinds taken by Oudinot's men, there remained enough for the numerous stragglers returning from Moscow on the following day.

The supreme command and indeed all officers who were able to appreciate the situation were extremely worried. We had before us the Beresina, on the opposite bank of which were gathered Tchitchakoff's forces, our flanks were threatened by Wittgenstein, Koutousoff was on our tail, and except for the debris of the Guard and Oudinot's and Victor's corps, reduced now to a few thousand combatants, the rest of the Grande Armée, recently so splendid, was composed of sick men and soldiers without weapons, whom starvation had deprived of their former energy. Everything conspired against us; for although, owing to a drop in the temperature, Ney had been able, a few days previously, to escape across the frozen Nieman, we found the Beresina unfrozen, despite the bitter cold, and we had no pontoons with which to make a bridge.

On the 25th of November, the Emperor entered Borisoff, where Marshal Oudinot awaited him with the 6000 men he had left. Napoleon, and the officers of his staff were astonished at the good order and discipline which obtained in 2nd Corps, whose bearing contrasted so markedly with that of the wretched groups of men whom they were leading back from Moscow. Our troops were certainly not so smart as they would have been in barracks, but every man had his weapons and was quite prepared to use them. The Emperor was so impressed by their turn-out that he summoned all the colonels and told them to inform their regiments of his satisfaction with the way they had conducted themselves in the many savage actions which had been fought in the province of Polotsk.

Chapter 17
The Crossing of the Beresina

You will recall that when the Bavarian General Comte de Wrède made his unauthorised departure from 2nd Corps, he took with him Corbineau's cavalry brigade, after assuring General Corbineau that he had orders to do so, which was not true. Well, this piece of trickery resulted in the saving of the Emperor and the remains of his Grande Armée.

General Corbineau, dragged unwillingly away from 2nd Corps, of which he was a part, had followed General Wrède as far as Gloubokoye, but there he had declared that he would go no further unless the Bavarian general showed him the order, which he claimed to have, instructing him to keep Corbineau with him. General Wrède was unable to do this, so Corbineau left him and headed for Dokshitsy and the headwater of the Beresina, then, going down the right bank of the river, he intended to reach Borisoff, cross the bridge and take the road to Orscha to look for Oudinot's Corps, which he thought was in the region of Bobr.

The Emperor, who had available the services of several thousand Poles belonging to the Duchy of Warsaw, has been blamed for not attaching, from the beginning of the campaign, some of them to every general or even every colonel to act as interpreters, for this would have avoided many mistakes. This was proved during the dangerous journey of several days which the Corbineau brigade had to undertake through unknown country, the language of whose inhabitants none of the Frenchmen could understand, for it so happened that among the three regiments which the General commanded was the 8th Polish Lancers, whose officers extracted from the local people all the necessary information. This was a tremendous help to Corbineau.

When he was about half a day's journey from Borisoff, some peasants told the Polish Lancers that Tchitchakoff's troops were occupying the town, information which dashed his hopes of crossing the Beresina; however these same peasants having persuaded him to turn round, led him to the village of Studianka, not far from Weselovo, four leagues above Borisoff, where there is a ford. The three regiments crossed the ford without loss and the General , going across country and avoiding some of Wittgenstein's troops who were moving towards Borisoff, eventually rejoined Oudinot on the 23rd of November at a place called Natscha.

This daring march undertaken by Corbineau was much to his credit, but more than that, it was a stroke of remarkable good fortune for the army, for the Emperor, realising the impossibility of re-building the bridge at Borisoff in the near future, resolved, after discussing the matter with Corbineau, to cross the Beresina at Studianka. Tchitchakoff, who had been told of the crossing at this point effected by Corbineau's brigade, had placed a strong division and many guns opposite Studianka, so Napoleon, to deceive him, employed a stratagem, which although very old, is almost always successful. He pretended that he was not interested in Studianka and that he intended to use one of two other fords which were below Borisoff, the most practicable of which was at the village of Oukolada. To this end he sent ostentatiously to the spot one of the still armed battalions, followed by a horde of stragglers, which the enemy might take for a full-strength division of infantry. At the tail of this column were numerous wagons, a few guns and the division of Cuirassiers. When they arrived at Oukolada these troops placed the guns in position, and did all they could to look as if they were about to build a bridge.

Told of these preparations, Tchitchakoff had no doubt that it was Napoleon's intention to cross the river at this point so as to reach the road to Minsk, which ran nearby. He therefore hurriedly sent down the right bank, to face Oukoloda, the entire garrison of Borisoff. Not only that, for some extraordinary reason, the Russian General, who had sufficient troops to protect both the upper and lower parts of the river, removed all of those which he had placed previously in a position to oppose a crossing at Studianka and sent them too down to Oukoloda. He had now abandoned the place where the Emperor intended to build a bridge, and had concentrated his force, uselessly, six leagues downstream.

In addition to the error of massing all his army below Borisoff,

Tchitchakoff made a mistake which a sergeant would not have made, and one for which his government never forgave him. The town of Zembin, which is opposite to the ford at Studianka, is built on a vast marsh, through which runs the road to Wilna. The road goes over twenty-two wooden bridges which the Russian general could have easily reduced to cinders before leaving the district, as they were surrounded by many stacks of dry reeds. If Tchitchakoff had done this, the French army would have been left without hope. It would have served it nothing to have crossed the river, for it would have been halted by the deep marshland surrounding Zembin; but the Russian general left the bridges intact, and foolishly went down the Beresina with all his men, leaving only about fifty Cossacks to keep an eye on the ford.

While the Russians, taken in by Napoleon's subterfuge, were deserting the real point of attack, Napoleon gave his orders. Oudinot and his army Corps were to go by night to Studianka, and there arrange for the building of two bridges, before crossing to the right bank and occupying the area between the town of Zembin and the river. Marshal Victor, leaving Natscha, was to form the rear-guard. He was to drive before him all the stragglers, and was to try to hold Borisoff for a few hours before going to Studianka and crossing the bridges. Those were the Emperor's orders, the execution of which in detail was frustrated by events.

On the evening of the 25th, Corbineau's brigade, whose commander knew the area well, proceeded up the left bank of the Beresina towards Studianka, followed by Castex's brigade and several battalions of light infantry; after which came the bulk of 2nd Corps. We were sorry to leave Borisoff where we had spent two happy days. We had perhaps a presentiment of the bad times which were to come.

At daybreak on the 26th of November we arrived at Studianka, where there were no signs of any preparation for defence on the opposite bank, so that, had the Emperor not burned the bridging equipment a few days previously at Orscha, the army could have crossed immediately. The river, which some have described as huge, is more or less as wide as the Rue Royale in Paris where it passes the Ministry of Marine. As for its depth, it is enough to say that the three regiments of Corbineau's brigade had forded it seventy-two hours previously without accident, and did so again on the day of which I write. Their horses never lost their footing and had to swim only at two or three places. At this time the crossing presented only a few minor inconveniences to the cavalry the artillery and the carts, one of which was that the riders and carters were wet up to their knees, which was not insupportable because, regrettably the cold was not sufficiently severe to freeze the river, which would have been better for us. The second inconvenience which arose from the lack of frost was that the marshy ground which bordered the opposite bank of the river was so muddy that the saddle-horses had difficulty in crossing it and the carts could sink in to their axles.

Esprit de corps is certainly very praiseworthy, but it should be moderated or forgotten in difficult circumstances. This did not happen at the Beresina, where the commanders of the artillery and the engineers both demanded sole responsibility for building the bridges, and as neither would give way, nothing was being done. When the Emperor arrived on the 26th, he ended this quarrel by ordering that two bridges should be built, one by the artillery and one by the engineers. Immediately beams and battens were seized from the hovels of the village and the sappers and the gunners got to work. Those gallant men showed a devotion to duty which has not been sufficiently recognised. They went naked into the freezing water and worked for six or seven hours at a stretch, although there was not a drop of "eau de vie" to offer them, and they would be sleeping in a field covered by snow. Almost all of them died later, when the severe frosts came.

While the bridges were being built and while my regiment and all the troops of 2nd Corps were waiting on the left bank for the order to cross the river, the Emperor, walking rapidly, went from regiment to regiment, speaking to the men and officers. He was accompanied by Murat. This brave and dashing officer who had so distinguished himself as the victorious French were advancing on Moscow, the proud Murat had been, so to speak, eclipsed since we had left that city, and during the retreat he had taken part in none of the fighting. One saw him following the Emperor in silence, as if he had nothing to do with what was going on in the army. He seemed to shed some of his torpor at the Beresina at the sight of the only troops who were still in good order, and who constituted the last hope of safety.

As Murat was very fond of the cavalry, and as of the many squadrons which had crossed the Nieman there remained none except those in Oudinot's corps, he urged the Emperor's footsteps in their direction.

Napoleon was delighted with the state of these units and of my regiment in particular, for it was now stronger than several of the brigades. I had more than 500 men on horseback, whereas the other colonels in the corps had scarcely 200, so I received some flattering comments from the Emperor, a great share of which was due to my officers and men.

It was at this time that I had the good fortune to be joined by Jean Dupont my brother's servant, a man of exemplary loyalty, devotion and courage. Left on his own after the capture of my brother early in the campaign, he had followed the 16th Chasseurs to Moscow and taken part in the retreat, while caring for my brother Adolphe's three horses, of which he had refused to sell a single one in spite of many offers. He reached me after five months of hunger and hardship, still carrying all my brother's effects, though he told me, with tears in his eyes, that having worn out his shoes and been reduced to walking barefoot in the snow, he had dared to take a pair of boots belonging to his master. I kept this admirable man in my service, and he was a great help to me when, some time later, I was wounded once more, in the midst of the most horrible days of the great retreat.

To return to the crossing of the Beresina. Not only did our horses cross the river without difficulty, but our "cantiniers" or sutlers, drove their carts across. This made me think that it might be possible, if one unharnessed some of the many carts which followed the army, to fix them in the river in a line, one after the other, to make a sort of causeway for the infantrymen, something which would greatly ease the flow of the mass of stragglers who the next day would be crowding round the entries to the bridges. This seemed to me to be such a good idea, that although I was wet to the waist, I recrossed the ford to offer it to the generals of the Imperial staff.

They accepted my suggestion, but made no attempt to pass it on to the Emperor. Eventually, General Lauristan, one of his aides-de-camp, said to me "I suggest that you yourself undertake the building of this footbridge, the usefulness of which you have so well explained". I replied to this wholly unacceptable proposition that I had at my disposal neither sappers nor infantrymen, nor tools, nor stakes, nor rope, and that in any case I could not leave my regiment, which being on the right bank, could be attacked at any time. I had offered him an idea which I thought was a good one, I could do no more and would now go back to my normal duties. Having said this I went back into the water and returned to the 23rd.

When the sappers and the gunners had finally completed the trestle bridges, they were crossed by the infantry and the artillery of Oudinot's corps, who, having reached the right bank, went to set up their bivouacs in a large wood, where the cavalry were ordered to join them. We could from there watch the main road from Minsk, down which Admiral Tchitchakoff had led his troops to the lower Beresina, and up which he would have to come to reach us, once he heard that we had crossed the river at Studianka.

On the evening of the 27th, the Emperor crossed the bridge with his guard and went to settle at a hamlet named Zawniski, where the cavalry were ordered to join him. The enemy had not appeared.

There has been much discussion about the disasters which occurred at the Beresina; but what no one has yet said is that the greater part of them could have been avoided if the general staff had paid more attention to their duty and had made use of the night 27th–28th to send over the bridge not only the baggage, but the thousands of stragglers who would be obstructing the passage the next day. It so happened that, after seeing my regiment well settled in their bivouac, I noticed the absence of the pack horse, which, as it carried the strong-box and the accounts of the regiment, could not be risked in the ford. I expected that its leader and the troopers of its escort had waited until the bridges were ready, but they had been so for some hours and yet these men had not arrived. Being somewhat worried about them, and the precious burden committed to their charge, I thought I would go in person and expedite their crossing, for I imagined that the bridges would be crowded. I hurried to the river where, to my great surprise, I found the bridges completely deserted. There was no one crossing them, although, by the bright moonlight, I could see not a hundred paces away, more than 50,000 stragglers or men cut off from their regiments, whom we called "rotisseurs". These men, seated calmly before huge fires, were grilling pieces of horse-flesh, little thinking that they were beside a river, the passage of which would, the next day, cost many of them their lives, whereas at present they could cross it unhindered in a few minutes, and prepare their supper on the other side. Furthermore, not one officer of the imperial household, not an aide-de-camp of the army general staff or that of a marshal was there to warn these unfortunate men and to drive them, if need be, to the bridges.

It was in this disorganised camp that I saw for the first time the soldiers returning from Moscow. It was a most distressing spectacle. All ranks were mixed together, no weapons, no military bearing! Soldiers, officers and even generals clad only in rags and having on their feet strips of leather or cloth roughly bound together with string. An immense throng in which were thrown together thousands of men of different nationalities gabbling all the languages of the European continent without any mutual understanding.

However, if one had used one of the regiments from Oudinot's corps or the Guard, which were still in good order, it would have been easy to herd this mass of men across the bridges, for, as I was returning to Zawniski, having with me only a few orderlies, I was able by persuasion and a bit of force to make several thousand of these wretched men cross to the right bank; but I had other duties to perform, and had to return to the regiment.

When I was passing by the general staff, and that of Marshal Oudinot, I reported the deserted state of the bridges and pointed out how easy it would be to bring the unarmed men across while there was no enemy opposition; all I got were evasive answers, each one claiming that it was a colleague's responsibility to see to such an operation.

On returning to the regimental bivouac, I was pleasantly surprised to see the corporal and the eight troopers who during the campaign had been in charge of our herd of cattle. These good fellows were desolate that the crowd of "rotisseurs" had set on their cattle, butchered and eaten them before their eyes without their being able to stop them. It was some consolation to the regiment that each trooper had taken from Borisoff enough food to last for twenty-five days.

My adjutant, M. Verdier, thought it his duty to go across the bridge to try to find the guardians of our accounts, but he got swallowed up in the crowd and was unable to get back. He was taken prisoner during the struggle on the next day, and I did not see him again for two years.

Chapter 18
Mélée with the Black Sea Cossacks

We now come to the most terrible event in the disastrous Russian campaign -- the crossing of the Beresina; which took place mainly on the 28th of November.

At dawn on this ill-fated day, the position of the two belligerents was as follows. On the left bank, Marshal Victor, having evacuated Borisoff during the night, had arrived at Studianka with 9th Corps, driving in front of him a mass of stragglers. He had left, to form his rear-guard, the infantry division of General Partouneaux, who had been told not to leave the town until two hours after him, and who should, in consequence, have sent out a small detachment of men, who could follow the main body and leave guides to signpost the route. He should also have sent an aide-de-camp to Studianka to reconnoitre the road and return to the division: but Partouneaux neglected all these precautions and simply marched off at the prescribed time. He came to a fork in the road, and he did not know which way to go. He must have been aware, since he had come from Borisoff, that the Beresina was on his left, and he should have concluded that to reach Studianka, at the side of this watercourse, it was the road on the left which he should take, but he did not do so, and following blindly some light infantry which had been ahead of him, he took the right hand road and landed in the middle of a large force of Wittgenstein's Russian troops.

Soon Partouneaux's division, completely surrounded, was forced, after a brave defence, to surrender. Meanwhile a simple battalion commander who was in charge of the divisional rear-guard, had the good sense to take the road to the left, by means of which he joined Marshal Victor at Studianka. The Marshal was greatly surprised to see the arrival of this battalion instead of the division of which it was the rear-guard, but his astonishment turned to dismay when he was attacked by Wittgenstein's Russians, whom he thought had been intercepted by Partouneaux. He could not then doubt that the General and all his regiments had been defeated and taken prisoner.

Fresh misfortunes awaited him, for the Russian General Koutousoff, who had been following Partouneaux from Borisoff with a strong body of troops, once he heard of his defeat, speeded up his march and came to join Wittgenstein in his attack on Marshal Victor. The Marshal, whose army corps had been reduced to 10,000 men, put up a stout resistance. His troops, even the Germans who were included among them, fought heroically though they were attacked by two armies, had their backs to the Beresina and had their movements hampered by the swarm of carts driven by undisciplined stragglers who were endeavouring, in a mob, to reach the river. Regardless of these circumstances they held off Koutousoff and Wittgenstein for the whole day.

While this confusion and fighting were going on at Studianka, the enemy, who aimed to gain control of both ends of the bridges, attacked Oudinet's Corps, which was in position before Zawniski, on the right bank. Some thirty thousand Russians, shouting loudly, advanced towards 2nd Corps, which was by now reduced to no more than eight thousand combatants. However, our men had not yet been in contact with those returning from Moscow, and had no idea of the disorder which ruled amongst them, so that their morale was excellent and Tchitchakoff was driven back before the very eyes of the Emperor, who arrived at that moment with a reserve of 3000 infantry and 1000 cavalry from the Old and the Young Guard. The Russians renewed their attack, and overran the Poles of the Legion of the Vistula. Marshal Oudinot was seriously wounded, and Napoleon sent Ney to replace him. General Condras, one of our best infantry officers, was killed. The gallant General Legrand received a dangerous wound.

The action took place in a wood of enormous pine trees. The enemy artillery could not therefore see our troops clearly, so that, although they kept up a vigourous bombardment, their cannon-balls did not hit us, but going over our heads, they broke off branches, some as thick as a man's body, which in their fall killed or injured a good number of our men and horses. As the trees were widely spaced, mounted men could move through them, although with some difficulty, despite which, Marshal Ney, on the approach of a strong Russian column, launched a charge against it with what remained of our division of Cuirassiers. This charge, carried out under such unusual conditions, was nevertheless one of the most brilliant which I have seen. Colonel Dubois, at the head of the 7th Cuirassiers, split the enemy column in two and took 2000 prisoners. The Russians, thrown into disarray, were pursued by the Light Cavalry and driven back to the village of Stakovo with great loss.

I was re-forming the ranks of my regiment, which had taken part in this engagement, when M. Alfred de Noailles, with whom I was friendly, arrived. He was returning from carrying an order from Prince Berthier, whose aide-de-camp he was; but instead of going back to the Marshal, he said as he left me, that he was going as far as the first houses of Stakovo to see what the enemy was doing. This curiosity proved fatal, for as he approached the village, he was surrounded by a group of Cossacks who knocked him off his horse and dragged him away by his collar while raining blows on him. I immediately sent a squadron to his aid, but this effort at rescue did not succeed, because a volley of fire from the houses prevented the troopers from getting into the village. Since that day nothing has been heard of M. de Noailles. It is likely that his superb furs and his uniform covered in gold braid having roused the cupidity of the Cossacks, he was murdered by these barbarians. M. de Noailles' family, knowing that I was the last person to speak to him, asked me for news about his disappearance, but I could tell them no more than what I have described. Alfred de Noailles was an excellent officer and a good friend.

This digression has diverted me from Tchitchakoff, who, after his defeat by Ney, did not dare to attack us again nor to leave the village of Stakovo for the rest of the day.

Having described briefly the position of the armies on the two banks of the Beresina, I shall tell you, in a few words what happened at the river itself during the fighting. The mass of unattached men who had had two nights and two days in which to cross the bridges, and who had, apathetically, failed to do so because they were not compelled, when Wittgenstein's cannon-balls began to fall among them, rushed in a body to get across. This huge multitude of men horses and carts piled up at the entrance to the bridges, trying to force their way on to them. Many of those who missed the entrance were pushed by the crowd into the Beresina where most of them were drowned.

To add to the disaster, one of the bridges broke under the weight of the guns and the heavy ammunition wagons which followed them. Everyone then headed for the second bridge, where the crowd was so thick that strong men were unable to withstand the pressure and a large number were stifled to death. When they saw that it was impossible to cross the overcrowded bridges, many of the cart drivers urged their horses into the river, but this method of crossing which would have been very successful if it had been carried out in an orderly manner on the two preceding days, failed in the great majority of instances, because driving their carts in a tumultuous mob, they crashed into one another and turned over. Some, however reached the opposite side, but as no one had prepared an exit by smoothing the slope of the river bank, which the general staff should have seen to, few vehicles could climb out, and many more people perished there.

During the night of 28th 29th November, the Russian cannons added to these scenes of horror by bombarding the wretched men who were trying to cross the river, and finally at about nine in the evening there was a crowning disaster, when Marshal Victor began his withdrawal, and when his divisions, in battle order, arrived at the bridge, which they could cross only by dispersing the crowds which blocked their way. We should perhaps draw a veil over these dreadful events.

At dawn on the 29th, all the vehicles remaining on the left bank were set on fire, and when finally General Éblé saw the Russians nearing the bridge, he set that on fire also. Several thousand unfortunates left at Studianka fell into the hands of Wittgenstein.

So ended the most terrible episode of the Russian campaign, an episode which would have been a great deal less terrible if we had made proper use of the time which the Russians allowed us after we had reached the Beresina. The army lost in this crossing 20 to 25,000 men.

Once this major obstacle had been crossed, the disorganised mass of men who had escaped from the disaster was still huge. They were directed to go along the road to Zembin. The Emperor and the Guard followed. Then came the remains of several regiments, and finally 2nd Corps, for whom Castex's brigade formed the last rear-guard.

I have already explained that the Zembin road, the only way left open for us, goes through an immense marsh by means of a great number of bridges which Tchitchakoff neglected to burn when he occupied this position a few days previously. We did not make the same mistake, for after the army had passed, the 24th Chasseurs and my regiment easily set them on fire by means of the stacks of dry reeds heaped up in the neighbourhood.

By ordering the burning of the bridges, the Emperor had hoped to rid himself for a long time of pursuit by the Russians, but fate was against us. The cold which at this time of year could have frozen the waters of the Beresina to give us a pathway across, had left the river running; but we had scarcely crossed over when there was sharp frost which froze it to the point where it would bear the weight of a cannon...and as it did the same to the marsh of Zembin, the burning of the bridges was of no value to us. The three Russian armies which we had left behind, could now pursue us without meeting any obstacle; but fortunately the pursuit was not very energetic, and Marshal Ney, who commanded the rear-guard and who had gathered together all the troops still capable of fighting, made frequent sallies against the enemy if they dared to approach too near.

Since Marshal Oudinot and General Legrand had been wounded, General Maison commanded 2nd Corps, which being, in spite of many losses, now numerically the strongest in the army, was always given the task of holding off the Russians. We kept them at a distance during the 30th of November and the 1st of December; but on the 2nd of December they pressed us so hard, in considerable numbers, that a serious engagement took place in which I received a wound, made even more dangerous because the temperature on that day registered 25 degrees of frost. I should perhaps limit myself to telling you that I was injured by a lance without going into further details, for they are so unpleasant that I still do not like to remember them. However, I said I would tell the story of my life, and so this is what happened at Plechtchenitsoui.

It so happened that a Dutch banker named Van Berchem, with

whom I had been a close friend at the college of Sorèze, had sent to me at the start of the campaign his only son, who having become French by the incorporation of his country into the Empire, had enlisted in the 23rd, although he was barely sixteen years old. He was a fine and intelligent young man, and I made him my secretary, so that he went everywhere fifteen paces behind me with my orderlies. That is where he was on the day in question, when 2nd Corps, for whom my regiment was acting as rear-guard while crossing a vast open plain, saw coming towards them a mass of Russian cavalry, who quickly surrounded them and attacked them on all sides. General Maison deployed his troops with such skill that our squares repelled all the charges made by the enemy regular cavalry.

The Russians then sent in a swarm of Cossacks, who came impudently to attack with their lances the French officers who stood before their troops. Seeing this, Marshal Ney ordered general Maison to chase them off, using what remained of the division of Cuirassiers and also Corbineau's and Castex's brigades. My regiment, which was still numerically strong, was confronted by a tribe of Cossacks from the Black Sea, wearing tall astrakhan hats, and much better clad and mounted than the usual run of Cossacks. We engaged them, but as it is not their custom to stand and fight in line, they turned round and made off at the gallop. However, not knowing the locality they headed for an obstacle which is very unusual in these enormous plains, a large, deep gully, which owing to the perfect flatness of the surrounding country could not be distinguished from any distance. This pulled them up short, and seeing that they could not get across with their horses, they bunched together and turned to present to us their lances.

The ground, covered by frost, was very slippery, and our over-tired horses could not gallop without falling. There was, therefore, no question of a charge, and my line advanced at a trot towards the massed enemy, who remained motionless. Our sabres could touch their lances, but as they are thirteen or fourteen feet long, we could not reach our foes, who could not retreat for fear of falling into the gulch, and could not advance without encountering our swords. We were thus face to face, regarding one another when, in less time than it takes to tell, this is what happened.

Anxious to get to grips with the enemy, I shouted to my troops to grab some of the lances with their left hands and pushing them to one sided get into the middle of this crowd of men, where our short weapons would give us an enormous advantage over their long spears. To encourage them to obey, I wanted to set an example, so dodging several lances, I managed to reach the front rank of the enemy. My warrant officers and my orderlies followed me, and soon the whole regiment. There then ensued a general mêlée; but at the moment when it started, an old white-bearded Cossack, who was in the rear rank and separated from me by some of his comrades, lent forward and thrusting his lance skillfully between the horses he drove the sharp steel into my right knee, which it pierced, passing through beneath the kneecap.

Enraged by the pain of this injury, I was pushing my way towards the man to take my revenge, when I was confronted by two handsome youths of about eighteen to twenty, wearing brilliant costumes, covered with rich embroidery, who were the sons of the chieftain of this clan. They were accompanied by an elderly man who was some sort of tutor, but who was unarmed. The younger of his two pupils did not draw his sword, but elder did and attacked me furiously. I found him so immature and lacking strength that I did no more than disarm him, and taking his arm pushed him behind me, telling Van Berchem to look after him. I had hardly done this when a double explosion rang in my ears and the collar of my cape was torn by a ball. I turned round quickly, to see the young Cossack officer holding a pair of double-barrelled pistols with which he had treacherously tried to shoot me in the back and had blown out the brains of the unfortunate Van Berchem!

In a transport of rage I hurled myself at this rash stripling, who was already aiming his second pistol at me. Seeing death in my face, he seemed momentarily paralysed. He cried out some words in French. But I killed him.

Blood calls for blood. The sight of young Van Berchem lying dead at my feet, the act I had just carried out, the excitement of battle and the pain of my wound, combined to induce a sort of frenzy. I rushed at the younger of the Cossack officers and grabbing him by the throat I had already raised my sabre when his elderly mentor, to protect his charge, laid the length of his body on my horses neck in a manner which prevented me from striking a blow and called out, "Mercy! In the name of your mother, have mercy! He has done nothing!"

On hearing this appeal, in spite of the scenes around me, I seemed to see the white hand I knew so well, laid on the young man's breast and to hear my mother's gentle voice saying,"Be merciful". I lowered my sabre and sent the youth and his guardian to the rear.

I was so disturbed by what had happened that I would have been unable to give any further orders to the regiment if the fighting had continued for any length of time, but it was soon finished. Many of the Cossacks had been killed and the remainder, abandoning their horses, slid into the depths of the ravine, where a number died in the huge snow-drift which the wind had created.

In the evening following this affair, I questioned my prisoner and his guardian. I learned that the two youngsters were the sons of a powerful chieftain, who, having lost a leg at Austerlitz, hated the French so much that being unable to fight them himself, he had sent his two sons to do so. I thought it likely that, as a prisoner, the cold and misery would be fatal to the one survivor. I took pity on him and set both him and his venerable mentor at liberty. On taking his leave of me the latter said, "When she thinks of her eldest son, the mother of my two pupils will curse you, but when she sees the return of her youngest, she will bless you and the mother in whose name you spared him".

The vigour with which the Russian troops had been repulsed in this last contact having cooled their ardour, we did not see them again for two days, which allowed us to reach Molodechno; but if the enemy allowed us a momentary truce the cold increased its attack. The temperature fell to 27 degrees of frost. Men and horses were falling at every stride, frequently not to rise again. Notwithstanding, I remained with the debris of my regiment, in the midst of which I made my nightly bivouac in the snow. There was nowhere I could go to be better off. My gallant officers and men regarded their commanding officer as a living flag. They endeavoured to preserve me and offered me all the care which our appalling situation permitted. The wound to my knee prevented me from sitting astride my horse, and I had to rest my leg on my horse's neck to keep it straight, which made me get even colder. I was in great pain but there was nothing that could be done.

The road was lined with the dead and dying, our march was slow and silent. What remained of the guard formed a little square, in which travelled the Emperor's carriage, in which was also King Murat.

On the fifth of December, after dictating his twenty-ninth bulletin, which created stupefaction throughout all of France, the Emperor left the army at Smorgoni to return to Paris. He was nearly captured at Ochmiana by some Cossacks. The Emperor's departure greatly affected the morale of the troops. Some blamed him and accused him of abandoning them. Others approved saying that it was the only way to preserve France from civil war and invasion by our so-called allies, the majority of whom were waiting only for a favourable opportunity to turn against us, but who would not dare to make a move if they heard that Napoleon had returned to France, and was organising fresh military forces.

Chapter 19
The Agonies of the Retreat in Winter

On his departure, the Emperor handed the command of the remains of the army to Murat, who in the circumstances proved une-
qual to the task, which it must be admitted was extremely difficult.
The cold paralysed the mental and physical activity of everyone; all
organisation had broken down. Marshal Victor refused to relieve
2nd Corps, who had formed the rear-guard since the Beresina, and
Marshal Ney had, unwillingly, to keep it there. Each morning a
multitude of dead were left in the bivouac where we had spent the
night. I congratulated myself on having, in September, made my
men equip themselves with sheepskin coats, a precaution which
saved the lives of many of them. The same applied to the supplies of
food which we had taken from Borisoff, for without these it would
have been necessary to dispute with the starving hordes over the
dead bodies of horses.

Writers have claimed that there were instances of cannibalism.
I have to say that there were so many dead horses lying along the
route that there was no need for anyone to resort to this. What is
more, it would be a great mistake to think that the countryside was
completely bare. There was shortage in localities close to the road,
which had been stripped by the army on its march to Moscow
but the army had passed in a torrent, without spreading out to the
sides. Since then the harvest had been gathered and the country
had recovered somewhat, so that it was only necessary to go for
one or two leagues from the road to find plenty. It is true, however,
that only a well organised detachment could do this without being
picked off by the parties of Cossacks which prowled around us.

I arranged, with some other colonels, the formation of forag-
ing parties, who came back not only with bread and a few cattle,
but with sledges loaded with salted meat, flour and oatmeal taken
from villages which had not been abandoned by the peasantry.
This proves that if the Duc de Bassano and General Hogendorp,

to whom the Emperor had confided, in June, the administration of Lithuania, had done their job properly during the long period which they spent at Wilna, they could have created large storage depots; but they were interested only in supplying the town, without bothering about the troops.

On the 6th of December, the cold increased and the temperature fell to nearly minus thirty; so that this day was even more deadly than its predecessors, particularly for troops who had not been conditioned gradually to the climate. Amongst this number was the Gratien division, consisting of 12,000 conscripts, who left Wilna on the 4th to come in front of us. The sudden transition from warm barracks to a bivouac in twenty-nine and a half degrees of frost, within forty-eight hours was fatal to nearly all of them. The rigour of the season had an even more terrible effect on the 200 Neapolitan cavalrymen who formed King Murat's bodyguard. They also came to join us after a long stay in Wilna but they all died on the first night which they spent on the snow.

The remnants of the Germans, Italians, Spaniards, Croats and other foreigners whom we had led into Russia, saved their lives by means which the French found repugnant: they deserted, went to villages adjoining the road and awaited, in the warmth of their houses, the arrival of the enemy. This often took some time, for, surprisingly, the Russian soldiers, used to spending the winter in draught-free houses, warmed by continuously burning stoves, are more susceptible to the cold than the inhabitants of other parts of Europe, and their army suffered heavy losses; which explains the slowness of the pursuit.

We did not understand why Koutousoff and his generals did no more than follow us with a weak advance-guard, instead of attacking our flanks and going to the head of our column to cut off all means of retreat, but they were unable to carry out this manoeuvre, which would have finished us, because their soldiers suffered as much from the cold as we did, many of them dying as a result. The cold was so intense that one could see a sort of steam coming from one's eyes and ears, which froze on contact with the air and fell like grains of millet onto one's chest, and one had to stop frequently to rid the horses of huge icicles which were formed by their breath freezing on the bits of their bridles.

There were, however, thousands of Cossacks, attracted by the hope of plunder, who braved the seasonal bad weather and hung around our columns, even attacking places where they saw baggage, though a few shots would drive them off. Eventually, in order to harass us without running any danger, for we had been forced to abandon our artillery, they mounted light cannons on sledges, and used them to fire on our men, until they saw an armed detachment advancing towards them, when they took to their heels. These sneak attacks did little real damage, but they became very unpleasant because of their constant repetition. Many of the sick and wounded were taken and despoiled by these raiders, some of whom had acquired an immense amount of booty, and the greed for enrichment attracted new enemies, who came from the ranks of our allies: these were the Poles.

Marshal de Saxe, the son of one of their kings, said rightly that the Poles were the biggest thieves in the world, and would rob even their own parents, so, not surprisingly, those in our ranks showed little respect for the property of their allies. On the march or in bivouac, they stole anything they saw; but as no one trusted them, petty thieving became more difficult, so they decided to operate on a grand scale. They organised themselves into bands, and at night they would don peasant headgear and slip out of the bivouac to meet at an agreed spot, then they would return to the camp shouting the Cossack war-cry of "Hourra! Hourra!" which so frightened men whose morale had been broken, that many of them fled abandoning their possessions and food. The false Cossacks, after stealing all they could would return to the camp before daylight and become once more Poles, ready to become Cossacks again on the next night.

When this form of brigandage was disclosed, several generals and colonels decided to put a stop to it. General Maison kept such a close watch in the lines of 2nd Corps, that one fine night our guards surprised a group of about fifty Poles at the moment when they were about to play their role of Cossacks. Seeing that they were surrounded these bandits had the impudence to claim that they were just having a joke, but as this was not the time nor place for laughter, General Maison had them all shot out of hand. It was some time before we saw robbers of this kind again, but they reappeared later.

On the 9th of December, we arrived at Wilna, where there were some stores; but as the Duc de Bassano and General Hogendorp had left for the Nieman, there was no one to give orders, so that there, as at Smolensk, the officials demanded proper receipts for the issue of food and clothing, which was virtually impossible because of the disorganization of almost all the regiments. We lost some precious time in this way General Maison broke into several stores and his men took some supplies, but the remainder was taken the next day by the Russians. Soldiers from other corps wandered round the town in the hope of being taken in by the inhabitants, but the people who six months previously had welcomed the French with open arms, closed their doors to us when they saw us in distress. Only the Jews would accommodate those who could pay for temporary shelter.

Admitted neither to the stores nor to private houses, the majority of famished men headed for the hospitals where, although there was not enough food for all of them, they were at least sheltered from the piercing cold. This respite was enough to decide 20,000 sick and wounded, among whom were two hundred officers and eight generals, to go no further. They had reached the end of their physical and mental resources.

Lieutenant Hernoux, one of the most vigourous and brave officers in my regiment, was so overcome by what he had been through that he lay down on the snow, refusing to move, until he died. Several soldiers, of all ranks, blew their brains out, to escape from their suffering.

During the night 9th-10th December, in thirty degrees of frost, some Cossacks came and began shooting at the gates of Wilna. Many people thought this was the entire army of Koutousoff, and in a panic they fled from the town. I regret to say that King Murat was among them. He left without giving any orders, but Marshal Ney stayed and organised the retreat as best he could. We quitted Wilna on the morning of the 10th, leaving behind not only a great number of men, but also an artillery park and a part of the army's funds.

We had scarcely left the town when the infamous Jews turned on the men whom they had taken into their houses, stripped them of their clothes and threw them out naked into the snow. Some officers of the Russian advance-guard, which was entering the town, were so indignant at this behaviour that they killed a number of them.

In the midst of this chaos Marshal Ney had urged onto the road to Kowno all those whom he could stir into movement, but he had gone no more than a league when he came to the hill of Ponari. This small slope which in other circumstances the army would have hardly noticed, now became a most serious obstacle because the ice with which it was covered made it so slippery that the draught-horses were unable to drag up it the carts and wagons, so that what remained of the army's money would have fallen into the hands of the Cossacks had not Marshal Ney ordered that the wagons should be opened and the soldiers allowed to empty the strong-boxes. This sensible measure gave rise later to assertions that the men had robbed the Imperial treasury.

Several days before our arrival at Wilna, the intense cold having killed many of our horses and made the rest unfit to ride, my troopers all went on foot. I would have very much liked to join them but my injury prevented this, so I took to a sledge to which was harnessed one of my horses. This new method of transport gave me the idea that I might by this means save the sick men, of whom I had a considerable number. There is no dwelling in Russia so poor that it does not have a sledge, and it was not long before I had a hundred or so, each one drawn by a troop horse, carrying two sick men. This method of travel seemed to General Castex to be so convenient that he authorised me to put all my men on sledges. The commander of the 24th did the same and so the remains of the brigade became a sledge-borne unit.

You may think that in doing this we deprived ourselves of any means of defence, but you would be wrong, for we were much more mobile with the sleds, which could go anywhere, and whose shafts held up the horses, than we would have been in the saddle of animals which fell down all the time.

As the road was covered with abandoned muskets, each of our Chasseurs took two of them and an ample provision of cartridges, so that if any Cossacks dared to approach, they were met by a volume of fire which quickly drove them off. Our troopers could also fight on foot if need be. In the evening we formed a big square with our sledges, in the middle of which we lit our fires. Marshal Ney and General Maison often came to spend the night here, where they were secure, since the only enemies present were the Cossacks. This was undoubtedly the first time anyone had seen a rear-guard mounted on sledges; but it was a success in the prevailing conditions.

We continued to cover the retreat until, on the 13th of December, we saw the Nieman once more, and Kowno (Kaunas), the last town in Russia. It was at this spot that five months earlier we had entered the empire of the Czars. How greatly had our circumstances changed since then! What appalling losses had we suffered!

On entering Kowno with the rear-guard, Marshal Ney found that the only garrison was a small battalion of Germans some 400 strong, whom he joined to the troops which he still had in order to defend the town for as long as possible, to give the sick and wounded the opportunity to cross into Prussia. When he heard that Ney had arrived, King Murat left for Gumbinnen.

On the 14th, Platov's Cossacks, followed by two battalions of Russian infantry, mounted on sledges together with several guns, appeared at Kovno which they attacked at a number of points; but Marshal Ney, helped by General Gérard, held them off until nightfall, when he took us across the frozen Nieman, and was the last to leave Russian territory.

We were now in Prussia, an allied country. Marshal Ney, worn out and ill, regarding the campaign as finished left us and went to Gumbinnen, where there was a gathering of all the marshals. From that moment the army had no overall commander and each regiment made its own way into Prussia. The Russians, who were at war with this country, would have been entitled to follow us there, but satisfied with having re-conquered their territory, and not sure whether they should present themselves to the Prussians as friends or enemies, they decided to await instructions from their government, and halted at the Nieman. We took advantage of their hesitation to head for the towns of old Prussia.

The Germans are usually humane; many of them had relatives or friends in the regiments which had gone with us to Moscow. We were received well enough, and I can promise you that having slept for five months in the open, I was delighted to find myself in a warm room and a comfortable bed, but this sudden transition from a glacial bivouac to long-forgotten repose made me seriously ill. Nearly all the army were affected in this way. A number of them died, including Generals Éblé and Lariboisière, the artillery commanders.

In spite of the adequate reception given to us, the Prussians remembered their defeat at Jena, and the way in which Napoleon had treated them in 1807 when he seized part of their kingdom. Secretly they hated us and would have disarmed and captured us at the first signal from their King. Already General York, who led the numerous Prussian units which the Emperor had so unwisely placed on the left wing of the Grande Armée, and who were stationed between Tilsit and Riga, had made a pact with the Russians and had sent back Marshal Macdonald, whom, from some remnant of conscience, he did not dare to arrest.

The Prussians of all classes approved of General York's treachery, and as the provinces through which the sick and disarmed French soldiers were then passing were full of Prussian troops, it is probable that the inhabitants would have sought to take hold of them had it not been that they feared for their King, who was in Berlin, in the midst of a French army commanded by Marshal Augereau. This fear and the repudiation by the King (the most honest man in his kingdom) of General York, who was tried for treason and condemned to death, prevented a general uprising against the French. We profited from this to reach the Vistula and leave the country.

My regiment crossed the river near the fortress of Graudenz at the same place at which we had crossed on our way to Russia; but this time the crossing was much more dangerous because the thaw had already begun some leagues upstream and the ice was covered by about a foot of water and one could hear frightening crackings which heralded a general break-up. Added to which, it was in the middle of a dark night that I was given the order to cross the river immediately, for the General had just been informed that the King of Prussia had left Berlin and taken refuge in Silesia, in the midst of a considerable armed force. The populace becoming restless it was feared that they would rise against us as soon as the thaw prevented us from crossing the river. We had to get across at all costs, but this was a very dangerous operation, for the Vistula is quite wide at

Graudenz, and there were many gaps in the ice which it was difficult to see by the light of the fires lit on both banks.

As there was no possibility of crossing with our sledges, we abandoned them. We led the horses and preceded by some men armed with poles to indicate the crevasses, we commenced the perilous journey. We had icy water half-way up our legs, which was not good for the sick and injured, but the physical discomfort was nothing compared to the anxiety produced by the cracking of the ice, which threatened at any moment to sink beneath our feet. The servant of one of my officers fell into a crevasse and did not reappear. We eventually reached the other side where we spent the night warming ourselves in some fishermen's huts, and the next day we witnessed a total thaw of the Vistula, which, had we delayed our crossing for a few hours, would have made us prisoners.

From the spot where we had crossed the Vistula, we made our way to the little town of Sweld, where my regiment had been in cantonment before the war, and it was there that I greeted the year 1813. The year which had ended was certainly the hardest of my life.

Chapter 20
Consolidation and Recruitment

The losses suffered by the Grande Armée during the campaign in Russia were enormous, but they have been exaggerated. I have seen a situation report, covered with notes in Napoleon's hand, which gives the figure of those who crossed the Nieman as 325,000, of whom 155,000 were French. Reports issued in February 1813 gave the number of French who returned across the Nieman as 60,000, added to this figure can be that of 30,000 prisoners returned by the Russians after the peace of 1814. Giving a total loss of French lives of 65,000.

The loss inflicted on my regiment was in proportion much smaller. At the beginning of the campaign we had 1018 men in the ranks and we received 30 reinforcements at Polotsk, so that I took into Russia 1048 troopers. Of this number I had 109 killed, 77 taken prisoner, 65 injured and 104 missing. This amounted to a loss of 355 men, so that after the return of the men whom I had sent to Warsaw, the regiment, which from the bank of the Vistula had been sent beyond the Elbe to the principality of Dessau, had in the saddle 693 men, all of whom had fought in the Russian campaign.

When he saw this figure, the Emperor, who from Paris was supervising the reorganising of his army, thought it was a mistake, and sent the report back to me with an order to produce a corrected version. When I returned the same figure once more, he ordered General Sébastiani to go and inspect my regiment and give him a nominal roll of the men present. This operation having removed all doubt, and confirmed my report, I received a few days later a letter from the Major-general couched in the most flattering terms and addressed to all officers and N.C.O.s and particularly to me, in which Prince Berthier stated that he had been directed by the Emperor to express his Majesty's satisfaction at the care we had taken of our men's lives, and his praise for the conduct of all our officers and N.C.O.s.

I had this letter read out before all the squadrons of the 23rd.

The year 1813 began very badly for France. The remains of our army, returning from Russia, had scarcely crossed the Vistula and started to reorganise, when the treachery of General York and the troops under his command forced us to retire beyond the Elbe, and shortly to abandon Berlin and all of Prussia, which rose against us, helped by the units which Napoleon had imprudently left there. The Russians speeded up their march as much as possible, and came to join the Prussians, whose King now declared war on the French Emperor.

Napoleon had in northern Germany no more than two divisions, commanded, it is true, by Augereau, but consisting mainly of conscripts. As for those French troops who had fought in Russia, once they were well fed and no longer slept on the snow, they recovered their strength, and could have been used oppose the enemy; but our cavalry were almost all without horses, very few infantrymen had kept their weapons, we had no artillery, the majority of the soldiers had no footwear and their uniform was in rags. The government had employed part of the year 1812 in making equipment of all sorts, but owing to the negligence of the war department, then in the hands of M. Lacuée Comte de Cessac, no regiment received the clothing allotted to it. The conduct of the administration in these circumstances deserves some comment.

When a regimental depot had got together, at great expense, the numerous items required by its active battalions or squadrons, the administration arranged, with forwarding agents, the transport of the supplies as far as Mainz, which was then part of the Empire. These goods were in no danger while crossing France to the bank of the Rhine; however M. de Cessac ordered a detachment of troops to escort them as far as Mainz. There they were handed over to foreign agents, who were supposed to forward them to Magdeberg, Berlin, and the Vistula, without any French supervision. This undertaking was carried out with so much bad faith and delay that the packages containing the supplies of clothing and footwear took six to eight months to go from Mainz to the Vistula, a distance they should have covered in forty days.

This had been no more than a serious inconvenience when the French armies were in peaceful occupation of Germany and Poland, but it became a calamity after the Russian campaign. More than two hundred barges laden with supplies for our regiments were ice-bound in the Bromberg canal, near Nackel, when we passed this point in January 1813, but as there was, in this immense convoy, no French agent, and as the Prussian bargees already considered us as enemies, no one told us that these vessels were loaded with goods. The next day the Prussians took possession of this huge quantity of clothing and footwear and used it to equip several of the regiments they sent against us. Although the result of this was that the increasing cold killed a large number of French soldiers, there are those who boast of our efficient administration!

The lack of order in the French army's line of march as it went through Prussia was due principally to the ineptitude of Murat, who had assumed command after the departure of the Emperor, and later to the feebleness of Prince Eugène de Beauharnais, the Viceroy of Italy.

When the time came for us to re-cross the Elbe and enter the territory of the Confederation of the Rhine, the Emperor, before removing his troops from Poland and Prussia, wanted to facilitate a return to the offensive by leaving strong garrisons in the fortresses which could assure the crossing of the Vistula, the Oder and the Elbe, such as Thorn, Stettin, Magdeberg, Danzig, Dresden, etc.

The position of France in the first months of 1813 was extremely critical, for in the south our armies in Spain had suffered some very serious reverses due to the weakening of their strength by the continual withdrawal of regiments, while the English ceaselessly sent reinforcements to Wellington, who had fought a brilliant campaign during 1812, and had captured Cuidad-Rodrigo, Badajoz and the fort of Salamanca, had won the battle of Arapiles, occupied Madrid and now threatened the Pyrenees.

In the north, the numerous battle-hardened soldiers whom Napoleon had led into Russia had nearly all died in action or of cold and starvation. The still intact Prussian army had just joined the Russians, and the Austrians were on the point of following their example. Finally, the sovereigns, and more importantly, the people of the Germanic Confederation, stirred up by the English, were wavering in their allegiance to France.

The greater part of the French nation still had the greatest confidence in Napoleon. Those who were well-informed blamed him, no doubt, for having the previous year led his army to Moscow, and in particular for having awaited the winter there, but the mass of the people, who were used to considering the Emperor as infallible and had no notion of the events of this campaign nor of the losses suffered by our men, saw only the glory which the occupation of Moscow reflected on our arms, and were more than willing to give the Emperor the means to heap victories round his eagles. Every department and every town gave patriotic gifts of horses, though the numerous levies of conscripts and money soon cooled this enthusiasm. Nevertheless the nation complied with reasonably good grace, and battalions and squadrons seemed to rise out of the ground, as if by some enchantment. It was remarkable that after all the levies of conscripts which had been made over the last twenty years, we had never recruited a finer body of men. There were several explanations for this.

To begin with, each of the eight hundred departments which then existed had, for several years, maintained a company of so-called departmental infantry, a sort of praetorian guard for the Prefects, who made a point of selecting men of a high physical standard for this duty. These men never left the principal towns of the department, where they were very well housed, fed and clad, and as they had very few duties to perform, they were able to build up their physical strength, for most of them led this life for six or seven years, during which time they were exercised regularly in the handling of arms, and in marches and manoeuvres. They lacked only the "baptism of fire" to become complete soldiers. These companies, depending on the importance of the department, were of 150 to 250 men. The Emperor sent them all to the army, where they were absorbed into the line regiments.

In the second place there was called into service a great number of conscripts from previous years, who had by protection, cunning or temporary illness obtained deferment, that is to say permission to remain at home until further orders. These older men were nearly all strong and vigourous.

These measures were legal; but what was not was the call-up of those who had already taken part in the ballot for conscription and whose names had not been drawn. These people, to whom this lottery had given the legal right to remain civilians, were nevertheless compelled to take up arms if they were less than thirty years old. This levy produced a large number of men fit to support the hardships of war. There was some objection raised to this measure, mainly in the Midi and the Vendée, but the greater part of the contingent fell into line, so great was the habit of obedience. This meekness on the part of the populace enticed the government into practices even more illegal and more dangerous withal, in that they struck at the upper class; for after forcibly enlisting men who had been exempted by lot, the same measure was applied to those who had quite legally paid for a replacement, and they were forced into the army, although some families had been financially strained and even ruined in an attempt to save their sons, for at that time replacements cost from 12 to 20,000 francs, which had to be paid in cash. There were even young men who had been replaced two or three times, but who were still forced to go, and it was not unknown for one to find himself serving in the same company as the man he had paid to be his substitute. This injustice was the result of advice given by Clarke, the Minister for War and Savary, the Minister of Police, who persuaded the Emperor that to prevent any disturbance during the war, it was necessary to remove the sons of influential families from the country and put them in the army, to serve, in some respects, as hostages. To reduce somewhat the odium felt by the upper class towards this imposition, the Emperor created, under the name of "Guards of Honour", four regiments of light cavalry, specially reserved for young gentlemen of good family. These units, which were given a brilliant Hussar's uniform, were commanded by general officers.

To these more or less legal levies, the Emperor added the men produced by an early conscription and a number of battalions formed from the seamen, sailors and gunners of the navy, all trained men, used to handling arms and bored with the monotonous life in port, keen to join their comrades in the army. There were more than thirty thousand of these seamen, and it did not take long for them to become first class infantry soldiers. Finally the Emperor, obliged to use every means to rebuild his army, of which the greater part had perished in the frozen wastes of Russia, further weakened his forces in Spain by taking not only several thousands of men to make up his guard, but several brigades and entire divisions composed of old soldiers, accustomed to hardship and danger.

For their part, the Russians and particularly the Prussians, were preparing for war. The German's natural laxity and sloth prevented them from acting quickly, for the debris of the French army which crossed the Elbe in 1812 stayed peacefully in cantonment on the left bank of the river for the first four months of 1813, without being attacked by the Russians and Prussians who were stationed on the opposite bank, and who did not feel themselves strong enough to do so, although Prussia had mobilised its landwehr, made up of all fit men, and Bernadotte, forgetting that he was born a Frenchman, had declared war on us, and had joined his Swedish troops to those belonging to the enemies of his native country.

During the period which we spent on the left bank of the Elbe, although the army received continual reinforcements, there was still very little in the way of cavalry except for some regiments, one of which was mine, so we had been allotted as cantonments several communes and the two little towns of Brenha and Landsberg, in pleasant country near Magdeberg. While we were there I had a great disappointment. The Emperor wished to speed the organisation of the new levies and thought that for this purpose the temporary presence of unit commanders at their regimental depots would be useful. So he decided that all colonels should return to France except those who had a certain number of men in their unit, the number fixed for the cavalry was four hundred, and I had more than six hundred mounted men. I was therefore forced to stay behind, when I so much longed to embrace my wife and the child which she had given me during my absence.

To the disappointment which I felt was added another vexation, the good General Castex, whom I had held in such high regard during the Russian campaign, was to leave us and join the mounted Grenadiers of the Guard. His brigade, and that of General Corbineau, who had been given the position of aide-de-camp to the Emperor, were both put in charge of General Exelmans. General Wathiez was to replace Castex, and General Maurin to replace Corbineau. These three generals had however gone to France after the Russian campaign and I was the only colonel left, so General Sébastiani, to whose corps the new division was to be attached, ordered me to take over the command, which added a great deal of work to my regimental duties, for I had to make frequent visits, in appalling weather, to the cantonments of the other three regiments. The wound to my knee, although it had healed, was still painful and I did not know if I would be able to remain on duty until the end of the winter, when after a month General Wathiez returned to take up the command of the division.

A few days later, without my having asked, I was ordered to go to France to organise the large number of recruits and horses which had been sent to my regimental depot. The depot was in the department of Jemmapes, at Mons in Belgium, which was then part of the Empire. I left immediately and travelled quickly. I realised that as I was authorised to go to France on duty, it would not be acceptable for me to request even the shortest period of leave to go to Paris, so I welcomed the offer made by Mme. Desbrières, my mother-in-law, to bring my wife and my son to Mons. After a year of separation, during which I had experienced so many dangers, it was with the greatest pleasure that I once more saw my wife, and held in my arms our little Alfred, now eight months old. This was one of the happiest days of my life. The joy which I felt on holding my little son was increased by the recollection that he very nearly became an orphan on the day of his birth.

I spent the end of April and the months of May and June at the depot, where I was extremely busy. Many recruits had been sent to the 23rd, men of good physique and from a warrior race, for they mostly came from the neighbourhood of Mons, the former province of Hainault, from where the Austrians used to draw their finest cavalrymen, at the time when they possessed the low countries. These are people who love and care well for horses, but as the horses which come from this district are a little too heavy for Chasseurs, I obtained permission to buy some in the Ardennes, from where we obtained a fair selection.

I found at the depot some good officers and N.C.O.s, several of whom had been in Russia and had gone to the depot to recover from injuries or illness, and the ministry sent me some young officers from the school of cavalry at Saint-Cyr. From this material I made up various squadrons, which, although not perfect, could mingle without difficulty with the old cavalrymen from Russia whom I had left on the banks of the Elbe, and throughout whom they would be spread on their arrival. As soon as a squadron was ready it was sent off to join the army.

Chapter 21
Lutzen & Bautzen

While I was busily engaged in rebuilding my regiment, as were many other colonels, mainly from the cavalry, who were in France for the same reason, hostilities broke out on the Elbe, which had been crossed by the allies.

The Emperor left Paris, and on the 25th of April he was at Naumbourg, in Saxony, at the head of 170,000 men, of whom only a third were French, a detachment of troops which had been sent to Germany having not yet arrived. The other two thirds of his army was formed of units from the Confederation of the Rhine, the majority of which were very reluctant to fight on his behalf. General Wittgenstein, who had gained some celebrity following our disaster at the Beresina, (although the weather did us far more harm than his manoeuvres), was in overall command of the Russian and German troops, a combined force of 300,000 men, which faced Napoleon's army on the 28th of April, in the region of Leipzig.

On the 1st of May there was a sharp engagement at Poserna, in an area where Gustavus Adolphus had died, during which Marshal Bessières was killed by a cannon-ball. The Emperor regretted his death more than did the army, which had not forgotten that it was the advice given to Napoleon by the Marshal, in the evening of the battle for Moscow, which had deterred him from achieving victory by committing his guards to the action; which had he done, it would have changed the outcome and led to the complete destruction of the Russian force.

The day after Bessières' death, while Napoleon was continuing his march towards Leipzig, he was attacked unexpectedly on the flank, by the Russo-Prussians, who had crossed the river Elster during the night. In this battle, which was given the name of the the Battle of Lutzen, there was some fierce fighting, in which the troops newly arrived from France showed the greatest courage, the

153

marine regiments being particularly notable. The enemy, soundly beaten, withdrew towards the Elbe, but the French, having almost no cavalry, were able to take few prisoners and their victory was incomplete. Nevertheless it produced a great moral effect in Europe, and above all in France, for it showed that our troops had retained their fighting qualities, and that only the frosts of Russia had overcome them in 1812.

The Emperor Alexander and the King of Prussia, after being present at Lutzen and witnessing the defeat of their armies, had gone to Dresden, from where they had to withdraw on the approach of the victorious Napoleon, who took possession of the town on the 8th of May, where he was shortly joined by his ally the King of Saxony. After a brief stay in Dresden, the French crossed the Elbe and pursued the Prusso-Russians, whose rear-guard they caught up with and defeated at Bischofswerda.

The Emperor Alexander, dissatisfied with Wittgenstein, assumed personal command of the allied armies, but having been defeated in his turn by Napoleon at Wurtchen, it seems likely that he recognised his lack of ability in this field, for he soon relinquished the position.

The Russo-Prussians having come to a halt and dug in at Bautzen, the French emperor ordered Ney to outflank their position, which resulted in a victory on the 21st of May, which lack of cavalry once more rendered incomplete though the enemy lost 18,000 men and fled in disorder.

On the 22nd, the French, in pursuit of the Russians, made contact with their rearguard at the pass of Reichenbach. What little cavalry Napoleon had was commanded by General Latour-Maubourg, a most distinguished soldier, who led it with such élan that the enemy were overwhelmed and abandoned the field after heavy losses. Those suffered by the French, though fewer, were most painful. The cavalry general, Bruyère, a fine officer, had both his legs carried away and died of this dreadful injury; but the saddest event of the day was the result of a cannon-ball which, after killing General Kirgener (brother-in-law of Marshal Lannes), mortally wounded Marshal Duroc, the grand marshal of the palace, a man liked by everyone, and Napoleon's oldest and best friend. Marshal Duroc survived for a few hours following his injury, and the Emperor who was at his side showed every sign of the deepest grief. Those who witnessed this melancholy scene, noted that the Emperor, who was forced to leave his friend by the demands of duty, parted from him in tears, having given him a rendez-vous in "A better world".

The French army now pressed on into Silesia, whose capital, Breslau (Wroclaw) it occupied on the 1st of June. The allies, and in particular the Prussians, much alarmed, realised that in spite of their boasts, they were unable, without help, to stop the French, and wanted to gain a respite in the hope that the Austrians would end their hesitation and join forces with them. They sent out envoys, given the task of soliciting an armistice which, subject to the mediation of Austria, would lead, they said, to a peace treaty. Napoleon thought that he should agree to this armistice, and so it was signed on the 4th of June, to last until the 10th of August.

While Napoleon was going from success to success, Marshal Oudinot was defeated at Luckau, and lost 1100 men. The Emperor hoped that during the armistice the numerous reinforcements from France which he was awaiting, particularly the cavalry which had been sorely missed, would make their appearance, and would take part in a new campaign if that became unavoidable. There were, however, several generals who regretted that the Emperor had not followed up his victory. They argued that if the armistice permitted us to build up our reserves, it did the same for the Russo-Prussians, who hoped that they would be joined by the Austrians, as well as by the Swedes, who were marching to their aid. The former were not yet ready, but they would have more than two months to organise and put into motion their numerous troops.

When at Mons I heard of the victories of Lutzen and Bautzen, I was sorry not to have been there, but my regrets were diminished when I found that my regiment had not been involved; it was, in fact, before Magdeburg on the road to Berlin. M.Lacour, a former aide-de-camp to General Castex had been posted as squadron commander to the 23rd, about the end of 1812, and he took command of the regiment in my absence. He was a brave man, who had acquired some education by reading, which gave him pretentions which were out of place in a military milieu; in addition to which his lack of experience as a commanding officer, resulted in the regiment suffering losses which should have been avoided, and of which I shall speak later. While I was at the depot, I gained as second squadron commander M. Pozac, a very fine officer in all respects who had been awarded a "Sabre of Honour" for his conduct at the battle of Marengo.

Towards the end of June, all the colonels who had been sent to France to organise the new forces, having completed this task, were ordered to return to their posts with the army, although hostilities would be suspended for some time. I was therefore forced to leave my family with whom I had passed so many happy days. Duty called and I had to obey.

I once more took the road to Germany, and went first to Dresden, to where the Emperor had summoned all the colonels in order to question them about the composition of the detachments they had sent to the army. There I learned something which annoyed me greatly. At the depot I had organised four superb squadrons of 150 men each. The two first of which (happily the smartest and best) had joined the regiment; the third had been taken, by Imperial decision, and sent to Hamburg to be incorporated in the 28th Chasseurs, one of the weakest regiments in the army. This was a lawful order, and I accepted it without complaint: but it was not the same when I was told that the 4th squadron which I had sent from Mons, having been noticed as it passed through Cassel, by Jérôme, the King of Westphalia, this prince had found it so desirable that he had, on his own authority, enrolled it in his Guard. I knew that the Emperor, very irritated that his brother had taken it upon himself to make off with some Imperial troops, had ordered him to send them on their way immediately, and I had hopes that I would receive them; but King Jérôme got hold of some of the Emperor's aides, who represented to his Majesty that as the King of Westphalia's Guard was composed entirely of Germans, who were not by any means to be relied upon, it was right that he should have a French squadron on whose loyalty he could count; in the second place the King had, at much expense, equipped the squadron with the brilliant uniform of Hussars of his Guard; and finally, that even without this squadron, the 23rd would still be the strongest regiment in the French cavalry. Whatever the reason, my squadron remained in the Westphalian guard, in spite of my loud protests.

I could not get over this loss, and found it supremely unjust that I should be deprived of the fruits of my trouble and labour.

I rejoined my regiment not far from the Oder in the region of Zagan, where it was in cantonment in the little town of Freistadt, as was Exelman's division, of which it was a part.

During our stay in this area, a curious incident occurred. A trooper by the name of Tantz, the only bad character in the regiment, having got thoroughly drunk, threatened an officer who had ordered him to be put in the police cell. Put before a court-martial he was found guilty, condemned to death and the sentence confirmed. Now when the guard, commanded by Warrant-officer Boivin, went to fetch Tantz to take him to the place where he was to be shot, they found him in the cell completely naked, on the pretext that it was too hot.

The warrant-officer, a brave fellow, but one whose brains did not match his courage, instead of making him dress, told him to wrap himself in a cloak. However, having arrived on the draw-bridge across the large moat which surrounded the château, Tantz threw the cloak in the faces of the guard, leapt into the moat which he swam across, and having reached the other side made off to join the enemy on the opposite bank of the Oder. We never heard anything more of him. I broke the warrant-officer for being so careless, but he soon regained his rank, by an act of bravery which I shall describe shortly.

The squadrons which I had recently added to the regiment, brought its strength up to 993 men, of whom almost 700 had fought in the Russian campaign. The newly arrived soldiers were a well-built body of men who had nearly all come from the departmental legion of Jemmapes, which made it easier to train them as cavalrymen; I incorporated the newcomers in the older squadrons. Both sides were preparing for the coming struggle but our opponents had made good use of their time, and had presented us with a powerful adversary by persuading the Austrians to take up arms against us.

The Emperor Napoleon, whom numerous victories had accustomed to taking little account of his enemies, believed himself to be once more invincible, when he saw himself in Germany at the head of 300,000 men, but he did not examine sufficiently closely the composition of the forces with which he was about to oppose the whole of Europe united against him.

The French army had received an intake of fine quality recruits, and had never looked better; but with the exception of some regiments, the majority of these new soldiers had never been in action, and the disasters of the Russian campaign had generated an uneasy feeling in the corps, the effects of which were still felt. Our superb army was better suited to being put on show to obtain terms, than to being engaged at this moment in combat. Nearly all the generals and colonels, who saw the regiments at close quarters, were of the opinion that they needed some years of peace.

If one were to pass from the French army to an examination of those of her allies, one would see nothing but apathy, ill-will and the wish for an opportunity to betray France. Everything should have led Napoleon to treat with his enemies, and to do this he should have first settled with his father-in-law, the Emperor of Austria, by giving back to him Dalmatia, Istria, the Tyrol and some of the other provinces which he had seized in 1805 and 1809. Some concessions of this sort offered to Prussia would have quietened the allies who, it seems, were willing to return to Napoleon the colonies which had been taken from France and to guarantee his occupation of all the provinces this side of the Rhine and the Alps, and also upper Italy; but in return he would have to give up Spain, Poland, Naples and Westphalia. These terms were acceptable; but at a conference with the diplomats sent to discuss them, Napoleon was rude to M. Metternich, the principal member of the delegation, and sent them away without any concessions. It is said that as he saw them leave the palace of Dresden, he remarked "We'll give them a sound thrashing". The Emperor seemed to forget that the enemy armies were almost three times the size of his own forces. He had in fact no more than 320,000 men in Germany, while the allies could put in the line almost 800,000 fighting men.

The Emperor's birthday was on the 15th of August, but he ordered that it should be celebrated in advance, because the armistice ended on the 10th. The rejoicings of Saint-Napoleon's day then took place in the cantonments. This was the last time that the French army celebrated the birthday of its Emperor! There was not much enthusiasm, for even the least perceptive of officers was aware that we were on the brink of a catastrophe, and the worries of the commanders affected the morale of their subalterns. However each one prepared to do his duty, though with little hope of success, in view of the great inferiority in numbers of our army as opposed to the innumerable troops of the enemy. Already, among our allies of the Confederation of the Rhine, the Saxon General Thielmann had deserted with his brigade to join the Prussians, after trying to hand over to them the fortress of Torgau. Among our troops there was much uneasiness and lack of confidence.

It was at this time that one heard of the return to Europe of General Moreau who, condemned to banishment after the conspiracy of Pichegru and Cadoudal, had retired to America. The hatred which Moreau had for Napoleon made him forget the duty he owed to his country. He soiled his reputation by ranging himself with the enemies of France; however, it was not long before he paid the price of this infamous conduct.

Now an immense semi-circle was formed around the French army. A body of 40,000 Russians was in Mecklemberg; Bernadotte, the Prince Royal of Sweden, occupied Berlin and the surrounding district with an army of 120,000 men, composed of Swedes, Russians and Prussians. Two great Russian and Prussian armies, 220,000 men strong, of whom 35,000 were cavalry, were in Silesia between Schweidnitz and the Oder; 40,000 Austrians were stationed at Lintz, and the main Austrian army of about 140,000 men was concentrated in Prague; finally, a short distance behind this front line of 560,000 combatants, an enormous body of reserves was ready to march.

The distribution of his troops made by Napoleon was as follows: 70,000 men were concentrated around Dahmen in Prussia, to oppose Bernadotte; Marshal Ney with 100,000 occupied part of Silesia. A corps of 70,000 was in the region of Zittau. Marshal Saint-Cyr with 16,000 men occupied the camp at Pirna and gave cover to Dresden. Finally the Imperial Guard, 20 to 25,000 strong was spread round this capital, ready to go wherever was necessary. Including the troops left in the garrisons of the forts, the troops at Napoleon's disposal were infinitely fewer than those of the enemy. This enumeration did not include the forces left in Spain and Italy.

Chapter 22
Action Against the Allies

The French Emperor had divided his army into 14 Corps, called infantry, although they each contained at least a brigade of light cavalry. The commanding generals were as follows:-

1 Corps. Gen. Vandamme. 2 Corps. Marshal Victor. 3 Corps. Marshal Ney. 4 Corps. Gen. Bertrand. 5 Corps. Gen. Lauriston. 6 Corps. Marshal Marmont. 7 Corps. Gen. Reynier. 8 Corps. Prince Poniatowski. 9 Corps. Marshal Augereau. 10 Corps. (confined in Danzig) Gen. Rapp. 11 Corps. Marshal Macdonald. 12 Corps. Marshal Oudinot. 13 Corps. Marshal Davout. 14 Corps. Marshal Saint-Cyr.

Finally came the Guard, under the direct orders of the Emperor.

The cavalry was divided into 5 Corps, commanded by 1. Gen. Latour-Mauberg, 2. Gen. Sébastiani, 3. Gen. Arrighi, 4. Gen. Kellermann. 5. Gen. Milhau. The cavalry of the Guard was commanded by general Nansouty.

The army, as a whole, approved of some of these appointments but disapproved of others. They disliked such important posts being given to Oudinot, who had made more than one mistake during the Russian campaign, to Marmont, whose rashness had lost the battle of Arpiles, to Sébastiani, who did not seem equal to the task, and finally it was regretted that for a campaign which was to decide the destiny of France, the Emperor had seen fit to try out the strategic talents of Lauriston and Bertrand. The first was a good artillery officer, and the second an excellent engineer, but neither had directed troops in the field, and so lacked the experience needed to command an Army Corps.

Napoleon, recalling that when he was named as commander-in-chief of the army of Italy, he had hitherto commanded only some battalions, which had not prevented him from successfully filling the post, probably believed that Lauriston and Bertrand could do the same thing. But men of such universal talent as Napoleon are rare, and he could not hope that his new corps commanders could follow his example. It is thus that the personal affection which he felt for these generals led him to commit once more the error which he had previously made in giving command of an army to the artilleryman Marmont.

The history of past wars shows quite clearly that to be commander-in-chief, theoretical knowledge will not suffice, and with a very, very few exceptions, it is necessary to have served in an infantry or cavalry unit and to have commanded one in the rank of colonel, to be competent to direct masses of men in the field. This is a basic training which very few men can acquire as generals or as commanders of an army. Louis XIV never confided the command of troops in the open country to Marshal de Vauban, who was, however, one of the most able men of his century, and one presumes that if he had been offered the post Vauban would have turned it down in order to concentrate on his own specialty, which was the attack and defence of fortresses. Marmont and Bertrand, lacked this modesty, and the affection which Napoleon had for them prevented him from listening to any observations on the subject.

King Murat, who had gone to Naples after the Russian campaign, rejoined the Emperor at Dresden. The coalition, that is to say the Austrians, Russians and Prussians, opened the campaign with an act of bad faith, unworthy of civilised nations. Although under the terms of the previous convention, hostilities should not have begun until the 16th of August, they attacked our outposts on the 14th, and put the greater part of their forces in motion after the defection of Jomini.

Until this time, only the two Saxon generals, Thielmann and Langueneau, had, shamefully, changed sides, but no general wearing French uniform had sullied it in such a manner. It was a Swiss, General Jomini, who was the first to do so. Jomini was a simple clerk, on a salary of 1200 francs, in the ministerial offices of the Republic of Helvetia, when, in 1800, General Ney was sent to Berne by the First Consul to discuss with the Swiss government the defence of their state, which was then our ally. The duties of the clerk Jomini, which involved dealing with confidential government documents, put him in contact with General Ney, who was thus in a position to appreciate his outstanding ability, and, yielding to his urgent requests, he arranged for him to admitted as lieutenant, and shortly captain, in the Swiss regiment which was being formed to serve with the French army. General Ney took an increasing interest in his protegé. He had him enrolled as a French officer, took him as an aide-de-camp and gave him the means to publish works which he had written on the art of war, works which, although over-valued, are not without some merit.

Thanks to protection of this kind, Jomini advanced rapidly to the rank of colonel and brigadier-general, and at the resumption of hostilities in 1813 was chief-of-staff to Marshal Ney. Seduced, however, by the extravagant promises made by the Russians, he deserted, in possession of much information about Napoleon's plans of campaign. It was fear that on hearing of this defection Napoleon would change these plans, that induced the allies to commence hostilities two days before the date agreed for the ending of the armistice. To the surprise of everyone, the Emperor Alexander rewarded the treacherous Jomini by taking him as an aide-de-camp, which is said to have outraged the delicate susceptibilities of the Austrian Emperor.

The information which Jomini was able to give the allies was a serious blow to Napoleon, for several of his units were attacked in the course of moving into position and had to give up a number of important points for lack of time to prepare their defence. However, the Emperor, whose plan it was to move into Bohemia, finding that his opponents were forewarned and on their guard against this, resolved to attack the Prussian army in Silesia, and re-engage in the offensive those troops which had been compelled to retreat before Blücher. In consequence Napoleon arrived at Löwenberg on the 20th of August, where he attacked a considerable force of the allies consisting of Prussians, Austrians and Russians. Various actions took place on the 21st, 22nd and 23rd, in the areas of Goldberg, Graditzberg and Bunzlau. The enemy lost 7000 men killed or taken prisoner, and retired behind the Katzbach.

During one of the numerous engagements which took place during these three days, Wathiez's brigade, which was pursuing the enemy, was held up by a wide and swift-flowing stream, a tributary of the Bobr. There was no way of crossing except by two wooden bridges about a quarter of a mile apart, which were covered by Russian artillery fire. The 24th Chasseurs, who had passed into the command of the gallant Colonel Schneit, having received the order to attack the left hand bridge, advanced to the assault with their usual courage, but it was a different matter when it came to the 11th (Dutch) Hussars, recently incorporated into the brigade. Ordered to take the right hand bridge, their Colonel M. Liégeard, the only Frenchman in the unit, called in vain on his troops to follow him, they were so overcome by fear that not one of them moved. As my regiment, which was in the second line, was being subjected to as much fire as the 11th Hussars, I hastened to the side of their colonel to give him some help in urging his men to attack the enemy artillery, which was the only way of stopping the cannonade, but when I saw that I would have no success, and that the cowardice of the Hollanders would result in many casualties in my regiment, I led my troops to the front of them and was about to move into the attack when I saw the bridge on the left collapse under the first section of men from the 24th, throwing them into the river where several men and horses were drowned. The Russians, during their withdrawal had prepared this trap by sawing so cunningly through the main timbers supporting the bridge that, unless one were warned, it was impossible to see what had been done.

The sight of this disaster made me fear that the same treatment had been given to the bridge towards which I was leading my men, so I called a halt in order to arrange an inspection. This was a dangerous undertaking, for not only was the bridge within range of the enemy guns, but it was also within range of the muskets of an infantry battalion. I was about to call for a volunteer for this perilous task, when warrant-officer Boivin, whom I had recently demoted for negligently allowing the Chasseur condemned to death to escape, got off his horse and coming to me said, rather than risking the life of one of his comrades, would I please permit him to carry out the mission, in order to redeem his mistake. Pleased with this courageous declaration, I said, "Go then, and you will recover your epaulets at the end of the bridge!"

Boivin went forward and, ignoring cannon-balls and bullets, he examined the superstructure of the bridge and its supports and returned to assure me that it was in order and that the regiment could cross. I thereupon reinstated him in his rank. He remounted his horse and placing himself at the head of the squadron which was about to cross the bridge he led the way towards the Russians, who did not wait for us to attack, but withdrew smartly. The month following, when the Emperor reviewed the regiment and awarded several promotions, I had Boivin made a sous-lieutenant.

Our new brigade commander, General Wathiez, was able during the these various actions to win the affection and regard of the troops. As for the divisional commander, General Exelmans, we knew only his reputation in army circles which was that of a man of outstanding bravery; but he was also regarded as being somewhat unreliable. We had proof of this in an event which occurred at the recommencement of hostilities.

At a time when the division was carrying out a withdrawal, to which my regiment was giving cover, General Exelmans, on the pretext that he was about to lay a trap for the Prussian advance guard, ordered me to place at his disposal my elite company and 25 of my best marksmen, whom he put under the command of Major Lacour; then he put these 150 men in a meadow surrounded by woodland, and after telling them not to move without his permission, he went off and completely forgot them. The enemy arrived, and seeing the detachment abandoned in this manner, they halted, fearing that it had been put there to lure them into an ambush. To reassure themselves, they sent some individual men to slip into the wood, on the right and left, and when they heard no sound of gunfire, they gradually built up the number until they had completely surrounded our troopers. It was in vain that several officers pointed out to Major Lacour that this movement was going to cut off his retreat; Lacour, brave but lacking initiative, stuck rigidly to the order he had been given, without considering that General Exelmans might have forgotten him and that it might be as well to send someone to remind him, and at least to reconnoitre the terrain over which he might be able to retreat. He had been ordered to stay there, and he would stay there even if his men were killed or taken prisoner!

While Major Lacour was carrying out his instructions in the manner of a simple sergeant rather than that of a senior officer, the division marched into the distance. General Walthiez and I, when we saw that the detachment did not return, and not knowing how to contact General Exelmans, who was galloping across country, had serious misgivings. I then asked permission from General Walthiez to return to Major Lacour, and on receiving it I left at the gallop with a squadron and arrived just in time to see a most distressing sight, particularly for a commanding officer who cared for his soldiers.

The enemy, having infiltrated both flanks and even the rear of our detachment, had mounted a frontal attack by a greatly superior force, so that some 700 to 800 Prussian lancers surrounded our 150 men, whose only way of retreat was over a wretched foot-bridge of wooden planks which joined the two steep banks of a nearby mill-stream. Our horsemen could cross here only one by one so that there was congestion, and the elite company lost several men. A number of riders then noticed a large farmyard which they thought might lead to the mill-stream, and in the hope of finding a bridge they entered it, followed by the rest of the detachment. The stream did in fact, run past the farmyard, but it there formed the mill-pool, the banks of which were lined by slippery flagstones, making access extremely difficult for horses. This gave the enemy a great advantage, and in an attempt to capture all the French who had entered this huge yard, they closed the gates.

It was at this critical moment that I appeared on the other side of the stream with the squadron which I had hurriedly brought with me. I ordered them to dismount, and while one man held four horses, the rest, armed with their carbines, ran to the footbridge, which was guarded by a squadron of Prussians. The Prussians being on horseback and having only a few pistols as firearms, were unable to reply to the sustained fire from the carbines of our Chasseurs, and were forced to remove themselves to a distance of several hundred paces, leaving behind some forty dead and wounded.

The troops who had been shut in the farmyard wanted to take advantage of this momentary respite to force the main gate and make a rush for it on horseback; but I called to them not to attempt it, because to join me they would have had to cross the footbridge, which they could do only one by one, and at this point they would offer a target to the Prussians who would undoubtedly charge and destroy them. The river banks were garnished by many trees, amongst which an infantrymen can easily withstand the attacks of cavalry, so I placed the dismounted men along the riverside and once they were in communication with the mill's yard, I passed a message to the men there to dismount also, take their carbines, and while a hundred of them held off the enemy by their fire, the remainder could slip behind this protective screen and pass the horses from hand to hand over the footbridge.

While this manoeuvre, covered by the fire from a cordon of 180 dismounted Chasseurs, was proceeding in an orderly fashion, the Prussian lancers, furious that their prey was about to escape, tried to disorganise our retreat by a vigourous attack, but their horses, caught up in the willow branches, amid the numerous holes and pools of water, could scarcely move at a walk over the muddy ground, and could never reach our foot-soldiers, whose well aimed fire, directed at close range, inflicted on them heavy losses.

The Prussian major who led this charge, forcing his way boldly into the centre of our line, killed with a pistol shot to the head, Lieutenant Bachelet, one of my good regimental officers. I greatly regretted his loss, which was, however promptly revenged by the Chasseurs of his section, for the Prussian major, hit by several bullets, fell dead beside him.

The death of their leader, the numerous casualties they had suffered, and above all the impossibility of getting at us determined the enemy to give up the enterprise and they withdrew. I was able to pick up the wounded and make my retreat without being followed. My regiment lost in this deplorable affair an officer and nine troopers killed, and thirteen who were made prisoner, among whom was Lieutenant Maréchal. The loss of these twenty-three members of the regiment I found all the more distressing because it served no useful purpose, and fell wholly on the finest soldiers in the unit, most of whom had been earmarked for decoration or promotion. I have never forgotten this undeserved setback. It resulted in our taking a poor view of General Exelmans, who got away with a reprimand from General Sébastiani and from the Emperor, who was influenced by his friendship with Murat. Old General Saint-Germain, a former commander, and almost the creator, of the 23rd Chasseurs, for whom he had retained much affection, having stated loudly that Exelmans deserved exemplary punishment, the two generals fell out and would have come to blows if the Emperor had not personally intervened. Major Lacour, whose incapacity had been largely responsible for this catastrophe, I no longer regarded with any confidence.

Chapter 23
The War of 1813

After the 21st, 22nd and 23rd of August, days on which we had defeated Field-marshal Blücher's corps, and forced him to retire behind the Katzbach, the Emperor gave orders for the follow-up on the next day. However, on hearing that the combined army of the allies, some 200,000 strong, commanded by Prince Schwartzenberg, had just emerged on the 22nd from the mountains of Bohemia and was heading for Saxony, Napoleon, taking his Guard as well as the cavalry of Latour-Maubourg and several divisions of infantry hastened by forced marches to Dresden, where Marshal Saint-Cyr had shut himself in with the troops he had hurriedly withdrawn from the camp at Pirna. On leaving Silesia the Emperor told Marshal Ney to follow him, and left Marshal Macdonald in charge of the large force which he left on the Bobr, that is to say the 3rd, 5th and 11th Infantry Corps and the 2nd cavalry, with a powerful element of artillery, making a total of 75,000 men. The control of such a great body of combatants was too much for Marshal Macdonald, as subsequent events will show.

You must have noticed that the larger the number of troops involved, the less detail I give of their movements: firstly because this could require an enormous work, which I might not be able to complete, and secondly because it could make the reading of these memoirs too wearisome. I shall therefore be even more concise in my description of events in the War of 1813, in which 600,000 to 700,000 men took part, than I have been in describing previous campaigns.

On the 25th of August, the allies having surrounded the town of Dresden, whose fortifications were not proof against a major attack, the position of Saint-Cyr became critical for he had no more than 17,000 French troops to resist the immense numbers of the enemy. The latter, badly served by their spies, were unaware of the approaching arrival of Napoleon, and full of confidence in their superior numbers, they delayed the attack until the following day. This confidence was increased when they were strengthened by two Westphalian regiments who had deserted from King Jérôme to join the Austrians.

The worried Marshal Saint-Cyr expected to be attacked on the morning of the 26th; but he was reassured as to the outcome of the struggle by the presence of the Emperor, who had arrived that very day at an early hour, at the head of the Guard and a numerous body of all arms. Soon after his arrival, the enemy, who still thought that they faced only Saint-Cyr's Corps, assaulted the town in force and captured several redoubts. The Russians and the Prussians, who now controlled the suburbs of Pirna, were attempting to break down the Freyberg gate when on the Emperor's orders it swung open to allow the emergence of a column of infantry of the Imperial Guard, the leading brigade of which was commanded by General Cambronne. It was as if the head of Medusa had appeared. The enemy recoiled horrified, their guns were captured at the double and the gunners killed on their mountings. Simultaneous sorties were made from all the gates of Dresden with the same results, and the allies, abandoning the redoubts they had taken, fled into the surrounding country where they were pursued by the cavalry to the foot of the hills. On this first day the enemy had 5000 men put out of action, and we took 3000 prisoners. The French had 2500 killed or wounded, amongst the latter there being five generals.

The next day it was the French army which took the initiative, although they had 87,000 fewer men than their adversaries. The action was at first fierce and sanguinary; but the rain which fell in torrents on the heavy soil soon covered the battle-field with pools of muddy water through which our troops moved with much difficulty on their advance towards the enemy. Nevertheless, advance they did, and the Young Guard had already driven back the enemy left, when Napoleon, having observed that Prince Schwartzenberg, the allies' commander-in-chief, had not given sufficient support to his left wing, overwhelmed it with an attack by Marshal Victor's infantry and Latour-Maubourg's cavalry.

King Murat, who was in command of this part of the line, was highly successful. He forced his way through the pass of Cotta and outflanking Klenau's corps, he separated it from the Austrian army and attacked it, sabre in hand, at the head of his Carabiniers and Cuirassiers. Klenau was unable to withstand this fearsome charge, almost all his battalions were compelled to surrender, and two other divisions of infantry suffered the same fate.

While Murat was defeating the enemy left, their right wing was routed by the Young Guard, so that after some three hours, victory was assured and the allies beat a retreat towards Bohemia.

As a result of this second day of heavy fighting, the enemy left on the field of battle 18 flags, 26 cannons and 40,000 men, of whom 20,000 were prisoners. The main losses were suffered by the Austrian infantry, who had two generals killed, three wounded and two taken prisoner.

It may be remarked that at this epoch percussion caps were virtually unknown, and the infantry of all nations still used flint-lock muskets, which it was almost impossible to fire once the priming powder became wet. Now, as it had rained without ceasing for the whole day, this contributed largely to the defeat of the enemy infantry by our cavalry, and gave rise to an extraordinary incident.

A division of Cuirassiers, commanded by General Bordesoulle, found itself facing a strong Austrian infantry division formed into a square. Bordesoulle called on the enemy general to surrender, which he refused to do. Bordesoulle then pointed out to the Austrian that not one of his men's guns was capable of being fired, to which he replied that his men could defend themselves successfully with their bayonets, as the cavalry, whose horses were in mud up to their hocks, would be unable to charge them down. "Then I will blast your square with my artillery" "But you don't have any guns, they are stuck in the mud." "If I show you my cannons, which are behind my first regiment, will you then surrender?" "I would have no alternative, for I would have no means of defence."

The French general then brought to within thirty paces of the enemy a battery of six guns, the gunners with their slow-matches in their hands prepared to fire on the square. At this sight the Austrian general and his division laid down their arms.

The rain having prevented the infantry of both armies from using their muskets and greatly slowed the movements of the cavalry, it was the artillery which, in spite of the difficulty of manoeuvering on the rain sodden ground, played a decisive rôle. In particular the French artillery, whose teams of horses Napoleon had doubled up, using animals from the headquarters wagons, which remained safely in Dresden. Our guns did great damage; it was one of their cannon-balls which struck Moreau.

It had been rumoured for some time that the once illustrious French general had returned to Europe and had joined the ranks of his country's enemies. Few people believed this, but it was confirmed in the evening following the battle of Dresden in a bizarre manner. Our advance-guard was in pursuit of the routed enemy when one of our Hussars saw, on entering the village of Notnitz, a magnificent Great Dane, which seemed to be searching in distress for its owner.

He took hold of the dog, and read on its collar the words "I belong to General Moreau." He was then told by the curé of the village that that General Moreau had undergone a double amputation in his house. A French cannon-ball had landed in the middle of the Russian general staff, it had struck one of the General's legs, and going through his horse had then struck the other. This had happened at the moment when the Austrian army had been defeated, and to prevent Moreau falling into French hands, the Emperor Alexander had arranged for him to be carried by some Grenadiers until, the pursuit having slackened, it was possible to dress his wounds and amputate both legs. The Saxon curé, who had witnessed this cruel operation, said that Moreau, who was well aware that his life was in danger, had repeatedly cursed the fate that had left him mortally wounded by a French missile, amongst the enemies of his country. He died on the 1st of September, and the Russians took away his body.

No one in the French army regretted the death of Moreau when it was known that he had taken arms against his country. A Russian envoy came to claim the dog on behalf of Colonel Rapatel, Moreau's aide-de-camp, who had stayed with him.

As Prince Schwartzenberg, the commander of the enemy troops defeated at Dresden, had given Teplice as the rallying point for the remains of his defeated armies, the Austrians retreated through the valley of Dippoldiswalde, the Russians and the Prussians on the Telnitz road and the remnants of Klenau's corps via Freiberg. Napoleon accompanied the French columns which were pursuing the vanquished enemy as far as Pirna, but just before he arrived in that town, he was taken by a sudden indisposition, due perhaps to the fact that he had spent five days constantly on horseback, exposed to incessant rain.

It is one of the misfortunes of princes that there are always to be found in their entourage people who, to demonstrate their attachment, claim to be alarmed at the slightest indisposition and exaggerate the precautions which should be taken, which is what happened on this occasion. The master-of-horse, Caulaincourt, advised the Emperor to return to Dresden, and the other great officers dared not give the much more sensible advice to continue to Pirna, which was no more than a league distant. The Young Guard was already there and the Emperor would have been able to have the rest which he required while remaining in a position to guide the movements of the troops in pursuit of the enemy, which he could not do from Dresden which was much further from the center of operations.

Napoleon then left to Marshals Mortier and Saint-Cyr the task of supporting General Vandamme, commander of 1st Corps, who, detached from the Grande Armée for three days, had defeated a Russian corps and now threatened the enemy rear. He had cut the road from Dresden to Prague and occupied Peterswalde, from where he dominated the Kulm basin and the town of Teplice, a most important point through which the allies had to make their retreat. However the return of the Emperor to Dresden nullified these successes and led to a disastrous reverse which contributed greatly to the fall of the Empire.

General Vandamme was fine and courageous officer who, already well-known from the earliest wars of the revolution, had been almost continually in command of various Corps during those of the empire; so that it was surprising that he had not yet been awarded the baton of a marshal; withheld perhaps because of his brusque and abrupt manner. His detractors said, after his defeat, that his desire to obtain this coveted honour had driven him, with no more than 20,000 men, to stand rashly in the path of 200,000 of the enemy, with the aim of barring their passage; but the truth is that having been informed by the Emperor's chief of staff that he would be supported by the armies of Marshals Saint-Cyr and Mortier, and been given a direct order to capture Teplice and so seal off the enemy's line of retreat, General Vandamme had perforce to obey.

Under the impression that he would be supported he descended boldly, on the 29th of August, towards Kulm from where, pushing enemy troops before him, he sought to reach Teplice; it is a certainty that if Mortier and Saint-Cyr had carried out the orders which they had been given, the Russian, Austrian and Prussian forces, stuck on the appalling roads, cut off from Bohemia and finding themselves attacked in front and in the rear, would have laid down their arms. Vandamme would have then been eulogised by the same people who have since blamed him.

However that may be, Vandamme arrived at Teplice on the morning of the 30th of August to be confronted by the division of Ostermann, one of the best of the Russian generals. Vandamme went confidently into the attack, as he saw, coming down from the heights of Peterwalde, and taking the route which he had taken the day previously, a body of troops which he took to be the armies of Mortier and Saint-Cyr, whose help the Emperor had promised him; but instead of friends these newcomers were two large Prussian divisions commanded by General Kleist, which, on the advice of Jomini, had passed between the corps of Mortier and Saint-Cyr without these two marshals taking any notice, such was the reluctance of Saint-Cyr to go to the aid of one of his colleagues. A reluctance which, on this occasion, spread to General Mortier. Neither of them budged and this at a time when their co-operation joined to the gallant efforts of Vandamme would have led to the total defeat of the enemy, whose columns of infantry, cavalry, artillery and baggage were piled up in disorder in the narrow passes of the high mountains which lie between Silesia and Bohemia.

In place of the help he was expecting, General Vandamme saw appear the two divisions of General Kleist, which instantly attacked him. Vandamme, continuing to fight the Russians of Ostermann in front of Teplice, turned round his rear-guard to face Kleist, whom he attacked furiously, but although the enemy was weakening, the huge reinforcements which they recieved, bringing their strength to around 100,000 men as opposed to Vandamme's remaining 15,000, made him think, in spite of his courage and tenacity, that he should retire towards the corps of Mortier and Saint-Cyr, whom he believed to be close at hand in accordance with what Prince Berthier had written to him on the Emperor's instructions.

On their arrival at the pass of Telnitz, the French found it occupied by General Kleist's divisions, who completely blocked their passage; but nevertheless, our battalions, preceded by the cavalry of General Corbineau who, in spite of the rough, mountainous terrain, had insisted on remaining the advance-guard, fell on the Prussians with such ferocity that they overcame them and broke through the pass after taking all the enemy guns, from which they took away only the horses because of the bad state of the roads.

Any soldier will be aware that such a success could be won only at the cost of many casualties, and after this savage engagement the strength of 1st Corps was greatly reduced. However, Vandamme, completely surrounded by forces ten times more numerous than his own, refused to surrender and placing himself at the head of two battalions of the 85th, the only ones left to him, he hurled himself into the midst of the enemy in a fight to the death. His horse was killed and a group of Russians seized him and made him prisoner. It is said that he was brought before the Emperor Alexander and his brother, the Grand Duke Constantin, and was rash enough to exchange insults with them. He was then taken to Wintka, on the frontier of Siberia, and did not see his country again until after the peace of 1814.

The battle of Kulm cost 1st Corps 2000 men killed and 8000 made prisoner, amongst whom was their commanding general. The 10,000 who were left managed to fight their way through the enemy lines to join Saint-Cyr and Mortier. Those two generals had gravely failed in their duty by not pursuing the beaten enemy and instead stopping - Saint-Cyr at Reinhards-Grimme and Mortier at Pirna - where they could hear the noise of the battle being fought by Vandamme.

It is surprising that from nearby Dresden Napoleon did not send one of his aides-de-camp, to make certain that Saint-Cyr and Mortier had gone to the aid of Vandamme, as he had ordered. The two marshals, having failed to carry out their orders, should have been court-martialled, but the French army, overwhelmed by the enormous number of enemies which Napoleon had raised against it, had reached such a point of exhaustion that had Napoleon wished to punish all those who failed in their duty, he would have had to dispense with the services

of almost all his marshals. He therefore did no more than reprimand Saint-Cyr and Mortier.

He had an increasing need to conceal his disasters, for it was
not only at Kulm that his troops had suffered a reverse, but at all
points of the immense line which they occupied.

Chapter 24
The Battle of Katzbach

It has been rightly said that in the last campaigns of the Empire, battles were rarely fought with any skill unless Napoleon himself was in command. It is regrettable that this great captain was not fully aware of this, and placed too much confidence in his lieutenants, of whom several were not up to the tasks which they presumed to undertake, as will be seen from some examples. Instead of ordering his corps commanders, when they were acting on their own initiative, to remain as much as possible on the defensive until he could come with a powerful reserve to crush the force facing them, the Emperor allowed them too much latitude, and as each one was jealous of his own reputation and wanted to have his personal Battle of Austerlitz, they often went ill-advisedly on the offensive and were defeated as a result.

This is what happened to Marshal Oudinot, to whom Napoleon had given a considerable army made up of the Corps of Bertrand and Reynier, in order to keep a watch on the numerous Prussian and Swedish troops stationed near Berlin under the command of Bernadotte, who had now become the Prince of Sweden. Marshal Oudinot was not as strong as his opponent and should have temporised, but the habit of advancing, the sight of the steeples of Berlin and the fear of not living up to the confidence Napoleon reposed in him, led him to push forward Bertrand's corps, which was repulsed, a setback which did not prevent Oudinot from persisting in his aim of taking Berlin. However he lost a major battle at Gross-Beeren and was forced to retire via Wittemberg, having suffered heavy losses.

A few days later, Marshal Macdonald, whom Napoleon had left on the Katzbach at the head of several army corps, thought that he also would take advantage of the liberty given him by the absence of the Emperor to attempt to win a battle, which would compensate for the bloody defeat which he had endured on the Trébia during the Italian campaign of 1799, but once more he was defeated.

Macdonald, although personally very brave, was constantly unfortunate in battle, not that he lacked ability but because, like the generals of the Austrian army, and in particular the famous Marshal Mack, he was too rigid and blinkered in his strategic movements. Before the battle he drew up a plan of action which was almost always sound, but which he should have modified according to circumstances; this, however, his stolid temperament did not permit. He was like a chess player who, when he plays against himself, can make all the right moves, but does not know what to do when a real opponent makes moves which he had not foreseen. So, on the 26th of August, the day on which the Emperor was winning a resounding victory at Dresden, Macdonald lost the battle of Katzbach.

The French army, 75,000 strong, of which my regiment was a part, was drawn up between Liegnitz and Goldberg, on the left bank of the little river named the Katzbach,(Kaczawa) which separated them from several Prussian Corps commanded by Field-Marshal Blücher. The area which we occupied was dotted with small wooded hills, which, although practicable for cavalry, made movement difficult, but, by the same token, offered much advantage to the infantry. Now, as the main body of Macdonald's troops consisted of this arm, and he had only 6000 cavalry of Sébastiani's Corps, and as the enemy had 15 to 20,000 horse on the immense plateau of Jauër,(Jawor) where the ground is almost everywhere level, it was plainly Macdonald's duty to await the Prussians in the position which he occupied. In addition to this, the Katzbach does not have a steep approach on the left bank, where we were, but on the other side it does, so that to reach the plateau of Jauër one has to climb a high hill covered with rocks and affording only a steep and stony road.

The Katzbach, which runs at the foot of this hill has no bridges except at the few villages and only some narrow fords, which become unpassable on the least rise in the water-level. This river covered the French army front, which was greatly in our favour; but Marshal Macdonald wanted to attack the Prussians, and he abandoned this highly advantageous position and put the Katzbach at his back by ordering his troops to cross it at several points. Sébastiani's cavalry, of which Exelmans' division, which included my regiment, formed a part, were instructed to cross the river by the ford at Chemochowitz.

The weather, which was already threatening in the morning, should have warned the Marshal to put off the attack to another day, or at least to act rapidly. He did neither, and wasted precious time in giving detailed orders so that it was not until two in the afternoon that his columns began to move, and no sooner had they done so than they were overtaken by a tremendous storm which swelled the Katzbach and made the ford so difficult that General Saint-Germain's Cuirassiers were unable to cross.

Having arrived on the other bank, we climbed, by a narrow gully, a very steep slope which the rain had made so slippery that the horses were falling at every step. We had to dismount and did not get back into the saddle until we had reached the great plateau which dominates the valley of the Katzbach. There we found several divisions of our infantry, which the generals had wisely placed near the clumps of trees which are scattered over this plain; for, as I have said, the enemy were far stronger than us in cavalry, and had a further advantage in that the rain had made it impossible for the infantrymen to fire their weapons.

When we had arrived on this vast open space, we were astonished to see no signs of the enemy. The complete silence that reigned there seemed to me to conceal some kind of a trap, for we were certain that on the previous night Marshal Blücher was in this position with more than 100,000 men. It was, in my view, necessary to reconnoitre the countryside thoroughly before going any further. General Sébastiani thought differently; so as soon as Rousel d'Urbal's division was formed up, he despatched them into the distance, with not only their own guns but those belonging to Exelmans' division, which we had dragged onto the plateau with so much difficulty.

As soon as Exelmans, who had been separated from his troops, rejoined us as we emerged from the gully, and saw that Sébastiani had made off with his guns, he hurried after him to reclaim them, leaving his division without orders. The two brigades of which it was composed were some five hundred paces from one another, facing the same way and formed into columns by regiment. My regiment was at the head of Wathiez's brigade and had behind it the 24th Chasseurs. The 11th Hussars were in the rear.

The plateau of Jauër is so huge that although the Roussel d'Urbal division, which had gone ahead, was made up of seven regiments of cavalry, we could scarcely see them on the horizon. A thousand paces to the right of the column of which I was a part, was one of the clumps of trees which dot the plain. If my regiment had been on its own I would certainly have had this wood searched by a platoon; but as Exelmans, who was very jealous of his authority, had established it as a rule that no one was to leave the ranks without his order, I had not dared to take the usual precautions, and for the same reason the general commanding the brigade had felt obliged to do the same. This passive obedience was nearly fatal.

I was at the head of my regiment which, as I have said, was leading the column, when I suddenly heard a great outcry behind me; this arose from an unforeseen attack by a numerous body of Prussian lancers who, emerging unexpectedly from the wood, charged the 24th Chasseurs and the 11th Hussars, whom they took on the flank and threw into the greatest disorder. The enemy charge being on the oblique, had first struck the tail of the column, then the centre and was now threatening the head. My regiment was about to be hit on the right flank. The situation was critical, for the enemy was advancing rapidly. Confident in the courage and skill of all ranks of my cavalrymen, I ordered them to form line facing right at the full gallop.

This movement, so dangerous in the presence of the enemy, was carried out with such speed and accuracy that in the blink of an eye the regiment was in line facing the Prussians who, as they approached us obliquely, exposed a flank, which our squadrons took advantage of to get among their ranks where they effected great carnage.

When they saw the success obtained by my regiment, the 24th recovered from the surprise attack which had at first disorganised them, and rallying smartly they repelled the part of the enemy line which faced them. As for the 11th Hussars, composed entirely of Hollanders whom the Emperor had believed he could turn into Frenchmen by a simple decree, their commander found it impossible to lead them into a charge. But we were able to do without the assistance of these useless soldiers, for the 23rd and the 24th were enough to rout the three Prussian regiments which had attacked us.

While our Chasseurs were pursuing them, an elderly enemy colonel who had been unhorsed, recognising my rank by my epaulets, and fearing that he might be killed by one of my men, came to take refuge beside me where, in spite of the excitement of the action, no one would dare to strike him while he was under my protection. Although he was on foot, in the clinging mud, he followed for a quarter of an hour the hurried movements of my horse, supporting himself by a hand on my knee and repeating all the time "You are my guardian angel". I was truly sorry for the old fellow, for although he was dropping with fatigue he was unwilling to leave me, so when I saw one of my men leading a captured horse, I had him lend it to the Prussian colonel , whom I sent to the rear in the charge of a trusted Sous-officier. You will see that this enemy officer was not slow in showing his gratitude.

The plateau of Jauër now became the theatre for a desperate struggle. From each of the woods there emerged a horde of Prussians, so that the plain was soon covered by them. My regiment, whose pursuit of their opponents I had been unable to slow down, found itself before long facing a brigade of enemy infantry, whose muskets put out of action by the rain, could not fire a shot at us. I tried to break the Prussian square, but our horses, bogged down in the mud to their hocks, could move only at a slow walk, and without the weight of a charge it is almost impossible for cavalry to penetrate the close-packed ranks of infantry who, calm and well led, present a hedge of bayonets. We could go close enough to the enemy to speak with them and strike their muskets with the blades of our sabres, but we could never break through their lines, something which we could have done easily if General Sébastiani had not sent our brigade artillery elsewhere.

Our situation and that of the enemy infantry was really rather ridiculous for we were eye to eye without being able to inflict the least harm, our sabres being too short to reach the enemy, whose muskets could not be fired. We remained in this state for a considerable time, until General Maurin, the commander of a neighbouring brigade, sent the 6th Regiment of Lancers to help us. Their long weapons, outreaching the bayonets of the Prussians killed many of them and allowed not only the Lancers but also the Chasseurs of the 23rd and 24th to get into the enemy square, where they did great carnage. During the fighting, one could hear the sonorous voice of Colonel Perquit shouting in a very pronounced Alsation accent "Bointez! Lanciers, Bointez!"

The victory which we had won on this part of the vast battle-field was snatched from us by the unexpected arrival of more than 20,000 of Prussian cavalry who, after overwhelming the Roussel d'Urbal division, which had been so unwisely sent alone more than a league ahead of us, now came to attack us with infinitely greater numbers.

The approach of this enormous body of enemy troops was signalled by the arrival of General Exelmans who, as I have said, had briefly left his division to go almost unaccompanied to claim back from General Sébastiani his battery of artillery, which that General had so inappropriately despatched to join that of Roussel d'Urbal. Having been unable to find General Sébastiani, he arrived close to the leading division only to witness the capture of Roussel d'Urbal's guns and also his own, and to find himself involved in the utter rout of his colleague's squadrons. We had a warning of some disaster in the sight of our General, his appearance altered by the fact that he had lost his hat and even his belt. We hastened to recall our soldiers, who were busy sabring the enemy infantry which we had just broken into, but while we were engaged in forming them up in good order we were completely overrun by the many Prussian squadrons who were pursuing the debris of d'Urbal's division.

Instantly, Sébastiani's cavalry division, consisting at the most of 5 to 6000 men was confronted by 20,000 enemy horsemen who, as well as outnumbering us, had the advantage of being almost all of them Uhlans, that is to say armed with lances, while we had only a few such squadrons. So in spite of the stiff resistance which we put up, the groups which we formed were broken up by the Prussians, who drove us steadily back to the edge of the plain and to the verge of the steep descent into the gorge, at the bottom of which ran the river Katzbach.

We were met here by two divisions of French infantry, together with which we hoped to make a stand; but the muskets of our men were so wet that they would not fire, and they had no other means of defence but a battery of six guns and their bayonets, with which they momentarily arrested the Prussian cavalry; but the Prussian generals having brought up some twenty cannons, the French guns were instantly disabled and their battalions crushed. Then, cheering loudly, the twenty thousand enemy cavalry advanced on our troops and drove them in confusion towards the Katzbach.

This river which we had crossed in the morning with so much difficulty although it was not very deep, had been transformed into a raging torrent by the pouring rain which had continued ceaselessly throughout the whole day. The water, surging between the two banks, covered almost entirely the parapet of the bridge at Chemochowitz and made it impossible to discover if the ford at that point was still passable. However it was by those two points we had crossed in the morning, and it was to them that we went. The ford proved impassable for the infantry and a number were drowned there, but the great majority were saved by the bridge.

I gathered together my regiment, as much as was possible, and having been formed into tightly packed half-platoons which could give each other mutual support, they entered the water in reasonably good order and gained the other bank with the loss of only two men. All the other cavalry units took the same route, for in spite of the confusion inseparable from such a retreat, the troopers realised that the bridge had to be left for the infantry. I must confess that the descent of the slope was one of the most critical moments in my life. The very steep hillside was slippery under our horses feet, and they stumbled at every pace over numerous outcrops of rock. In addition, the constant hail of grape-shot which was hurled from the enemy guns made our position highly precarious. I came out of this without any personal accident, thanks to the courage, determination, and skill of my excellent Turkish horse, which by walking along the edge of precipices like a cat on a roof, saved my life, not only on this occasion but on several others. I shall mention this admirable creature later.

The French infantry and cavalry who had been driven down from the Jauër plateau thought themselves safe from their enemies once they had crossed the river, but the Prussians had sent a strong column to a bridge upstream of that at Chemochowitz, where they had crossed the Katzbach, so that having arrived on the bank which we had quitted in the morning, we were astonished to be attacked by squadrons of Uhlans. However, in spite of the surprise, several regiments, among which Marshal Macdonald in his report mentioned mine, unhesitatingly attacked the enemy. Nonetheless, I do not know what would have happened without the arrival of the division of General Saint-Germain. He had remained on the left bank of the river in the morning, and having in consequence taken no part in the fighting, found himself in full readiness to come to our aid. This division composed of two regiments of carabiniers, a brigade of Cuirassiers, and with six twelve pounders, fell furiously on the enemy and drove back into the river all those who had crossed with the aim of cutting off our retreat, and as there is nothing so terrible as troops who, having suffered a setback, resume the offensive, the troopers of Exelmanns' and d'Urbal's divisions slaughtered all whom they could reach.

This counter-attack did us much good, for it halted the enemy who, for that day, did not dare to follow us across the Katzbach. However, the French army suffered an immense disaster, for Marshal Macdonald having crossed the river by all the bridges and fords which there were between Liegnitz and Goldberg, that is to say on a line of more than five leagues, now found nearly all these crossing points cut off by flooding, the French army was extended in a long line with the Prussians at their back and facing an almost uncrossable river, so that the frightful scenes which I had witnessed on the Jauër plateau were reproduced at all points of the field of battle. Everywhere the rain prevented our infantry from firing and aided the attacks of the Prussian cavalry, four times more numerous than ours. Everywhere retreat was made highly perilous by the difficulty of crossing the flooded Katzbach. Most of those who tried to swim across were drowned, Brigadier-General Sibuet being among their number. We were able to save only a few pieces of artillery.

Chapter 25
Executions & Tartars

After the unhappy affair at the Katzbach, Marshal Macdonald, in an attempt to re-unite his troops, indicated as rallying points the towns of Bunzlau, Lauban, and Gorlitz. A pitch-dark night, rutted roads and continuous torrential rain made movement slow and very difficult; and many soldiers, particularly those of our allies, went astray or lagged behind.

Napoleon's army lost at the battle of the Katzbach 13,000 men killed or drowned, 20,000 prisoners and 50 cannons. A veritable calamity. Marshal Macdonald, whose faulty tactics had led to this irreparable catastrophe, although he forfeited the confidence of the army, was able to retain his personal esteem by the frankness and loyalty with which he admitted to his mistakes; for the day following the disaster he called together all the generals and colonels, and after engaging us to do all we could to maintain order, he said that every officer and man had done his duty, and there was only one person who was responsible for the loss of the battle, and that was himself; because, in view of the rain, he should not have left a well-broken terrain to go and attack, in a vast open space, an enemy who squadrons greatly outnumbered our own, nor, during a rain-storm, have put a river at his back. This contrite admission disarmed the critics, and everyone buckled to in order to help save the army, which retreated towards the Elbe via Bautzen.

Fate now seemed to be against us; for a few days after Marshal Oudinot had lost the battle of Gross-Beeren, Macdonald that of the Katzbach and Vandamme that of Kulm, the French forces suffered another major reverse. Marshal Ney, who had succeeded Oudinot in command of the troops who were destined to march on Berlin, not having a sufficiently powerful force to accomplish this difficult task, was defeated at Jutterbach (Jüterbog) by the turncoat Bernadotte, and compelled to quit the right bank of the Elbe.

The Emperor came back to Dresden with his Guard. The various units under the command of Macdonald took up positions not far from that town, while Marshal Ney, having pushed back the Swedes to the right bank, concentrated his troops on the left bank at Dassau and Wittemberg. For almost a fortnight, between the end of September and the beginning of October, the French army remained almost motionless around Dresden. My regiment was in bivouac close to Veissig on the heights of Pilnitz, which were occupied by a division of infantry supported by the cavalry of Sébastiani and Exelmans.

Although there was no official armistice, the weariness of both sides led to a de facto suspension of hostilities, from which both parties profited to prepare for new and more terrible conflicts.

While we were in camp at Pilnitz, I received a letter from the colonel of Prussian cavalry to whom I had lent a horse after he had been captured and injured by the men of my regiment at the start of the battle of the Katzbach. This senior officer, named M. de Blankensée, who had been freed by his own troops when things turned against us, was nonetheless grateful for what I had done, and to prove it he sent me ten Chasseurs and a lieutenant belonging to my regiment who had been left wounded on the battlefield and taken prisoner. M. de Blankensée had seen that their wounds were dressed, and after caring for them for a fortnight he had obtained permission to have them led to the French outposts, with a thousand thanks to me, for having, as he assured me, saved his life. I believe he was right, but I was still touched by this expression of thanks from one of the leaders of our opponents.

During the time we were in this camp there took place a strange event which was witnessed by all the regiments. A corporal of the 4th Chasseurs, while drunk, had shown disrespect to an officer, and a Lancer of the 6th whose horse had bitten him and would not let go had struck it in the belly with some scissors which led to its death. Certainly the two men deserved to be punished, but only by proper disciplinary procedures. General Exelmans condemned them both to death on his own authority, and having ordered that the division should mount their horses, he drew them up in a huge square, one side of which was left open, where two graves were dug, to the side of which the two convicted men were led.

I had been away all night and returned to the camp in time to see these lugubrious preparations. I had no doubt that the prisoners had been tried and condemned, but I soon learned that this was not the case, and drawing near to a group formed by General Exelmans, the two brigadiers and all the regimental commanders, I heard M. Devence, Colonel of the 4th Chasseurs, and Colonel Perquit of the 6th Lancers beg General Exelmans to pardon the two culprits. General Exelmans refused to do so.

I have never been able to see an act which I consider unjust without expressing my indignation. It was perhaps wrong of me, but I addressed Colonels Devence and Perquit saying that it was an affront to their dignity that men of their regiments should be paraded through the camp as criminals when they had not had a proper trial, and I added "The Emperor has given no one the power of life or death, and has reserved for himself the right to grant pardon".

General Exelmans was sufficiently influenced by the effect produced by my outburst to announce that he would pardon the Chasseur of the 4th, but that the Lancer would be shot; that is to say he would pardon the soldier who had been disrespectful to his officer, but condemn to execution the one who had killed a horse.

In order to carry out this execution each regiment was asked to provide two N.C.O.s but as they did not carry muskets, they would have to use those belonging to other soldiers. When this order reached me, I did not reply to my regimental sergeant-major, who took my meaning; so that no one from the 23rd presented himself to take part in the execution. General Exelmans noticed this but said nothing. Eventually a shot rang out, and all those present muttered with indignation. Exelmans ordered that, as was usual, the troops would be marched past the corpse. The march began. My regiment was second in the column and I was in some doubt whether I should make it march past the unlucky victim of Exelmans' severity when a great burst of laughter was heard from the 24th Chasseurs, who were in front of me and had already arrived at the scene of the execution. I sent a warrant officer to find out the cause of this unseemly mirth in the presence of the dead, and I soon discovered that the dead man was in remarkably good health!

The truth was that all that had happened was a theatrical performance staged to scare any soldiers who were tempted to indiscipline; a performance which included shooting a man with blanks. To keep the operation secret from the rank and file, our chief had formed the firing squad of sous-officiers, to whom he had issued the blank cartridges. However, to complete the illusion it was necessary for the troops to view the body, and Exelmans had told the Lancer who was to play the part to throw himself on his face at the sound of the shots and pretend to be dead, then to leave the army the next night, dressed as a peasant and with a sum of money which he had been given for the purpose; but the soldier who was a sharp-witted Gascon, had realised perfectly well that General Exelmans was exceeding his authority, and had no more right to have him shot without trial than he had to dismiss him from the army without a proper discharge, and so he remained standing when the shots were fired and refused to leave the camp without a pass which would guarantee him from arrest by the gendarmerie.

When I learned that it was this discussion between the General and the dead man which had produced the shouts of laughter from the 24th Chasseurs at the head of the column, I thought it better that my regiment did not take part in this comedy which seemed to me to be as much contrary to discipline as the misdemeanors it was supposed to punish or prevent. I therefore turned my squadrons about, and setting off at the trot I left this unhelpful scene and, returning to the camp, I ordered them to dismount. My example was followed by all the brigadiers and regimental commanders of the division, and Exelmans was left alone with the "dead man", who set off calmly down the road to the bivouac, where he tucked into a meal with his comrades amid much more laughter.

During our stay on the plateau of Pilnitz, the enemy, and above all the Russians, received many reinforcements, the main one, led by General Benningsen was of not less than 60,000 men, and was composed of the corps of Doctoroff and Tolstoï and the reserve of Prince Labanoff. This reserve came from beyond Moscow and included in its ranks a large number of Tartars and Baskirs, armed only with bows and arrows.

I have never understood with what aim the Russian government brought from so far and at such great expense these masses of irregular cavalry, who having neither sabres nor lances nor any kind of firearm, were unable to stand up against trained soldiers, and served only to strip the countryside and starve the regular forces, which alone were capable of resisting a European enemy. Our soldiers were not in the least alarmed at the sight of these semi-barbarous Asiatics, whom they nick-named cupids, because of their bows and arrows.

Nevertheless, these newcomers, who did not yet know the French, had been so indoctrinated by their leaders, almost as ignorant as themselves, that they expected to see us take flight at their approach; and so they could not wait to attack us. From the very day of their arrival in sight of our troops they launched themselves in swarms against them, but having been everywhere repulsed by gunfire, the Baskirs left a great number of dead on the ground.

These losses far from calming their frenzy, seemed to excite them still more, for without any order and in all directions, they buzzed around us like a swarm of wasps, flying all over the place and being very hard to catch, but when our cavalry did catch them they effected a fearful massacre, our lances and sabres being immensely superior to their bows and arrows. All the same, as the attacks by these barbarians were incessant and the Russians supported them with detachments of Hussars to profit from the confusion which the Baskirs could create at various points on the line, the Emperor ordered the generals to be doubly watchful, and to make frequent visits to our advance posts.

Now both sides were preparing to renew hostilities which, as I have already said, had not been suspended by any agreement, but simply de facto. All was completely peaceful in my camp, and I had as usual taken off my coat and was preparing to shave in the open air before a little mirror nailed to a tree, when I was given a slap on the shoulder. As I was in the middle of my regiment, I turned round sharply to see who had used this familiarity with his commanding officer. I found myself facing the Emperor, who, wishing to examine some neighbouring positions without arousing the enemy, had arrived with only one aide-de-camp. As he was not accompanied by a detachment of his Guard, he was followed by squadrons chosen in equal numbers from all the regiments in the division, and having, on his orders, taken command of this escort, I spent the entire day at his side, and have nothing but praise for his kindliness.

When we were preparing to return to Pilnitz, we saw a horde of Baskirs hurrying towards us, with all the speed of their little Tartar horses. The Emperor, who had never before seen troops of this sort, stopped on a hillock and asked for the capture of some prisoners. To this end, I ordered two squadrons of my regiment to hide behind a clump of trees, while the remainder continued their march. This well-known ruse would not have deceived Cossacks, but it succeeded perfectly with the Baskirs, who have not the slightest notion of tactics. They passed close to the wood without sending anyone to inspect it, and were continuing to follow the column when they were unexpectedly attacked by our squadrons who, falling on them suddenly, killed a great number and took some thirty prisoners.

I had these brought to the Emperor, who, after examining them expressed his surprise at the spectacle of these wretched horsemen who were sent, with no other arms than bows and arrows, to fight European soldiers armed with sabres, lances, guns and pistols. These Tartar Baskirs had Chinese features and wore extravagant costumes. When we got back to the camp, my Chasseurs amused themselves by giving wine to the Baskirs who, delighted with this novel reception got drunk and expressed their joy by such extraordinary grimaces and capers that all the watchers, including Napoleon, were in fits of laughter.

On the 28th of September, after reviewing our army corps, the Emperor treated me with quite exceptional benevolence, for although he very rarely gave more than one reward at a time, he created me an officer of the Legion of Honour, a Baron, and awarded me a grant of money. He loaded favours on the regiment, saying that it was the only one of Sébastiani's corps which had maintained good order at the Katzbach, had captured some enemy guns and had driven off the Prussians whenever they met them.

The 23rd Chasseurs owed this distinction to the high praise of its conduct received by the Emperor from Marshal Macdonald who, after the debacle at the Katzbach, had sought refuge in the ranks of my regiment and had taken part in the fierce charges it made to drive the enemies back across the river.

After the review, when the troops were on the road to their camp, General Exelmans came to the front of the regiment and loudly complemented them for the recognition given by the Emperor to their courage. Then, turning to me, he embarked on a veritable, and exaggerated, eulogy of their colonel.

The French army now was concentrated in the area of Leipzig. All the enemy forces also proceeded to the town, around which their great number allowed them to form a huge circle, which contracted every day, and whose aim was obviously to hem in the French troops and cut off all means of retreat.

On the 14th of October there was a sharp encounter between the Austro-Russian advance-guard and our own; but after an indecisive result, both sides returned to their previous positions, and the action ended with one of the most ridiculous features of war, a cannonade which went on until nightfall, with no result but the loss of many men's lives.

The Emperor, after leaving at Dresden a garrison of 25,000 men commanded by Marshal Saint-Cyr, came to Leipzig, where he arrived on the morning of the 15th.

Chapter 26
The Battle of Leipzig

The exact details of the battle of Leipzig will never be known, partly because of the extent and complexity of the area over which fighting continued for several days, and partly because of the immense number of troops of different nations which took part in this memorable encounter. It is principally the documents relating to the French army which are missing, because several commanders of army corps and divisions, and some members of the general staff, having been killed or left in enemy hands, most of their reports have never been finished, and those which have been, reflect the inevitable haste and disorder surrounding their compilation. At Leipzig I was the colonel of a regiment, a part of a division whose movements I was bound to follow, so it was not possible for me to know what was happening elsewhere in the manner which it had been in previous campaigns, when as an aide-de-camp to various marshals, I was able to acquire a general view of operations while carrying orders to different parts of the battlefield. I must therefore, more than ever, limit my description to what is absolutely necessary for an understanding of the main events of the battle of Leipzig, the outcome of which had such a profound influence on the destinies of the Emperor, of France and of Europe.

The iron circle within which the allies were preparing to enclose the French army, had not yet completely surrounded Leipzig, when the King of Wurtemburg, a man of violence but honourable, thought it his duty to warn Napoleon that the whole of Germany, incited by the English, was about to rise against him, and that he had barely sufficient time to retire with the French troops behind the river Main, before all of the German Confederation abandoned him to join his enemies. He added that he himself, King of Wurtemburg, could not avoid doing likewise, as he was forced to accede to the demands of his subjects, who clamoured for him to go with the torrent of German public opinion and, breaking with Napoleon, range himself with the enemies of France.

The Emperor, shaken by this advice from the most able and most faithful of his allies, is said to have considered retiring towards the mountains of Thuringia and Hesse, to get behind the river Saale and there wait for the allies to attack him, where they would be at a disadvantage on the difficult terrain, heavily wooded and full of narrow passes.

This plan could have saved Napoleon; but it had to be executed quickly, before the enemy armies were completely united and near enough to attack us during the retreat. However, when it came to deciding to abandon a part of his conquests, the Emperor could not make up his mind. He was most unwilling to have it thought that he considered himself defeated because he sought refuge behind these inaccessible mountains. The over-boldness of this great captain was our undoing; he did not stop to consider that his army, weakened by numerous losses, contained in its ranks many foreigners who were waiting only for a favourable opportunity to betray him, and that it was liable to be overwhelmed by superior forces in the great open plains of Leipzig. He would have been wiser to lead it to the mountains of Thuringia and Hesse, which offered good defensive positions, and so nullify some of the numerical advantage of the royal coalition. In addition, the approach of winter and the need to feed their many troops would have soon compelled the enemies to separate, while the French army, its front and its flanks protected by the extreme difficulty of mounting an attack in a country bristling with natural obstacles, would have had behind it the fertile valleys of the Main, the Rhine and the Necker.

Such a position would at least have given us some time and perhaps tired the allies to the point of desiring a peace; but the confidence which Napoleon had in himself and in the valour of his troops overcame these considerations, and he elected to await his enemies on the plains of Leipzig.

This fatal decision had hardly been taken, when a second letter from the King of Wurtemburg informed the Emperor that the King of Bavaria, having suddenly changed sides had made a pact with the allies, and that the two armies, the Austrian and the Bavarian, in cantonment on the banks of the Inn, had joined into a single unit under the command of General de Wrède and were marching to the Rhine; and finally that, to his regret, he was compelled by force to join his army to theirs. In consequence, the Emperor could expect that soon 100,000 men would surround Mainz, and threaten the frontier of France.

At this unexpected news, Napoleon thought he should return to the project of retiring behind the Saale and the mountains of Thuringia; but it was too late, for already the main forces of the allies were in contact with the French army, and too close for it to be possible to carry out a retreat without being attacked in the course of this difficult operation. So the Emperor decided to stand and fight. It was a disastrous decision, for the effective strength of the French troops and their allies amounted to no more than 157,000 men, of whom only 29,000 were cavalry, while Prince Schwartzenberg, the enemy generalissimo, disposed of a force of 350,000, of whom 54,000 were cavalry.

This huge army consisted of Russians, Austrians, Prussians, and Swedes, whom the former French Marshal Bernadotte was leading against his fellow countrymen and one-time brothers in arms. The total number of those engaged amounted to 507,000 without counting the troops left in fortresses.

The town of Leipzig is one of the most commercial and richest in Germany. It stands in the middle of a great plain which extends from the Elbe to the Harz mountains, to Thuringia and to Bohemia. Its situation has made it almost always the principal theatre for the wars which have bloodied Germany. A little river named the Elster, which is so small and shallow that one could call it a stream, runs from south to north through water-meadows in a slight valley as far as Leipzig. This water-course divides into a great number of branches which are a real obstacle to the usual operations of war, and require a multiplicity of bridges for communication between the villages which edge the valley.

The Pleisse, another river of the same sort but even smaller than the Elster runs about a league and a half from the latter, which it joins under the walls of Leipzig.

To the north of the town is a small stream called the Partha which winds through a narrow valley and has at every pace fords or little bridges across it.

Leipzig, being at the confluence of these three streams and almost surrounded to the north and west by their multiple branches is the key to the terrain through which they run. The town, which is not very large, was at this period surrounded by an old wall in which were four large gates and three small ones. The road to Lutzen via Lindenau and Markranstadt was the only one by which the French army could communicate freely with its rear.

It is in the area of ground between the Pleisse and the Partha that the heaviest fighting took place. There, a noticeable feature is a small isolated hillock called the Kelmberg, known also as the Swedish redoubt, because in the thirty years war, Gustavus Adolphus built some fortifications at this spot, which dominates the surrounding countryside.

The battle of Leipzig began on the 16th of October 1813 and lasted three days; but the fighting on the 17th was infinitely more savage than that on the 16th and 18th.

Without wishing to go into the details of this memorable encounter, I think I should indicate the principal positions occupied by the French army, which will give a general idea of those of the enemy, since each of our army corps had facing it one and sometimes two of the enemy.

King Murat was in control of our right wing, the extremity of which was bounded by the Pleisse near the villages of Connewitz, Dölitz, and Mark-Kleeberg which were occupied by Prince Poniatowski and his Poles. Next to him and behind the market-town of Wachau was the corps of Marshal Victor. Marshal Augereau occupied Dösen.

These various corps of infantry were flanked and supported by several masses of Marshals Kellermann's and Michaud's cavalry.

The centre, under the direct command of the Emperor, was at Liebert-Wolkwitz. It was made up of the infantry corps of General Lauriston and Marshal Macdonald, having with them the cavalry of Latour-Maubourg and Sébastiani. My regiment which was part of this last general's corps, was positioned facing the hillock of Kelmberg, or the Swedish redoubt.

The left wing, commanded by Marshal Ney, comprised the infantry Corps of Marshal Marmont, and of Generals Souham and Reynier, supported by the cavalry of the Duc de Padoue. They occupied Taucha.

A body of 15,000 men under the command of General Bertrand was sent from Leipzig to guard the crossings of the Elster and the road to Lutzen.

At Probstheyda, behind our centre, was the reserve commanded by Marshal Oudinot and consisting of the Young and the Old Guard and Nansouty's cavalry.

The venerable King of Saxony, who had been unwilling to desert his friend the Emperor of France, remained in the town of Leipzig with his guard and several French regiments who were there to maintain order.

During the night of 15th–16th, Marshal Macdonald's troops were moved to concentrate in Liebert-Wolkwitz, leaving the area of the Kelmberg: but as there was no wish to abandon this position to the enemy before dawn, I was told to keep it under surveillance until first light. This was an operation of some delicacy, since I had to advance with my regiment to the foot of the hillock, while the French army retired for half a league in the opposite direction. I ran the risk of being surrounded and perhaps captured with all my men by the enemy advance-guard, whose scouts would not fail to climb to the top of the hillock as soon as the dawn light allowed them to see what was going on in the vast plains below them, which were occupied by the French army.

The weather was superb and, although it was night, one could see reasonably well by the light of the stars; but as in these circumstances it is much easier to see what is overhead than to see what is below one's feet, I brought my squadrons as close as possible to the hillock so that its shadow would conceal the riders, and after ordering silence and immobility, I awaited events.

The event which fortune had in store was one which could have changed the future of France and the Emperor and made my name for ever celebrated.

Half an hour before first light, three riders, coming from the direction of the enemy, climbed, at walking pace, the hillock of Kelmberg, from where they could not see us, although we could see clearly their silhouettes and hear their conversation. They were speaking in French, the one being Russian and the other two Prussians. The first, who seemed to have some authority over his companions, ordered one of them to go and inform their majesties that there were no Frenchmen at this spot, and they could climb up, for in a few minutes it would be possible to see the whole of the plain; but they should do this right away, in case the French sent sharpshooters to the area.

The officer to whom these words were addressed observed that the escort was still a long way off. "What does it matter?" was the reply, "There is no one here but us". At these words my troops and I redoubled our attention, and soon we saw on the top of the hillock some twenty enemy officers, of whom one dismounted.

Although on setting up an ambush, I had no expectation of making any great capture, I had, however warned my officers that if we saw anyone on the Swedish redoubt, at a signal from me two squadrons would go round it, one to left and one to right, in order to encircle any enemy who had risked coming so close to our army. I had high hopes, when the over-keenness of one of my troopers ruined my plan. This man having accidently dropped his sabre, immediately took his carbine, and fearing that he would be late when I gave the order to attack, he fired into the middle of the group, killing a Prussian major.

You may imagine how, in an instant, all the enemy officers, who had no other guard but a few orderlies, seeing themselves on the point of being surrounded, made off at the gallop. We dared not follow them too far for fear of falling ourselves into the hands of the approaching escorts. We did manage to capture two officers, from whom we could get no information, but I learned later from my friend, Baron de Stoch, who was a colonel in the guard of the Grand Duke of Darmstadt, that the Emperor Alexander of Russia and the King of Prussia had been among the group of officers who almost fell into French hands, an event which would have changed the destiny of Europe. However, fate having decided otherwise, there was nothing left for me to do but to withdraw smartly with my regiment to the French lines.

On the 16th of October at eight o'clock in the morning, the allied batteries gave the signal for the attack. A lively cannonade was directed at our lines and the allied army marched towards us from every point. The fighting commenced on our right, where the Poles, driven back by the Prussians, abandoned the village of Mark-Kleeberg.

At our centre the Russians and the Austrians attacked Wachau and Liebert-Wolkwitz six times and were repeatedly repulsed with great losses. The Emperor regretting, no doubt that he had abandoned that morning the Swedish redoubt which the enemy had occupied and from where their gunners rained down grape-shot, ordered its recapture, which was promptly carried out by the 22nd Light Infantry aided by my regiment.

Having obtained this first success, the Emperor, not being able to outflank the enemy wings because their superior numbers allowed them to present too long a front, decided to keep them occupied while he attempted to break through their centre. To this end, he sent Marshal Mortier to Wachau with two divisions of infantry, and Marshal Oudinot with the Young Guard. General Drout with sixty cannons aided the attack, which was successful.

For his part, Marshal Victor overcame and routed the Russian Corps commanded by Prince Eugène of Wurtemberg; but after suffering considerable losses, the Prince was able to rally his Corps at Gossa.

At this moment General Lauriston and Marshal Macdonald debouched from Liebert-Wolkwitz and the enemy was overthrown. The French then took possession of the wood of Grosspossnau. Geberal Maison was wounded in the taking of this important point.

It was in vain that the numerous Austrian cavalry commanded by General Klenau and aided by a host of Cossacks tried to restore the situation, they were defeated by General Sébastian's cavalry. This was a very fierce encounter; my regiment took part; I lost several men and my senior Major was wounded in the chest by a lance, having failed to protect himself by carrying his rolled cape.

Prince Schwartzenberg, seeing his line badly shaken, advanced his reserves to support it, which decided the Emperor to order a massive cavalry charge which involved the two corps of Kellermann and Latour-Maubourg as well as the Dragoons of the

Guard. Kellermann overcame a division of Russian Cuirassiers, but taken on the flank by another division he had to fall back to the heights of Wachau after taking several enemy flags.

King Murat then advanced the French infantry and the fighting was renewed. The Russian Corps of the Prince of Wurtemberg was once more overwhelmed and lost twenty-six guns. This treatment resulted in the enemy centre yielding and it was about to give way when the Emperor of Russia who had witnessed the disaster, rapidly advanced the numerous cavalry of his guard which, encountering the squadrons of Latour-Maubourg in the state of confusion which always follows an all-out charge, repelled them in their turn and took back twenty-four of the guns which they had just captured. It was during this charge that General Latour-Maubourg had his leg carried away by a cannon-ball.

So far neither side had secured a marked advantage and Napoleon, to achieve a victory, had just launched against the enemy centre the reserve consisting of the infantry and cavalry of the Old Guard and a body of fresh troops newly arrived from Leipzig, when a regiment of enemy cavalry which had either deliberately or accidently got behind French lines created some alarm amongst the moving troops, who halted and formed a square so as not to be taken by surprise, and before it was possible to find out the cause of this alert, night had everywhere suspended military operations.

There had been other events on our extreme right. For the whole day General Merfeld had tried fruitlessly to secure a passage across the Pleisse, defended by Poniatowski's Corps and his Poles; however, towards the end of the day, he managed to take the village of Dölitz, which compromised our right wing; but the infantry Chasseurs of the Old Guard came from the reserve at the Pas de Charge and chased the Austrians back across the river, taking some hundreds of prisoners, among whom was General Merfeld who found himself for the third time in French hands.

Although the Poles had allowed the capture of Dölitz, the Emperor, to boost their morale, thought he should give the baton of a marshal of France to their leader, Prince Poniatowski, who did not enjoy the honour of bearing it for very long.

On the other side of the river Elster, the Austrian General Giulay had taken the village of Lindenau after seven hours of fierce fighting. The Emperor when told of this serious event, which compromised the way of retreat for the major part of his troops, ordered an attack by General Bertrand, who re-took the position by a vigourous bayonet charge.

On our left, the impatience of Ney nearly led to a major catastrophe. The Marshal who commanded the left wing which had been placed in position by the Emperor, seeing that by ten o'clock in the morning no enemy troops had appeared, sent, on his own authority, one of his army corps, commanded by General Souham, to Wachau, where there seemed to be an active engagement; but while this ill-considered movement was being carried out, the Prussian Marshal Blücher, who had been delayed, arrived with the Silesian army and captured the village of Möckern. Then Ney, deprived of a part of his force, and having at his disposal only Marmont's division, was compelled to withdraw to the walls of Leipzig and do no more than defend the suburb of Halle.

The French lost many men in this engagement, which also had a very disturbing effect on those of our soldiers who were in positions in front of or to one side of Leipzig, for they heard the sound of cannon and small-arms fire coming from behind them. However, at about eight in the evening, the fighting ceased in all parts and the night was peaceful.

Chapter 27
Cossacks & Arrows

This first day led to no decisive victory; but the French had the advantage, since with very much smaller numbers, they had not only held their own against the coalition, but had driven them off some of the ground they had occupied the day before.

The troops on both sides were preparing to renew the fighting on the following morning; but contrary to their expectations, the 17th passed without any hostile movement on the part of either side. The coalition was awaiting the arrival of the Russian Polish army, and the troops which were being brought by the Prince Royal of Sweden, Bernadotte, which would greatly increase their strength.

For his part Napoleon, now regretting his rejection of the peace offers which had been made to him two months previously during the armistice, hoped to have some result from a peace mission which he had sent the previous evening to the allied sovereigns through the Austrian General Comte de Merfeld, who had recently been taken prisoner.

Here could be seen a strange sequence of events. It was the Comte de Merfeld who sixteen years previously had come to ask General Bonaparte, then the commander of the army in Italy, for the armistice of Léoben. It was he who had brought back to Vienna the peace treaty concluded between the Austrian government and the Directorate, represented by General Bonaparte. It was he who had carried to the French emperor, on the night following the Battle of Austerlitz, the proposal for an armistice made by the Austrian Emperor; now, as a remarkable turn of fate had brought General Merfeld once more into the Emperor's presence at a moment when he in his turn was in need of an armistice and peace, he had high hopes that this intermediary would return with the result he desired. However things had gone too far for the allied sovereigns to treat with Napoleon, from whom such a plea denoted the weakness of his position. So, although unable to conquer us on the 16th, they hoped to overcome us by a renewed effort with their superior numbers, and relied heavily on the defection of the German units which were still with us, and whose leaders, all members of the secret society, the Tugenbund, took advantage of the lull in hostilities of the 17th to agree on the manner in which they would execute their treacherous designs. The Comte de Merfeld's mission did not even receive a reply.

On the morning of the 18th, the coalition began its attack. The 2nd Cavalry Corps, of which my regiment was a part, was placed as it had been on the 16th, between Liebert-Wolkwitz and the Kelmberg. The fighting, which broke out everywhere, was fiercest towards our centre, at the village of Probstheyda, which was attacked simultaneously by a Russian and a Prussian Corps who were driven off with tremendous losses. The Russians vigourously attacked Holzhausen, which Macdonald defended successfully.

About eleven o'clock, a cannonade was heard from behind Leipzig, in the direction of Lindenau, and we learned that at this point our troops had broken through the ring within which the enemy believed they could contain the French army, and that General Bertrand's corps was marching towards Weissenfeld in the direction of the Rhine, without the enemy being able to stop him. The Emperor then ordered to evacuation of the equipment to Lutzen.

Meanwhile, the Leipzig plateau, around Connewitz and Lössnig, was the scene of a massive engagement; the earth shook with the noise of a thousand cannon, and the enemy tried to force a passage across the Pleisse. They were driven back, although the Poles managed to ruin some of the bayonet charges made by our infantry. Then the 1st French Cavalry Corps, seeing the Austrian and Prussian squadrons going to the aid of their allies, emerged from behind the village of Probstheyda and hurled themselves at the enemy, whom they overwhelmed and drove back to their reserves which were led by Prince Constantine of Russia. Defeated again at this spot the allies built up an immense force in order to capture Probstheyda, but this formidable mass had such a hot reception from some divisions of our infantry and the infantry

Chasseurs of the Old Guard that they promptly withdrew. We lost there Generals Vial and Rochambeau. The latter had just been made a Marshal of France by the Emperor.

Bernadotte had not yet attacked the French and seemed, it was said, to waver; but at last urged on or even threatened by the Prussian Marshal Blücher, he decided to cross the Partha above the village of Mockau, at the head of his troops and a Russian corps which had been placed under his command. When a brigade of Saxon Hussars and Lancers which was positioned at this point saw the Cossacks who preceded Bernadotte approaching they marched towards them as if to give battle; but then, turning round suddenly and forgetting about their aged King, our ally who was in the midst of Napoleon's troops, the infamous Saxons aimed their muskets and cannons at the French.

This force led by Bernadotte, following the left bank of the Partha, headed for Sellerhausen which was defended by Reynier, whose corps was almost entirely made up of German contingents. Reynier having seen the desertion of the Saxon cavalry, distrusted their infantry, which he had placed next to the cavalry of Durette in order to restrain them; but Marshal Ney, with misplaced confidence, ordered him to deploy the Saxons and send them to assist a French regiment which was defending the village of Paunsdorf. The Saxons had gone only a little distance from the French, when seeing the Prussian ensigns in the fields of Paunsdorf they ran towards them at top speed, led by the shameless General Russel, their commander. Some French officers could not believe such treachery, and thought that the Saxons were going to attack the Prussians; so that General Gressot, Reynier's chief-of-staff rushed towards them to moderate what he thought was an excess of zeal, only to find himself confronted by enemies! This defection of an entire army corps produced a frightening gap in the French centre, and had the additional effect of raising the allied morale. The Wurtemberg cavalry promptly followed the example of the Saxons.

Not only did Bernadotte welcome the perfidious Saxons into his ranks, but he used their artillery to bolster up his own, which the former Marshal France now aimed at Frenchmen.

The Saxons had scarcely entered the enemy ranks when they celebrated their treachery by firing at us a hail of projectiles, many of which were directed to my regiment, for I lost some thirty men, among whom was Captain Bertain, an excellent officer who had his head taken off by a cannon-ball.

So now it was Bernadotte, a man for whom French blood had procured a throne, who was attempting to deliver to us the coup de grace.

Amid this general disloyalty, the King of Wurtemberg presented an honourable exception, for as I have said, he had informed Napoleon that circumstances forced him to renounce his friendship; but even after he had taken this final step, he ordered his troops not to attack the French without giving them ten days warning, and although he was now an enemy of France, he dismissed from his army the general and several officers who had handed over their troops to the Russians at the battle of Leipzig, and withdrew all their decorations from the turncoat regiments.

Probstheyda, however, continued to be the theatre of a most murderous struggle. The Old Guard, deployed behind the village, held itself in readiness to hasten to the aid of its defenders. Bulow's Prussian corps having attempted to push forward, was heavily defeated; but we lost in the action General Delmas, a distinguished soldier and a man of high principles who, having been involved with Napoleon since the creation of the Empire, had spent ten years in retirement, but asked to be returned to active service when he saw his country in danger.

Facing a terrible cannonade, and continual attacks, the French line remained steadfastly in position. Towards our left, Marshal Macdonald and General Sébastiani were holding the ground between Probstheyda and Stötteritz, in spite of numerous attacks by Klenau's Austrians and the Russians of Doctoroff, when they were assailed by a charge of more than 20,000 Cossacks and Baskirs, the efforts of the latter being directed mainly at Sébastiani's cavalry.

With much shouting, these barbarians rapidly surrounded our squadrons, against which they launched thousands of arrows which did very little damage because the Baskirs, being entirely irregulars, do not know how to form up in ranks and they go about in a mob like a flock of sheep, with the result that the riders cannot shoot horizontally without wounding or killing their comrades who are in front of them, but shoot their arrows into the air to describe an arc which will allow them to descend on the enemy. This system does not permit any accurate aim, and nine tenths of the arrows miss their target. Those that do arrive have used up in their ascent the impulse given to them by the bow, and fall only under their own weight, which is very small, so that they do not as a rule inflict any serious injuries. In fact the Baskirs, having no other arms, are undoubtedly the world's least dangerous troops.

However, since they attacked us in swarms, and the more one killed of these wasps, the more seemed to arrive, the huge number of arrows which they discharged into the air of necessity caused a few dangerous wounds. Thus, one of my finest N.C.O.s. by the name of Meslin had his body pierced by an arrow which entered his chest and emerged at his back. The brave fellow, taking two hands, broke the arrow and pulled out the remaining part, but this did not save him, for he died a few moments later. This is the only example which I can remember of death being caused by a Baskir arrow, but I had several men and horses hit, and was myself wounded by this ridiculous weapon.

I had my sabre in my hand, and I was giving orders to an officer, when, on raising my arm to indicate the point to which he was to go, I felt my sabre encounter a strange resistance and was aware of a slight pain in my right thigh, in which was embedded for about an inch, a four foot arrow which in the heat of battle I had not felt. I had it extracted by Dr.Parot and put in one of the boxes in the regimental ambulance, intending to keep it as a memento; but unfortunately it got lost.

You will understand that for such a minor injury I was not going to leave the regiment, particularly at such a critical time. The reinforcements brought by Bernadotte and Blücher were determinedly attacking the village of Schönfeld, not far from where the Partha enters Leipzig. Generals Lagrange and Friederichs who were defending this important point, repelled seven assaults and seven times drove the allies out of houses they had captured. General Friederichs was killed during this action; he was a fine officer who among his other qualities, was the most handsome man in the French army.

Nevertheless, it looked as if the allies might take Schönfeld until Marshal Ney went to the aid of the village, which remained in

French hands. Marshal Ney received a blow on his shoulder which forced him to leave the field of battle.

By nightfall the troops of both sides were, in most parts of the line, in the same positions which they had occupied at the beginning of the battle. In the evening my troopers and those of all the divisions of Sébastiani's cavalry tethered their horses to the same pickets which they had used for the three preceding days, and almost all the battalions occupied the same bivouacs. So this battle which our enemies have celebrated as a great success, was in fact indecisive, since being greatly inferior in numbers, having almost all the nations of Europe against us and harbouring a crowd of traitors in our ranks, we had not yielded an inch of ground. The English general, Sir Robert Wilson, who was in Leipzig in the rôle of British representative and whose testimony cannot be suspected of partiality, said of this battle:-

"In spite of the defection of the Saxon army in the middle of the battle, in spite of the courage and perseverance of the allied troops, it proved impossible to take from the French any of the villages which they regarded as essential to their position. Night ended the fighting, leaving the French, and in particular the defenders of Probstheyda, in the well-earned position of having inspired in their enemies a generous measure of respect."

After sunset, when it was beginning to grow dark, I was ordered to put a stop, at the front of my regiment, to the useless exchange of fire which usually goes on after a serious engagement. There is some difficulty in separating men on both sides who have been fighting each other, the more so because, to prevent the enemy from knowing what is going on, and making use of it to fall unexpectedly on our advance-posts, one cannot use drums or trumpets to instruct the infantrymen to cease fire and to form up to rejoin their regiments. A warning is given to platoon commanders, in quiet tones, and they then send sous-officiers to look silently for the small, scattered groups. As the enemy were doing the same, the firing gradually grew less and soon stopped entirely.

To make sure that no sentinel was forgotten and that this little withdrawal to bivouac was carried out in good order, it was my custom to have it supervised by an officer. The one who was on duty on this evening was a Captain Joly, a brave and well-trained officer, but inclined to be obstinate. He had given evidence of this trait some months before the battle when, given the job of distributing some officer's remounts which had been presented, on the Emperor's instructions, to those who had taken part in the Russian campaign, M. Joly, ignoring my advice and that of his friends, had selected for himself a magnificent light grey, which neither I nor my friends would have because of its striking colour, and which I had at first reserved for the trumpeters. So on the evening of the battle of Leipzig, while M. Joly, in carrying out his duty, was riding at a walk behind the lines of infantry, his horse stood out so clearly, in spite of the failing light, that it was picked out by the enemy and both horse and rider were seriously wounded. The captain had a musket ball through his body and died during the night in a house in the suburb of Halle, to where, on the previous evening, I had sent Major Pozac.

Although the latter's wound was not dangerous, he was grieved to think that the French army would probably leave and he would become a prisoner of the enemy, who would deprive him of the sabre of honour which he had been awarded by the First Consul after the battle of Marengo when he was still only a sous-officier; but I calmed his anxieties by taking charge of the precious sabre which was given into the care of one of the regimental surgeons, and handed back to Pozac when he returned to France.

Chapter 28
After Leipzig

The calm of the night having replaced in the fields of Leipzig the terrible battles which they had just witnessed, the leaders of both sides could examine their positions.

That of the Emperor Napoleon was the least favourable. If one could blame this great man for not retreating behind the Saale eight days before the battle, when he could have still avoided risking the safety of his army, which was threatened by infinitely more numerous forces, there is now even more reason to disapprove of his judgement when, at Leipzig, one sees him completely surrounded on the field of battle by his enemies. I use the word "completely" because, on the 18th, at eleven in the morning, Lichtenstein's Austrian corps seized the village of Kleinzschocher, on the left bank of the Elster, and for a time the route from Leipzig to Weissenfels, the only way of escape for the French, was cut and Napoleon's army entirely encircled.

It is true that this situation did not last for more than half an hour, but would Napoleon not have been wiser to avoid all the consequences which might have arisen from such an event by taking shelter behind the mountains of Thuringia and the river Saale before all the enemy forces could combine to surround him?

We now come to a very critical situation. The French had held on to their positions for the three days of the battle, but this success had been achieved only at the expense of much blood, for in killed and wounded we had 40,000 casualties. It is true that the enemy had suffered 60,000, a figure greatly to their disadvantage, which was attributable to the persistence with which they attacked our entrenched positions. As, however, they had many more men than we did, having lost 40,000 we were proportionately much more weakened than they were.

In addition to this, the French artillery had fired during the three days 220,000 rounds, of which 95,000 were fired on the 18th, and there were no more than 16,000 rounds left in the reserves, that is to say enough to continue in action for only two hours. This shortage of ammunition which should have been foreseen before we engaged a powerful enemy so far from our frontiers, prevented Napoleon from renewing the battle, which he might possibly have won, and forced him to order a retreat.

This was a movement which it was very difficult to carry out, because of the nature of the terrain which we occupied, which was full of water-meadows and streams and traversed by three rivers, creating many narrow defiles which would have to be negotiated under the eyes and within close range of the enemy, who might easily throw our ranks into disorder during this perilous march.

There was only one means of assuring our retreat, and that was the construction of a large number of pathways and footbridges across the meadows, ditches and small streams, together with larger bridges across the Partha, the Pleisse and principally, over the Elster, which was joined by these various tributaries at the gates and even within the town of Leipzig. Now, nothing could have been easier than the creation of these indispensable means of passage, for the town and suburbs of Leipzig, barely a musket-shot away, offered a ready source of planks and beams, girders, nails and rope etc. The whole army believed that numerous crossing places had been made since their arrival before Leipzig and that these had been increased on the 16th and above all on the 17th, when the whole day had passed without any fighting. Well! For a number of deplorable reasons and by unbelievable negligence, nothing whatsoever had been done, and among those official documents which we possess relating to this famous battle, one can find nothing, absolutely nothing, which would show that any measures had been taken to facilitate, in case of a retreat, the movement of the many columns which were in action beyond the obstructions formed by the rivers and the streets of Leipzig and its suburbs. None of the officers who escaped from the disaster, nor any of the authors who have written about it have been able to show that any of the senior staff of the army took steps to establish new crossing points or to ensure free use of those which existed. Only General Pelet, who is a great admirer of Napoleon and who, for this reason, is sometimes given to exaggeration, writing fifteen years after the battle, states that M.

Odier, the deputy quartermaster of the Imperial Guard, told him several times that he was present when one morning (he does say on what day) the Emperor ordered a general on his staff to look into the construction of bridges and made him specially responsible for the task. General Pelet does not disclose the name of the general to whom the Emperor gave this order, although it would be most important to know it.

M. Fain, Napoleon's secretary, says in his memoirs "The Emperor ordered the construction in the neighbouring marshes of new pathways which would ease the passage of this long defile".

I do not know how much credit history will give to the accuracy of these assertions; but even supposing them to be true, there are those who think that the head of the French army should have done more than give an order to a general staff officer, who perhaps did not have at his disposal sappers or the necessary material, and that he should have given the responsibility for creating new crossing points to several officers, at least one from every regiment in each army corps, for it is plain that no one was doing anything. Here now is the truth of the matter, which is known to very few people.

The Emperor had for head of his general staff, Marshal Prince Berthier, who had never left him since the Italian campaign of 1796. He was capable, precise and loyal but having often suffered the effects of the imperial temper, he had developed such a fear of Napoleon's outbursts that he had decided never to take the initiative on any matter, never to ask any questions, and simply to carry out those orders he received in writing. This system which maintained good relations between the Major-general and his chief, was harmful to the interests of the army; for no matter how great the Emperor's energy and ability, it was impossible for him to see everything and undertake everything; and so if he overlooked something of importance nothing was done.

It seems that this is what happened at Leipzig, where, when almost all the marshals and generals had on several occasions, and particularly on the last two days, pointed out to Berthier how necessary it was to provide adequate ways out in the event of a retreat, his invariable reply had been "The Emperor has not ordered it." No materials were supplied, and so not a plank nor beam had been placed across a rivulet when, during the night of 18th-19th the Emperor ordered a retreat to Weissenfels and the river Saale.

The allies had suffered such heavy losses that they felt it impossible to renew the struggle. They did not dare to attack us afresh, and were on the point of retiring themselves when they noticed the heavy equipment of the army heading for Weissenfels via Lindenau, and realised that Napoleon was preparing to retreat. Whereupon they took steps to place themselves in a position to profit from any opportunities which this movement might present to them.

The most unhappy moment of a retreat, particularly for a unit commander, is that when he has to leave behind those wounded whom he is compelled to abandon to the mercy of the enemy, who frequently does not have any and robs and murders those who are too badly injured to follow their comrades. However, since the worst of all things is to be left lying on the ground, I took advantage of the night to have my men pick up all the wounded from my regiment, whom I put in two adjoining houses, firstly to shield them from the drunken fury of the enemy, who would occupy the suburb, and secondly to allow them to help one another and keep up their spirits. An assistant surgeon, M. Bordenave, offered to remain with them. I accepted his offer, and after the peace I recommended this estimable doctor, whose care saved the lives of many men, for the award of the Legion of Honour.

The troops now began their march away from the battlefield where they had shown so much courage and shed so much blood. The Emperor left his bivouac at eight in the evening and went to the town where he stayed at a hostelry in the horse market, named "The Prussian Arms", and after giving some orders he went to visit the aged King of Saxony, whom he found preparing to follow him.

This King, a devoted friend, expected that to punish his unshakable adherence to the French Emperor, the allied sovereigns would seize his kingdom, but what grieved him more was the thought that his army had been dishonoured by deserting to the enemy. Napoleon was unable to comfort the good old man, and it was with difficulty that he persuaded him to remain in Leipzig, in the heart of his state, and send an envoy to the confederates to ask for terms.

When this emissary had left, the Emperor said adieu to the old King, the Queen and the Princess their daughter, a model of virtue who had followed her father even to face the guns of the enemy. The separation was made more unhappy when it was learned that the allies would make no promises about the fate reserved for the Saxon monarch, who would thus be at their mercy. He ruled over some fine provinces, an invitation to his enemies to be implacable.

About eight in the evening the retreat began, with the corps of Marshals Victor and Augereau, the ambulances, a part of the artillery, the cavalry and the Imperial Guard. While these troops filed through the suburb of Lindenau, Marshals Ney, Marmont and General Reynier guarded the suburbs of Halle and Rosenthal. The Corps of Lauriston, Macdonald and Poniatowski entered the town in succession and took up positions at the barriers which pierced the walls, all was thus arranged for a stubborn resistance by the rear-guard to allow the army to retreat in good order. Nevertheless, Napoleon wished to spare Leipzig the horrors which always result from fighting in the streets, and so he permitted the magistrates to address a request to the allied sovereigns asking them to allow, by an armistice of a few hours, the peaceful evacuation of the town. This proposal was rejected and the allies, hoping that the rear-guard might be thrown into a confusion by which they could profit, did not hesitate to expose to the risk of total destruction one of the finest towns in Germany.

Several French generals then suggested, indignantly, to Napoleon that he could assure the retreat of his army by massing it in the centre of the town and then setting fire to all the suburbs except that of Lindenau, by which our troops could leave while the fire held up the enemy.

In my opinion the allies' refusal to consent to an arrangement which would allow the retreat to be carried on without fighting, gave us the right to employ all possible means of defence, and fire being the most effective in such a situation, we should have used it; but Napoleon could not bring himself to do so, and this excessive magnanimity cost him his throne, for the fighting which I am about to describe resulted in the loss of almost as many men as the three days of battle in which we had just been involved, and worse even than that, it disorganised the army which would otherwise have arrived in France still a potent force. The stiff resistance which for three months the weak remnants put up against the allies is evidence enough of what we might have done if all the French fighting men who had survived the great battle had crossed the Rhine in good order with their weapons. France would probably have repelled the invaders.

That, however is not what happened, for while Napoleon with what I regard as misplaced generosity, refused to burn an enemy town in order to ensure the unopposed retreat of part of his army, the infamous Bernadotte, dissatisfied with the ardour displayed by the allies in destroying his fellow Frenchmen, launched all the troops under his command against the suburb of Taucha, captured it and from there reached the avenues of the town.

Encouraged by this example, Marshal Blücher and his Prussians, the Austrians and the Russians did the same and attacked from all sides the tail-end of the French, who were retreating towards the bridge at Lindenau. Finally, for good measure, a lively fusillade broke out near this bridge, the only way for our troops to cross the Elster. This fusillade came from the battalions of the Saxon guard who had been left in the town with their King, and who, regretting not to have deserted with the other regiments of their army, wanted to show their German patriotism by attacking from behind the French who were passing the château where their monarch was in residence. It was in vain that the venerable prince appeared on the balcony, amidst the firing, crying out "Kill me, you cowards! Kill your King, so that I may not witness your dishonour!" The wretches continued to slaughter the French, while the King, going back to his apartments, took the flag of his Guard and threw it in the fire.

A parting stab in the back was given to our troops by a battalion of men from Baden who, being notorious cowards, had been left in the town during the battle to split logs for the fires of the bakery. These worthless Badeners, sheltered by the walls of the big bakery, fired from its windows on our soldiers, of whom they killed a great many.

The French fought back bravely from house to house and although the whole of the allied force was massed in the town filling the avenues and main streets our troops disputed every foot of ground as they retired towards the big bridge across the Elster at Lindenau.

The Emperor had difficulty in getting out of the town and reaching the outskirts through which the army was marching. He stopped and dismounted at the last of the smaller bridges, known as the mill bridge and it was then that he ordered the big bridge to be mined. He sent orders to Marshals Ney, Macdonald and Poniatowski to hold the town for a further twenty-four hours, or at least until nightfall, to allow the artillery park, the equipment and the rear-guard time to go through the suburb and across the bridges; but the Emperor had scarcely remounted his horse and gone a thousand paces down the road towards Lützen when suddenly there was a massive explosion.

The big bridge across the Elster had been blown up. Macdonald, Lauriston, Reynier and Poniatowski, with their troops as well as 200 artillery pieces were still on the streets of Leipzig and all means of retreat were now cut off. It was a total disaster!

To explain this catastrophe, it was said later that some Prussian and Swedish infantrymen, for whom the Badeners had opened the Halle gate, had gradually worked their way to the region of the bridge where having joined some of the Saxon guard they had occupied some houses from which they started to fire on the French columns. The sapper charged with the responsibility of detonating the mine was deceived by this fire into thinking that the enemy had arrived and that the time had come for him to carry out his mission, and so he put a light to the fuse. Others blamed a colonel of the engineers named Montfort who, at the sight of some enemy infantrymen, had taken it on himself to order the detonation of the explosives. This last version was adopted by the Emperor and M. de Monfort was put on a charge and made a scapegoat for the fatal event, but it later became clear that he had nothing to do with it. However this may be, the army laid the blame once more on the Major-general Prince Berthier. It was justly claimed that he should have put the protection of the bridge in the hands of an entire brigade, whose general should have been made personally responsible for giving the order to blow it up, when he thought the moment had come to do so.

Prince Berthier defended himself with his usual response "The Emperor had not ordered it!"

After the destruction of the bridge, some of the French whose retreat was thus cut off, jumped into the Elster in the hope of swimming across. Several of them succeeded in doing so, Marshal Macdonald being among them; but the greater number, including among others Prince Poniatowski, were drowned, because after crossing the river they were unable to climb the muddy bank, which was lined by enemy soldiers.

Those of our soldiers who were trapped in the town and its suburbs aimed only to sell their lives as dearly as possible. They barricaded themselves behind the houses and fought all day and part of the night, but when their ammunition was exhausted they were forced to retire into their improvised defences where they were nearly all slaughtered! The carnage did not end until two o'clock in the morning.

The number of those massacred in the houses is given as 13,000, while 25,000 were taken prisoner. The enemy collected 250 cannons.

After describing in general the events which followed the battle of Leipzig, I shall now describe some of those which related particularly to my regiment and Sébastiani's cavalry corps to which it belonged. Seeing that we had for three consecutive days repelled the enemy attacks and maintained our positions on the field of battle, the men were greatly surprised and disgusted when, on the evening of the 18th we learned that because of shortage of ammunition we were about to retreat. We hoped that at least (and that appeared to be the Emperor's intention) we would go no further than across the river Saale to the proximity of the fortress of Erfurt, where we could renew our stocks of ammunition and recommence hostilities. So we mounted our horses at eight in the evening on the 18th of October, and abandoned the battlefield on which we had fought for three days and where we left the bodies of so many of our gallant comrades.

We had hardly left our bivouac when we ran into some of the difficulties arising from the failure of the general staff to make any arrangements for the withdrawal of such a large body of troops. At every minute the columns, particularly the artillery and cavalry, were held up by the need to cross wide ditches, bogs, and streams over which it would have been easy to put small bridges. Wheels and horses sank into the mud and the night being very dark there was congestion everywhere; our progress was therefore extremely slow, even when we were in the open country, and often completely arrested in the streets of the suburbs and the town. My regiment which was at the front of the column formed by Excelmans' division, which led this wearisome march, did not reach the bridge at Lindenau until four in the morning on the 19th. When we had crossed over, we were far from foreseeing the appalling catastrophe which would occur in a few hours.

Day broke. The fine, wide road was covered by troops of all arms, which showed that the army would still be of considerable strength on arriving at the Saale. The Emperor passed, but as he galloped along the side of the marching column, he did not hear the cheers which usually greeted his presence. The army was displeased with the little effort which had been made to secure its retreat since leaving the battlefield. What would the troops have said if they had known of the inadequate arrangements made at the Elster, which they had just crossed, but where so many of their comrades would lose their lives?

It was during a halt at Markranstadt, a little town some three leagues from Leipzig, that we heard the explosion of the mine which destroyed the bridge; but instead of being alarmed, we rejoiced, for we all believed that the fuse would not have been lit until after the passage of all our columns, and in order to prevent that of the enemy.

During the few hours of rest which we had at Markranstadt, without being aware of the catastrophe which had occurred at the river, I was able to review our squadrons in detail and find out what losses we had suffered during the three days of conflict. I was dismayed! For they came to 149 men, of whom 60 were killed, among whom were two captains, three lieutenant and eleven N.C.O.s. A very large fraction of the 700 men with which the regiment had arrived on the battlefield on the morning of October the 16th. Nearly all the wounded had been hit by cannon-balls or grapeshot which, sadly, gave them little hope of recovery. My losses might have been doubled if I had not, during the battle, taken precautions to shield my regiment from cannon fire, as much as possible. This requires some explanation.

There are circumstances where the most humane of generals finds himself in the painful position of having to expose his troops openly to enemy fire; but it often happens that certain commanders deploy their men uselessly in front of enemy batteries, and take no steps to avoid casualties, although sometimes this is very easy, particularly for cavalry, who because of the rapidity of their movements can go swiftly to the point where they are required and take up the desired formation. It is when large masses of cavalry are involved on extensive battlefields that these measures of preservation are most required, and where, however, they are least employed.

At Leipzig, on the 16th of October, Sébastiani, commanding the 2nd Cavalry Corps, having placed his three divisions between the villages of Wachau and Liebert-Wolkwitz, and indicated to each divisional general roughly the position he should occupy, Exelman found himself placed on undulating ground intersected, as a result, by small ridges and hollows. The Corps formed a line of considerable length. The enemy cavalry, being a long way from us, could not take us by surprise. I took advantage of the hollows in the ground where our brigade was positioned to conceal my regiment which though formed up and ready for action, saw the greater part of the day pass without losing a single man, for the cannon-balls went over their heads while neighbouring corps suffered considerable casualties.

I was congratulating myself on having done this when General Exelmans, on the pretext that everyone should be equally exposed to danger, ordered me, in spite of the representations of my brigade commander, to take the regiment a hundred paces forward. I obeyed, but in a short time I had a captain, M. Bertin, killed and some twenty men put out of action. I then had recourse to a different tactic: this was to send some troopers, well spaced out, to subject the enemy gunners to carbine fire. The enemy then advanced some infantrymen to counter this, and the two groups being involved in a fire-fight between the lines, the artillery could not use their guns for fear of hitting their own men. It is true that our gunners were in the same boat, but the cessation of gunfire in a minor corner of the battlefield was to our benefit, since the enemy had many more guns than we did. In addition to this, our infantry and that of the enemy being in action at the village of Liebert-Wolkwitz, the cavalry of both sides had to await the outcome of this savage fighting; it served no useful purpose for them to demolish one another by cannon fire, rather than leave the fighting to the infantrymen, who were for the most part only frightening the birds. My example was followed by all the regimental commanders of the other brigades, and the cannons opposite them too ceased fire, sparing the lives of many men. A greater number would have been spared if General Exelmans had not come and ordered the withdrawal of the men on foot, which was the signal for a hail of cannon-balls hurled at our squadrons. Fortunately the day was almost over.

It was now the evening of the 16th. All the colonels of cavalry belonging to 2nd Corps had found this method of sparing their men so effective that by common accord we all used it in the battle of the 18th. When the enemy started firing their cannons, we sent out our foot-soldiers, and as they would have captured the guns if they were not defended, the enemy had to send infantrymen to defend them, and so the guns were silenced on both sides. The commanders of the enemy cavalry which faced us, having probably realised what we were up to, started doing the same, so that on the third day the guns attached to the cavalry of both parties were much less used. This did not prevent vigourous cavalry engagements, but at least they were directed to the taking or holding of positions, in which we did not spare ourselves, but the cannonades aimed at stationary targets, which too often replace cavalry to cavalry actions, do nothing but kill good men for no useful purpose. This was something which Exelmans did not grasp, but as he was on the move all the time from one wing to the other, as soon as he had left a regiment the colonel sent out his foot-soldiers and the guns were silent.

All the cavalry generals, including Sébastiani, were so much persuaded of the advantages of this method, that eventually Exelmans was ordered not to irritate the enemy gunners by firing our guns at them, when the cavalry was only standing-to and had neither an attack nor a defence to undertake. Two years later I used the same tactics at Waterloo against the English guns and I lost far fewer men than I would have done otherwise: but now let us return to Markranstadt.

Chapter 29
We Attack Ott's Hussars

It was while the Emperor and the divisions which had come out of Leipzig were halted at this spot, that we heard the dreadful news of the destruction of the bridge at Lindenau, which deprived the army of almost all its artillery and half of its men, who were taken prisoner; and which delivered some thousands of our wounded comrades to the assaults and knives of the brutish enemy, full of liquor and encouraged to massacre by their unscrupulous officers! There was widespread grief! Each regretted the loss of a relative, a friend, some comrade in arms! The Emperor seemed appalled! However, he ordered Sébastiani's cavalry to retrace their steps to the bridge, in order to gather and protect any stragglers who had been able to cross the river at some point, after the explosion.

In order to speed this help, my regiment and the 24th who were the best mounted in the corps were told to go ahead of the column and leave at a rapid trot. As General Wathiez was indisposed, and I was the next in seniority, I had to take command of the brigade.

When we had reached half way to Leipzig, we heard much gunfire, and as we approached the avenues we could hear the despairing cries of the unfortunate French, who having no means of retreat and no cartridges for their firearms, were unable to defend themselves, and hunted from street to street and house to house, were overwhelmed by numbers and disgracefully butchered by the enemy, mainly the Prussians, the Badeners and the Saxon guards.

It would be impossible for me to express the fury felt then by the two regiments which I commanded. All longed for vengeance and regretted that this was denied them, since the Elster, with its broken bridge, separated us from the assassins and their victims. Our anger was increased when we came across about

218

2000 Frenchmen, most of them without clothes and nearly all wounded, who had escaped death only by jumping into the river and swimming across in the face of the shots being fired at them from the opposite bank. Marshal Macdonald was among them; he owed his life to his physical strength and his ability as a swimmer. The Marshal was completely naked and his horse had been drowned, so I quickly found some clothes for him and lent him the spare horse which always came with me, which allowed him to go immediately to rejoin the Emperor at Markranstadt and to give him an account of the disaster of which he had been a witness, and in which one of the principal episodes had been the death of Prince Poniatowski, who had perished in the waters of the Elster.

The remainder of the French who had managed to cross the river had been obliged to discard their arms in order to swim, and had no means of defence. They ran across the fields to avoid falling into the hands of four or five hundred Prussians, Saxons and Badeners who, not satisfied with the blood-bath of the massacres in the town, had made a footbridge of beams and planks across the remaining arches of the bridge, and had come to kill any of our unfortunate soldiers whom they could find on the road to Markranstadt.

As soon as I caught sight of this group of assassins, I instructed Colonel Schneit of the 24th to combine with my regiment to form a vast semi-circle round them, and then sounded the charge. The result was horrifying! The bandits, taken by surprise, put up very little resistance and there ensued a massacre, for no quarter was given.

I was so enraged at these wretches, that before the charge started I had promised myself that I would run my sabre through any of them I could catch, however when I found myself in their midst and saw that they were drunk and leaderless except for two Saxon officers who were fear-stricken at our vengeful approach, I realised that this was not a fight but an execution, and that it would not be a good thing for me to take part in it. I feared that I might find pleasure in killing some of these scoundrels, so I put my sabre back in its scabbard and left to our soldiers the business of exterminating these assassins, two thirds of whom were laid dead.

The remainder, including two officers and several Saxon guards, fled towards the debris of the bridge, hoping to recross the footbridge; but as they could cross only one by one and our Chasseurs were hard on their heels, they entered a large nearby inn and began to shoot at my men, helped by some Prussians and Badeners on the opposite bank.

As it seemed likely that the noise of firing would attract larger forces to the bank from where, without crossing the river, they could destroy my regiment by small-arms and cannon fire, I decided to bring matters to a conclusion, and ordered the majority of the Chasseurs to dismount and taking their carbines and plenty of ammunition to attack the rear of the inn and set on fire the stables and the hay loft. The assassins shut in the inn, seeing that they were about to be caught in the flames, tried to make a sortie; but as soon as they appeared in the doorway our Chasseurs shot them with their carbines.

It was in vain that they sent one of the Saxon officers to me to intercede; I was pitiless, and refused to treat as soldiers surrendering after an honourable defence, these monsters who had murdered our comrades who were prisoners of war. So the four to five hundred Prussians, Badeners and Saxons who had crossed the footbridge were all killed! I sent this information to General Sébastiani, who halted midway the other brigades of the Light Cavalry. .

The fire which we had lit in the forage store of the inn soon spread to the neighbouring houses. A major part of the village of Lindenau, which lines both sides of the road, was burned, delaying the repair of the bridge and the passage of enemy troops, bent on pursuing and harrying the retreating French army.

The mission being completed, I led the brigade back to Markranstadt, together with the 2000 French, who had escaped from the calamity at the bridge. Among them were several officers of all ranks; The Emperor questioned them on what they knew about the blowing up of the bridge and about the massacre of the French prisoners of war. It seems likely that this sorry tale made the Emperor regret that he had not taken the advice given him in the morning, to bar the enemy advance by setting fire to the suburbs, and even, if need be, the town of Leipzig itself, most of whose inhabitants had fled during the three day's battle.

In the course of this return to the bridge of Lindenau, the brigade which I was commanding suffered only three casualties, one of which was a member of my regiment; but it was one of my finest sous-officiers. He had been awarded the Legion of Honour and was named Foucher. A bullet wound, received at the inn had gone through both thighs, leaving four holes; but in spite of this serious injury the brave Foucher made the retreat on horseback, refused to enter the hospital at Erfurt, which we passed a few days later and remained with the regiment until we reached France. It is true that his friends and all the men in his platoon took great care of him, but he thoroughly deserved it.

As I left Leipzig, I was concerned about the fate of the wounded from my regiment, whom I had left behind, including Major Pozac; but luckily the distant suburb in which I had put them was not visited by the Prussians.

You have seen that during the last day of the great battle, an Austrian Corps tried to cut off our retreat by capturing Lindenau, through which passes the main road leading to Weissenfels and Erfurt, and how, on the Emperor's orders, they had been driven off by General Bertrand, who, after re-opening this route, had made his way to Weissenfels, where we rejoined him.

After the losses occasioned by the destruction of the bridge at Lindenau, it was impossible to think of stopping what remained of the army at the Saale, so Napoleon crossed the river.

A fortnight before the battle, this water-course had offered him an impregnable position, which he had spurned to risk a general engagement in open country, putting behind him three rivers and a large town, which presented obstructions at every step. The great captain had relied too much on his "star" and on the incapacity of the enemy generals.

In the event, they made such serious mistakes that in spite of an immense superiority in numbers, they were not only unable, during a battle lasting three days, to take from us a single one of the villages we were defending. I have heard the King of Belgium, who was then serving with the Russian army, say to the Duc d'Orleans that on two occasions the allies were in such confusion that the order for a retreat was given: but then the situation changed and it our army which had to submit to the fortune of war.

After crossing the Saale, Napoleon thanked and dismissed those officers and soldiers of the Confederation of the Rhine, who either from some sense of honour or from lack of opportunity were still in our ranks. He even carried magnanimity so far as to allow them to retain their arms, although he was entitled to treat them as prisoners of war, since their sovereigns had joined the forces of our enemies. The French army continued its retreat to Erfurt, without anything happening but an encounter at Kosen, where a single French division defeated an Austrian army corps and took prisoner its commanding general the Comte de Giulay.

Led on always by the hope of a fighting return to Germany, and by the help which he would receive in such a case from the fortresses which he was now forced to leave behind him, Napoleon put a numerous garrison into Erfurt. He had left in Dresden 25,000 men, under the command of Saint-Cyr; at Hamburg 30,000 under Davout, and many strongholds on the Oder and the Elbe, manned in accordance with their importance. These garrisons comprised a loss in manpower to add to that due to the forts of Danzig and the Vistula.

I shall not repeat what I have already said about the disadvantages of deploying too many of one's troops to man forts which one is forced to leave behind. I shall merely point out that Napoleon left in the forts of Germany 80,000 men, not one of whom returned to France until after the fall of the empire, which they might perhaps have prevented, had they been defending our frontiers.

The arsenal at Erfurt was able to make good the loss of our artillery. The Emperor, who up till now had borne his reverses with stoical resignation, was however upset by the departure of his brother-in-law, the King Murat, who, with the excuse that he was going to defend his kingdom of Naples, abandoned Napoleon, to whom he owed everything. Murat, at one time so brilliant in war, had done nothing much during this campaign of 1813. It is certain that, although he was in our ranks, he was carrying on a correspondence with M. de Metternich, the prime minister of Austria, who dangling before his eyes the example of Bernadotte, guaranteed, in the name of the allied sovereigns, the protection of his kingdom if he would join Napoleon's enemies. Murat left the French army at Erfurt and had scarcely arrived in Naples when he began preparations for war against us.

It was also at Erfurt that the Emperor learned of the audacious scheme of the Bavarians, his former allies, who, after deserting his cause, and joining with an Austrian Corps and several groups of Cossacks, had set off under the command of General the Comte de Wrède, whose ambition it was not only to stop the French army, but to make it captive, along with its Emperor.

General de Wrède marching parallel to us but at two days distance had already reached Wartzbourg with 60,000 men. He detached 10,000 to Frankfort and with the remaining 50,000 he went to the little fort of Hanau in order to bar the passage of the French. General de Wrède, who had fought on our side in Russia, thought that he would find the French army in the deplorable state to which cold and hunger had reduced those retreating from Moscow by the time they reached the Beresina, but we soon showed him that in spite of our misfortunes, we still had soldiers in good heart, and quite capable of defeating Austro-Bavarians.

General de Wrède, who did not know that the troops which we had fought at Leipzig, though following us were a long way behind, had become very bold and believed he could trap us between two fires. It was not possible for him to do so, though as several enemy corps were trying to mount an attack on our right by going through the mountains of Franconia, while the Bavarians stood in front of us the situation could have become serious.

Napoleon rose to the challenge and marched briskly towards Hanau, whose approaches are protected by thick forests and notably by the well-known pass of Gelnhausen, through which runs the river Kinzig. This river, whose banks are very steep, runs between two mountains which are separated by a narrow gap which allows the passage of the river, beside which has been made a fine main road, cut into the rock, and running from Fulde to Frankfort-on-main via Hanau.

Sébastiani's cavalry corps which had been the advance-guard from Weissenfels to Fulde, where one enters the mountains, should have been replaced by infantry at this point. I have never understood for what reason this well known principle of warfare was not followed in these grave circumstances; but to our astonishment, Exelmans' cavalry division continued to march in front of the army, led by my regiment and the 24th Chasseurs. I was in command of the brigade. We learned from the peasants that the Austro-Bavarian army already occupied Hanau, and that a strong division was facing the French, to dispute the passage of the defile.

My position, as commander of the advance-guard, was now very difficult; for how could I, without a single infantryman and with cavalry packed between two high mountains and an uncrossable torrent, fight troops on foot whose scouts, climbing up the rocks would shoot us at close range? I sent at once to warn the divisional general, but Exelmans could not be found. However I had been ordered to advance and I could not stop the divisions which were following me, so I continued my march until at a bend in the valley my scouts told me that they were in sight of a detachment of enemy Hussars. The Austro-Bavarians had made the same mistake as our leaders; for if the latter had sent cavalry to attack a long and narrow pass, where no more the ten or twelve horsemen could ride abreast, our enemies had sent cavalry to defend a position where a hundred sharpshooters could hold up ten regiments of cavalry. I was highly delighted to see that the enemy had no infantry, and as I knew from experience that when two opposing columns meet at a narrow spot, victory always goes to the one which, hurling itself at the head of the enemy, drives it back into the troops behind it, I launched at the gallop my elite company, of which only the leading platoon could engage the enemy; but they did so with such élan that the head of the Austrian column was overwhelmed and the rest thrown into such complete confusion that my troopers had only to take aim.

We continued the pursuit for more than an hour. The enemy regiment in front of us was that of General Ott. I had never seen such well turned out Hussars. They had come from Vienna, where they had been fitted with completely new uniforms, Their outfit, although a little theatrical, looked very handsome: the pelisse and dolman in white and the trousers and the shako in lilac; all clean bright and shining. One might have thought they were going to a ball, or to play in a musical comedy. This brilliant appearance contrasted somewhat with the more modest toilette of our Chasseurs, many of whom were still dressed in the worn clothing in which they had bivouacked for eighteen months, in Russia, Poland, and Germany, and whose distinguishing colours had been dimmed by the smoke of cannon and the dust of battlefields. However, under those threadbare garments were brave hearts and sturdy limbs. So the white pelisses of Ott's Hussars became horribly bloodstained, and this pretty regiment lost in killed and wounded more than 200 men without one of our Chasseurs having the smallest sabre cut, the enemy having always fled without ever turning to fight. Our Chasseurs took a large number of excellent horses and gold-braided pelisses.

Up until then everything had gone well, but as I galloped after the victors who pursued the vanquished, I was a bit worried about the end of this strange encounter, for the diminishing height of the mountains which bordered the Kinzig indicated that we were nearing the end of the valley, and it was likely that we would find ourselves in a small plain, full of infantry whose volleys and cannon fire would make us pay dearly for our success: but happily there was no such thing, and as we emerged from the pass we saw not a single infantryman, but only some cavalry, part of which comprised the main body of that section of Ott's regiment of Hussars, which we had so roughly manhandled and who in their panic continued their headlong flight, taking with them some fifteen squadrons, who retired to Hanau.

General Sébastiani then deployed his three divisions of cavalry which were soon supported by the infantry of Marshals Macdonald and Victor and several batteries. Then the Emperor with part of his guard, appeared and the rest of the French army followed.

It was now the evening of the 29th of October; we established our bivouacs in a nearby wood; we were only a league from Hanau and the Austro-Bavarian army.

Chapter 30
The Battle of Hanau

Here now are the reasons why Exelmans dropped behind when we were going through the pass. Before we entered the valley, the scouts had brought to him two Austrian soldiers absentees from their unit, who were scrounging and drinking in an isolated village. Exelmans was having them questioned in German by one of his aides, when he was surprised to hear them reply in fluent French. One of these men, half drunk, and thinking it would do him good, announced that they were Parisians. As soon as he uttered these words, the general, furious that Frenchmen should take up arms against their fellow countrymen, ordered them to be immediately shot. The poor lad who had boasted of being French was about to be put to death, when his companion, sobered by this fearful spectacle, protested that neither of them had ever set foot in France, but having been born in Vienna to parents who, although they came from Paris, were naturalised Austrians, they were regarded as Austrian subjects and had been forced to join the regiment assigned to them. To prove this he showed his army record which confirmed the fact. Exelmans, yielding to the advice of his aides-de-camp, agreed to spare the innocent man.

At this stage, hearing the sound of firing, the General wished to reach the head of the column which I was commanding; but on his arrival at the mouth of the pass, he found it impossible to get through and take a place in the ranks because of the speed with which the two regiments were galloping after the enemy. After trying many times he was so jostled that he fell with his horse into the Kinzig and nearly drowned.

The Emperor, who was preparing for battle, took advantage of the night to reduce the amount of wheeled transport by sending all the baggage off to the right, in the direction of Coblentz, escorted by some battalions of infantry and the cavalry of Lefebvre-Denouettes and Milhau. This was a great relief to the army.

On the morning of the 30th, the Emperor had at his disposal only the infantry Corps of Macdonald and Victor, amounting to 5000 men, supported by Sébastiani's cavalry division.

In the direction from which we were coming, a large forest, through which the road runs, covers the approach to Hanau. The tall trees of this forest allow movement without much difficulty. The town of Hanau is built on the other side of the river Kinzig.

General de Wrède, although not lacking in military skill, had, however, made the serious mistake of placing his army where it had the river at its back, which deprived it of the support which it could have received from the fortifications of Hanau, with which he could not communicate except by the bridge of Lamboy, which was his only road of retreat. It is true that the position he occupied barred the way to Frankfort and to France, and he felt certain that he could prevent us from forcing a passage.

On the 30th of October at dawn the battle began, like a great hunting party. Some grape-shot and some small-arms fire from our infantry, together with a charge in open order by Sébastiani's cavalry, scattered the first line of the enemy, somewhat unskillfully placed at the extreme edge of the wood; but as one penetrated a little further, our squadrons could not operate except in the few clearings which they came across, only the Light Infantry followed in the steps of the Bavarians, whom they pursued from tree to tree to the end of the forest. At that point they had to stop, faced by an enemy line of forty thousand men, whose front was covered by eighty guns.

If the Emperor had had with him all the troops which he brought from Leipzig, a vigorous attack would have made him master of the Lamboy bridge, and General de Wrède would have paid dearly for his temerity, but Marshals Mortier and Marmont and General Bertrand, as well as the artillery, were held up by various passes, mainly that of Gelnhausen, and had not yet arrived. Napoleon had no more than ten thousand troops. The enemy should have taken advantage of this to attack us in force, but they did not dare, and this hesitation gave time for the artillery of the Imperial Guard to arrive.

As soon as General Drouet, their commander, had fifteen pieces in the field, he began firing, and his line grew in size until he had fifty cannons, which he advanced, firing continuously, although he still had very few troops behind him to give support; however it was not possible for the enemy to see through the thick smoke from the guns, that the gunners had little to back them up. Eventually the infantry Chasseurs of the Imperial Old Guard appeared, just as a gust of wind blew away the smoke.

At the sight of their busbies, the Bavarian infantry recoiled in fear. General de Wrède in an effort to stop this disorder at all costs, ordered all his cavalry, Austrian, Bavarian and Russian, to charge our artillery, and in an instant our battery was surrounded by a swarm of horsemen. but at the voice of their commander, General Drouet, who, sword in hand, set them an example in resistance, the French gunners, taking their muskets, remained calmly behind their guns, from where they fired point-blank at the enemy. Nevertheless, the great number of the latter would have eventually triumphed, had not, on the Emperor's order, all Sébastiani's cavalry, along with all that of the Imperial Guard, mounted Grenadiers, Dragoons, Chasseurs, Mamelukes, Lancers and Guards of Honour, hurled themselves furiously on the enemy cavalry, killing a great number and dispersing the rest.

Then, falling on the Bavarian infantry squares, they broke them and inflicted tremendous losses, at which stage the Bavarian army, put to rout, fled to the bridge over the Kinzig and to the town of Hanau.

General de Wrède was a brave man, so, before admitting himself beaten by forces half as numerous as his, he resolved to make another effort, and gathering all the troops remaining to him, he made a surprise attack on us. Suddenly a fusillade broke out and the forest rang once more to the sound of artillery; cannon-balls whistled through the trees, from which great branches fell with a crash. The eye sought in vain to pierce the depths of the wood; one could hardly see the flash of the guns, which lit, at intervals, the shade cast by the foliage of the huge beeches, beneath whose canopy we fought.

Hearing the noise made by this attack, the Emperor sent from his position the infantry Grenadiers of his Old Guard, led by General Friant who soon overcame this last effort of the enemy, who now hastily left the field of battle to re-group under the protection of the fort of Hanau, which they abandoned during the night, leaving behind a great number of wounded. The French occupied the fort.

We were no more than two short leagues from Frankfort, a considerable town, with a stone bridge across the Main. The French army would need to go along the bank of this river to reach Mainz and the frontier of France, which was a day's march from Frankfort; so Napoleon detached Sébastiani's corps and a division of infantry to go and occupy Frankfort, and to take over and destroy the bridge. The Emperor and the bulk of the army bivouacked in the forest.

The main road from Hanau to Frankfort runs along the right bank of the river Maine. General Albert, a friend of mine, who commanded the infantry which accompanied us, had been married, some years previously, at Offenbach, a charming little town, built on the left bank exactly opposite the spot where, after emerging from the woods of Hanau, we rested our horses on the immense and beautiful plain of Frankfort.

Finding himself so close to his wife and their children, General Albert was unable to resist the temptation to have news of them, and to reassure them of his well-being after the dangers he had encountered at the battles of Leipzig and Hanau. To do this he exposed himself to more risk, perhaps, than he had run during either of these sanguinary affairs, for advancing on horseback and in uniform to the edge of the river, in spite of our warnings, he hailed a boatman who knew him; but while he was chatting with this man, a Bavarian officer ran up with a picket of infantry who, aiming their weapons, prepared to shoot at the French general. However, a large body of citizens and boatmen crowded in front of the soldiers and prevented them from firing, for General Albert was very well liked in Offenbach.

As I looked at this town, to where I had come while fighting for my country, I did not dream that one day it would be my refuge from the proscription of a French government, and that I would spend three years there in exile.

After leaving the forest of Hanau to go on his way to Frankfort, the Emperor had hardly gone two leagues when he learned that fighting had broken out once more behind him. This was because

229

the Bavarian general who, following his defeat the day before, had expected to be chased, with the Emperor at his heels, had taken reassurance from seeing the French army more concerned to reach the Rhine than to pursue him, and had launched a brisk attack on our rear-guard. However Macdonald, Marmont and Bertrand, who with their troops had occupied Hanau during the night, having allowed the Bavarians to attack them on that side of the Kinzig, received them with their bayonets, overwhelmed and massacred them. General de Wrède was seriously injured, and his son-in-law, Prince d'Oettingen was killed.

The command of the enemy army then devolved onto the Austrian General Fresnel who ordered a retreat, and the French army continued on its way peacefully towards the Rhine. We recrossed the river on the 2nd and 3rd of November 1813, after a campaign which included brilliant victories and disasterous defeats, the main cause of which, as I have said, was the mistake made by Napoleon when, instead of making peace in June, following the victories of Lutzen and Bautzen, he quarreled with Austria, which involved the Confederation of the Rhine, that is to say all of Germany, so that he soon had the whole of Europe ranged against him.

After we had returned to France, the Emperor spent only six days at Mainz, and then went to Paris, preceded by twenty-six flags taken from our enemies. The army disapproved of this rapid departure on the part of Napoleon. It was accepted that there were important political reasons which called him to Paris, but it was thought that he should have divided his time between his capital and the need to re-organise his army, and that he should have gone from one to the other to encourage the activity of each, for he should have learned by experience that in his absence little or nothing was done.

The last cannon shots which I heard in 1813 were fired at the battle of Hanau, where I nearly spent the last day of my life. My regiment carried out five charges, two on infantry squares, one on artillery and two on Bavarian cavalry; but the greatest danger I ran was when an ammunition wagon, loaded with mortar bombs, caught fire and exploded close to me. I have told how, on the Emperor's order, all the cavalry were in action at a particularly difficult moment. Now, in these circumstances, it is not good enough for a unit commander to send his troops blindly forward, a thing I have seen done on several occasions, but he must pay the closest attention to the ground over which his squadrons are about to pass, in case he sends them into bogs and marshes.

I was therefore, a few paces ahead, followed by my regimental staff and with my trumpeter at my side, who at a given command would signal to the various squadrons the obstacles which they would find in their way. Although the trees were widely spaced, the passage through the forest was difficult for the cavalry because the ground was littered with dead and wounded men and horses, arms, cannons and ammunition wagons, abandoned by the Bavarians. You can understand that in these conditions when one is galloping through shot and shell to reach the enemy one cannot always take much care of oneself, and I relied greatly on the intelligence and suppleness of my excellent and brave Turkish horse, Azolan. The little group which followed me had been much reduced by a blast of grape-shot which had wounded several of my orderlies and I had beside me only the trumpeter, a charming and good young man, when I heard from all along the line, cries of "Look out, Colonel!" And I saw ten paces away Bavariana ammunition wagon which one of our shells had set on fire.

A huge tree which had been knocked down by cannon-balls barred my way forward, and to go round it would have taken too long. I shouted to the trumpeter to duck, and crouching on my horse's neck, I urged him to jump the tree. Azolan leapt a long way, but not far enough to clear all the leafy branches in which his legs became entangled. The wagon was now in flames and the powder about to catch. I thought I was done for when my horse, as if he realised our common danger, started bounding four or five feet into the air, getting always further from the wagon, and as soon as he was clear of the branches he galloped off with such speed that he really seemed to be "Ventre à terre".

I was shaken when the explosion occurred, but it seemed I was out of range of the bursting shells for neither I nor my horse were touched.

Sadly it was not so for my poor young trumpeter, for when we resumed our march after the explosion we saw his body, mutilated by the shell fragments, and his horse also cut to pieces.

My brave Azolan had already saved my life at the Katzbach. I now owed him my life for the second time. I made much of him, and as if to show his pleasure he whinnied at the top of his voice. It is at times like these that one has to believe that some animals are more intelligent than is generally thought.

I greatly regretted the death of my trumpeter, who by his courage and his behaviour had made himself liked by all the regiment. He was the son of a teacher at the college in Toulouse, and had had a good education. He delighted in producing Latin quotations, and an hour before his death, the poor lad, having noticed that almost all the trees in the forest of Hanau were beeches, whose branches stretched out to make a sort of roof, had thought it a suitable occasion to declaim one of Virgil's eclogues, beginning: "*Tityre, tu patulae recubans sub tegmine fagi....*"; which greatly amused Marshal Macdonald who happened to be passing and who exclaimed, "There's a jolly lad whose memory isn't upset by his surroundings; I'll bet it's the first time anyone has recited Virgil to the sound of enemy cannon fire!"

"Those who live by the sword, perish by the sword" says the scripture, and if this is not applicable to every soldier, it was to a great many under the Empire. For example, M. Guindet, who killed Prince Louis of Prussia in the fighting at Saalefeld, was himself killed at the battle of Hanau. It was no doubt the fear of meeting a similar fate which led the Russian General Czernicheff to run away from danger.

You may remember that in the first months of 1812, this officer, then a colonel, an aide-de-camp and favourite of the Emperor Alexander, came to Paris where he abused his position to corrupt two poor employees in the Ministry of War , who were executed for having sold to him situation reports on the French army, and that the Russian Colonel only escaped the penalty of the law by secretly fleeing the country. On his return to Russia, M.de Czernicheff, although he was a courtier rather than a soldier, was given the rank of general officer and the command of a division of 3000 Cossacks, the only Russian troops who appeared at Hanau where their leader played a rôle which made him a laughing stock among the Austrians and Bavarians who were present at this engagement.

Czernicheff, as he marched towards us, spoke loudly of victory, believing that he had to face only soldiers who were sick and disorganised; but he changed his tune when he saw himself in the presence of the hardy and vigorous troops returning from Leipzig. General de Wrède had great difficulty in persuading him to enter the line, and as soon as he heard the fearsome cannonade of our artillery, he and his 3000 Cossacks trotted bravely off the field, to the cat-calls of the Austro-Bavarian troops, who witnessed this shameful conduct. When General de Wrède went personally to make some scathing observations, M. de Czernicheff replied that his regiment's horses needed feeding and that he was taking them for this purpose to nearby villages. This excuse was regarded as so ridiculous that for some time afterwards the walls of German villages were decorated by caricatures of M. de Czernicheff feeding his horses with bunches of laurels gathered in the forest of Hanau.

Once across the Rhine, the soldiers who made up the remains of the French army expected to see an end to their hardships as soon as they set foot on the soil of their motherland; but they were much mistaken, for the government, and the Emperor himself, had so much counted on success, and had so little foreseen that we might leave Germany, that nothing had been made ready at the frontier to receive and re-organise the troops. So, from the very day of our arrival at Mainz, the men and the horses would have gone short of food if we had not spread them out and lodged them with the inhabitants of nearby villages and hamlets; but since the first wars of the revolution, they had lost the habit of feeding soldiers, and complained vociferously, and it is true that the expense was too great for the communes.

As it was necessary to guard, or at least to watch over the immensely long frontier formed by the Rhine from Basle to Holland, we settled, as best we could the numerous sick and wounded in the hospitals of Mainz. All fit men rejoined the core of their regiments, and the various units of the army, which for the most part consisted only of a small cadre, were spread along the river. My regiment, together with what was left of Sébastiani's cavalry corps, went down the Rhine by short marches; but although the weather was perfect and the countryside charming, we were all deeply unhappy, for one could foresee that France was going to lose possession of this fine land, and that her misfortunes would not stop there.

My regiment spent some time in Cleves, next a fortnight in the little town of Urdingen, and then went on to Nimeguen. During this sad journey we were painfully affected by the sight of the inhabitants on the opposite bank, the Germans and the Dutch, tearing down the French flag from their steeples and replacing it with the flags of their former sovereigns. In spite of these gloomy reflections, all the colonels tried to re-organise the few troops which remained to them, but what could one do without clothing, equipment or replacement of arms?

The need to provide food for the army compelled the Emperor to keep it dispersed, whereas to re-organise it would require the creation of large centres of concentration. We were therefore in a vicious circle. However, the allies, who should have crossed the Rhine a few days after us, to prevent our re-organisation, felt themselves still so weakened as a result of the hard blows we had delivered during the last campaign, that they needed time to recover.

They left us in peace for the months of November and December, the greater part of which I spent on the bank of the Rhine, in the ghost of the army corps commanded by Marshal Macdonald.

I was eventually ordered, as were the other cavalry colonels, to take all my dismounted men to my regimental depot for the task of building up new squadrons. The depot of the 23rd was still at Mons, in Belgium, and that is where I went. It was there that I saw the end of the year 1813, so filled with great events and in which I had had encountered many dangers and undergone so many trials.

Before I end my chronicle of the year, I ought to summarise briefly the final events of the campaign of 1813.

Chapter 31
We Lose Germany, Spain & Italy

The German fortresses in which the retreating French had left garrisons were soon surrounded and in some cases besieged. Almost all surrendered. Four only were still holding out at the end of 1813.

The first of these was Hamburg, commanded by the intrepid Marshal Davout, who held on to this important fort until after the abdication of the Emperor, when the French government recalled the garrison to France; the second was Magdeburg, where General Le Marois, an aide-de-camp to the Emperor, also held out until the end of the war; the third was Wittemburg, defended by the elderly General Lapoype, and which was taken by assault on the 12th of the following January; and finally Erfurt, which had to capitulate for lack of food.

All the other fortresses beyond the Rhine, which the Emperor had wanted to keep, the most important of which were Dresden, Danzig, Stettin, Zamosk, Torgau and Modlin, were already in the hands of the enemy.

The circumstances surrounding the taking over of the first two of these fortresses do not reflect much honour on the allies. After the battle of Leipzig, Napoleon withdrew with the remains of his army, leaving at Dresden a corps of 25,000 men commanded by Marshal Saint-Cyr, who tried by force of arms to cut a passage through the enemies who blocked his way. He drove them back several times but eventually overcome by stronger forces and short of food he was compelled to accept the honourable capitulation which was offered to him. This stipulated that the garrison would keep its arms, would not be made prisoners of war and would march back to France in day-long stages.

The Marshal wanted his troops to move as a corps and to bivouac all together at the same place, which would allow them to defend themselves in case of treachery; but the enemy generals pointed out that owing to the exhaustion of the countryside, it would be impossible to provide at any one place twenty-five thousand rations, and the French marshal had to accept this. He then agreed that his force should be divided into several small columns of 2 or 3000 men who would travel one or even two days apart.

For the first few days all went well, but as soon as the last French column had left Dresden, having handed over the fort and the munitions of war, the foreign generals announced that they did not have the authority to sign the capitulation without the agreement of their generalissimo, Prince Schwartzenberg, and as he did not approve, the agreement was null and void. They offered to allow our troops to return to Dresden in exactly the same state as they had been previously, that is to say with only enough food for a few days, a shortage which they had concealed from the enemy for as long as they occupied the place, and which, as it was now known to them, made the offer worthless.

Our troops were indignant at this odious lack of good faith, but what action could be taken by isolated detachments of 2 or 3000 men, whom the enemy had taken the precaution of surrounding by battalions of their own, before they could hear of the breakdown of the capitulation? Any resistance was impossible and our men were forced to lay down their arms.

To the treachery practised on the field of battle, was now added that of the breaking of agreements of capitulation. This did not prevent the Germans from celebrating a victory, for they regarded any measures, however despicable, as justified in order to defeat Napoleon. This new morality was put into operation at Danzig.

General Rapp had defended this place for a long time but having run out of food he was compelled to surrender on condition that the garrison would be allowed to return to France. However, in spite of a treaty signed by the Prince of Wurtemberg, the commander of the army which conducted the siege, the conditions were violated and the garrison of 16,000 men were sent as prisoners to Russia where most of them died.

One of the most remarkable stories of this siege concerns a Captain de Chambure, who asked for and obtained permission to form an independent company, chosen from hand-picked volunteers. They engaged on the most daring ventures, going out at night and surprising enemy posts, getting into their entrenchments, into their camps, destroying their siege-works under the nose of their batteries, spiking their guns and going far into the country to capture or pillage their convoys. Chambure, having gone out one night with his men, surprised a Russian cantonment, set fire to an ammunition dump, destroyed several stores and killed or wounded one hundred and fifty men, for the loss of three of his own; and returned to the fort in triumph.

Now, however, let us return to examine the position of the French armies in December 1813.

Spain, the principal cause of all the catastrophes which marked the end of Napoleon's reign, had been stripped, in the course of the year, of all its best troops, which the Emperor had sent to reinforce the army in Germany. However, the effective strength of those who remained in the Iberian peninsula amounted to more than 100,000 men. A number which, although inadequate, would have contained the enemy if Napoleon had left the command to Marshal Soult; but as he most earnestly wished to make of his brother Joseph a general who could defend the kingdom which he had given him, it was to this prince, an estimable man but no soldier, that the Emperor entrusted the command of the armies of Spain. He gave him, it is true, as chief of staff and military advisor, Marshal Jourdan; but the Marshal was prematurely aged and had not been involved in active warfare since the first campaigns of the revolution. He was so worn out, both mentally and physically, that he inspired no confidence in the troops. So, in spite of the talents displayed by the generals who served under the orders of King Joseph, the Anglo-Portuguese army commanded by Lord Wellington and helped by Spanish guerrillas, caused us irreparable losses.

The French, under pressure at every point, had already been compelled to abandon Madrid, the two Castiles, and to recross the Ebro, to concentrate their main forces round the town of Vittoria. Attacked in this position by three times their number, they lost a battle; a loss which was made all the more disastrous by the fact that King Joseph and Marshal Jourdan had made no arrangements for the carrying out of a retreat, so that it became chaotic. The King's suite, the artillery parks, the many coaches of a crowd of

Spaniards, who having taken sides with Joseph, sought to escape the vengence of their compatriots, the wagons of the treasury, of the military administration, etc., etc., all found themselves piled up in confusion, so that the roads were obstructed and the regiments had great difficulty in moving. However they did not lose their formation, and in spite of vigorous attacks by the enemy, the greater part of the army managed to reach Salvatierra and the road to Pamplona, by which the retreat was made.

The battle of Vittoria demonstrated the talent and courage of General Clausel, who rallied the army and gave it some direction. It was, however, an unhappy day. The French lost 6000 men killed, wounded or taken prisoner and left in the hands of the enemy a large part of their artillery and almost all their baggage.

Despite this set-back, the troops whose morale was excellent, could have remained in Navarre with the aid of the fortress of Pamplona and the Pyrenees mountains, but King Joseph ordered the continuation of the retreat and the crossing of the Bidassoa, where our rear-guard, commanded by General Foy, was ordered to blow up the bridge. So, from the end of June, we abandoned that part of the Spanish frontier; nevertheless, Marshal Suchet still held out in Aragon (The region of Zaragossa) and Catalonia, and in the kingdom of Valencia; but the results of the battle of Vittoria had so much weakened us that when Wellington sent reinforcements to central Spain Suchet found it necessary to leave the town and the kingdom.

These events were taking place at a time when Napoleon was still triumphant in Germany. As soon as he was told of the state of affairs across the Pyrenees, he hastily revoked the powers which he had given to King Joseph and Marshal Jourden, and appointed Marshal Soult commander of all the armies in Spain.

Soult, after re-organising the divisions, made a great effort to help the French garrison left in Pamplona, but in vain. They were forced to capitulate and Marshal Soult had to take his troops back across the Bidassoa. The fortress of San-Sebastian, governed by General Rey, held out for a long time; but was eventually taken by assault by the Anglo-Portuguese, who, ignoring the laws of humanity, robbed, raped and massacred the unfortunate inhabitants of this Spanish town, although they were their allies. The

English officers made no attempt to stop these atrocities, which went on for three days, to the shame of Wellington, his generals and the English.

Marshal Soult defended the Pyrenees foot by foot and beat Wellington on several occasions; but the greater numbers at the latter's disposal allowed him unceasingly to take the offensive, so that he was able eventually to cross our frontier and set up his headquarters in Saint-Jean de Luz, the first town in France and a town which had never previously been lost, even during the defeats suffered by Francis I, or the disastrous wars of the end of the reign of Louis XIV.

It was evident that after the defection of the German troops at Leipzig, Marshal Soult could not hope to keep in the army of the Pyrenees several thousand soldiers from across the Rhine. They all went over to the enemy in a single night, thus augmenting Wellington's strength.

However, Marshal Soult, after concentrating several divisions below the ramparts of Bayonne, once more attacked the Anglo-Portuguese. On the 9th of December, at Saint-Pierre de Rube, there was a battle which lasted for five days, and was one of the bloodiest of the war, for it cost the enemy 16,000 lives and the French 10,000, but we were able to remain in position around Bayonne.

Before these events in the Pyrenees, Marshal Suchet, having learned of the reverses suffered by Napoleon in Germany, realised that it would be impossible for him to remain in the middle of Spain, and prepared to return to France. To do this he withdrew to Tarragon, where after taking the garrison into his army he blew up the ramparts. The retreat, although harried by the Spanish, was carried out in good order, and by the end of December 1813, Suchet and the troops under his command were established in Gerona.

To complete this examination of the position of the French armies at the end of 1813, one needs to recall that in the spring of that year, the Emperor, who distrusted Austria, had built up in the Tyrol and in his kingdom of Italy, a large army, the command of which he had given to his step-son Eugène de Beauharnais, the viceroy of the country. This prince was a good man, very gentle and greatly devoted to the Emperor, but although much more of a soldier than King Joseph of Spain, he lacked many of the qualities required to lead an army. The Emperor's affection for Eugène led him astray in this matter.

It was on the 24th of August, the day when the armistice between Napoleon and the allies was due to expire, that the Austrians abandoned their neutrality and declared themselves our enemies. The Italian troops continued to serve with us, but the Dalmatians (Croats) left us to join the Austrians. Prince Eugène had under his command a number of excellent lieutenants, but the fighting was never very strenuous because the commanders on both sides realised that the events in Germany would determine the outcome of the campaign. There were however, a number of actions, with various results. In the end the larger forces of the Austrians, who were shortly joined by an English contingent which disembarked in Tuscany forced the viceroy to lead the Franco-Italian army beyond the Adige.

In November came news of the defection of Murat the King of Naples. The Emperor to whom he owed everything, could not at first believe it. It was, however, only too true. Murat had joined forces with the Austrians, against whom he had fought for so long, and his troops already occupied Bologna. Such is the volatility of the Italians that everywhere they welcomed with acclamation the Austro-Neapolitans, whom they had previously detested and whom they would soon hate even more. By December, the vice-roi's army of only 43,000 men, occupied Verona and its surroundings.

The Emperor, seeing the whole of Europe combined against him, could not fail to realise that the first condition which a peace would demand of him would be the re-installment of the Bourbons on the throne of Spain. He decided therefore to do of his own volition what he would be forced to do later: he set free King Ferdinand, who had been detained at Valancay, and ordered Suchet's army to retire behind the Pyrenees.

Thus, at the end of 1813, we had lost all of Germany, all of Spain, and the greater part of Italy. Wellington's army, which had crossed the Bidassoa and the western Pyrenees, was encamped on French soil and threatening Bayonne, Navarre and Bordeaux.

Chapter 32
The Allies Advance

I began the year 1814 at Mons. Where I did not undergo such physical dangers as I had done in previous years, but where I suffered much more mentally.

As I had left, at Nimeguen, all the troopers of my regiment who still had horses, I had none at Mons, where the depot was situated, except dismounted men, for whom I was trying to get horses from the Ardennes, when events prevented this.

On the 1st of January, the enemies, after hesitating for three months before invading France, crossed the Rhine at several points, the two most important of these being firstly at Kaub, a market town situated between Bingen and Coblentz, where a rocky gorge greatly reduces the width of the river, and then at Basle where the Swiss handed over the stone bridge, in violation of their neutrality, a neutrality which they maintain or abandon according to their interests.

It is estimated that some five to six hundred thousand allied soldiers entered a France exhausted by twenty-five years of war, half of whose troops were prisoners in foreign lands, and many of whose provinces were ready to defect on the first suitable occasion. Amongst which was that containing the department of Jemmapes, of which Mons was the principal town.

This huge area of rich country which had been annexed to France, firstly "de facto" by the war of 1792, and then by right after the treaty of Amiens, had been so accustomed to this union that after the disasters of the Russian campaign, it had shown great enthusiasm and made considerable sacrifices to help the Emperor to put his troops back on a sound footing. Men, horses, equipment, clothing, it had complied with all demands without a murmur; but the losses we had suffered in Germany had discouraged the Belgians, and I found the attitude of the populace had completely changed. They loudly regretted the paternal government of the house of Austria, under which they had lived for so long, and were most anxious to separate themselves from France, whose continual wars were ruining their trade and industry. In a word, Belgium awaited only a favourable moment to revolt, an event which would be the more serious for us because, by its geographical situation the province was in the rear of the weakened army corps which we still had on the Rhine. The Emperor sent some troops to Brussels, whom he placed under the command of General Maisons, a capable and very determined man. Maisons, having, visited several departments, recognised that Jemmapes, and particularly the town of Mons, was the most disaffected. There was there, open discussion of the possibility of taking up arms against the weak French garrison, something which its commander general "O". could not have prevented, for the old general, stricken by gout, and lacking in energy, who had been born in Belgium, seemed afraid to earn the dislike of his compatriots. General Maisons suspended him from duty and gave me the command of the department of Jemmapes.

My job was made more difficult because, after the inhabitants of Liége, those who live in Borinage are the boldest and most turbulent in all Belgium, and to control them I had only a small unit of 400 conscripts, a few gendarmes and 200 unmounted cavalrymen from my regiment, among whom there were some fifty men who were born in the area and who, in case of trouble, would join the insurgents. I could rely entirely only on the other 150 Chasseurs, who born in France, and having been in action with me, would have followed me anywhere.

There were some good officers; those in the infantry, and in particular the battalion commander, were very willing to back me up.

I could not, however, disguise the fact that if it came to blows, the two sides were not equally matched. From the hotel where I stayed I saw every day 3 or 4,000 peasants and workmen from the town, armed with big sticks who gathered in the main square to listen to speeches from former Austrian officers, all of them wealthy nobles, who had quitted the service on the union of Belgium with France, and now spoke out against the Empire, which had loaded them with taxes, taken their children to send them to the wars, etc.,etc. These speeches were listened to with all the more attention, in that they were delivered by great landed proprietors, and addressed to their tenants and employees, over whom they wielded much influence.

Add to this that each day brought news of the advance of our enemies, who were approaching Brussels, driving before them the debris of Marshal Macdonald's Corps. All the French employees left the department to take refuge in Valenciennes and Cambrai. Finally the mayor of Mons, M. Duval of Beaulieu, an honourable man, thought it his duty to warn me that neither my feeble garrison nor myself were safe in the midst of an excited and numerous population, and that I would be wise to leave the town, a move which would not be opposed since my regiment and I had always lived at peace with the inhabitants.

I was aware that this proposition came from a committee composed of former Austrian officers, which had instructed the mayor to put it to me, in the hope that I would be intimidated. I resolved then to show my teeth, I said to M. Duval that I would be most grateful if he would summon the town council and the leading citizens, and that I would then give my reply to the proposals which he had brought me.

Half an hour later, all the garrison were armed, and when the municipal council accompanied by the wealthiest citizens had assembled in the square, I mounted on horseback, in order to be heard by all, and after I had told the mayor that before talking with him and his council, I had an important order to give to my troops, I told my men about the suggestion which had been made that we should abandon, without a struggle, the town which had been put in our care.

They were most indignant, and said so loudly! I added that I could not conceal the fact that the ramparts were broken down at several points, and a lack of artillery would make defence difficult against regular troops, though if need be we would do our best; but that if it was the inhabitants of the town and the countryside who rose against us, we would not confine ourselves to defence, we would attack with all the means at our disposal, for we would be dealing with revolutionaries. As a consequence I was ordering my men to take over the church tower, from where, after a delay of half an hour and three rolls on the drums they would fire on the occupants of the square, while patrols would clear the streets by shooting, mainly at those who had left their work in the country to come and do us harm. I added that if it came to fighting, I would order, as the best means of defence, the setting on fire of the town, in order to keep the inhabitants busy, and I would shoot at them continually to prevent its extinction.

This speech may seem a little drastic, but consider the critical position in which I found myself; with no more than 700 men, few of whom had seen action, no expectation of reinforcements, and surrounded by a multitude which increased in size by the moment, for the officer in charge of the detachment sent to the church tower told me that the roads leading to the town were full of miners from the pits of Jemmapes, heading for the town of Mons. My little troupe and I were at risk of being wiped out if I had not taken decisive action. My address had produced a marked effect among the rich noblemen, the promoters of this disturbance, and also among the townspeople, who began to disperse; but as the peasants did not budge, I brought up two ammunition wagons to issue a hundred cartridges to each soldier, and when they had loaded their weapons, I ordered the three rolls on the drums, the prelude to the fusillade.

At this frightening sound, the huge crowd which filled the square began to run in tumult to the neighbouring streets, where each one rushed to find shelter, and a few moments later the leaders of the Austrian party, with the mayor at their head, came to clutch at my hand and beg me to spare the town. I agreed on the condition that they would send immediately to tell the miners and workmen to go back to their homes. They hastened to comply, and the elegant young men who were the best mounted, jumped on their fine horses and went out through all the city gates to meet the mob which they sent back to their villages without any opposition.

This passive obedience confirmed me in my opinion that the disturbance had powerful backers, and that my garrison and I would have been held prisoner, had I not frightened the leaders by threatening to use all means, even fire rather than hand over to rioters the town confided to my charge.

The Belgians are very fond of music, and it so happened that there was a concert to be given that evening, to which I and my officers had been invited, as was M.de Laussat the prefect of the department.

We agreed that we should go there as usual, which was the right decision, for we were received with cordiality, at least on the surface. While talking to the nobles, who had been behind the disturbance, we put it to them that it was not for the populace to decide by rebellion the fate of Belgium, but rather for the contending armies; and it would be folly on their part to incite the workmen and peasants to shed their blood, in order to hasten by a few days a solution which would presently become evident.

An elderly Austrian general, who had retired to Mons, his birthplace, then said to his compatriots that they had been wrong to plot the seizure of the garrison, for that would have resulted in much damage to the town, as no soldiers would lay down their arms without a fight. They all agreed that this assessment was correct, and from that day forward the garrison and the townsfolk lived peacefully together as in the past. The people of Mons even gave us a few days later a striking demonstration of their support.

As the allied armies advanced, a crowd of partisans, mainly Prussians, disguised themselves as Cossacks, and driven by the desire for plunder they grabbed anything which had belonged to the French administration, and had no hesitation in seizing the goods of even non-military French citizens.

A large band of these imitation Cossacks, having crossed the Rhine and spread out on the left bank, had reached as far as the gates of Brussels, and had pillaged the imperial château of Tervueren, from where they took all the horses of the stud farm which the Emperor had installed there; then, splitting into smaller groups, these marauders infested Belgium. Some of them came to the department of Jemmapes, where they tried to stir up the populace, but when they did not succeed in doing so, they put this down to the fact that Mons, the principal town of the region, had not supported them because of the terror inspired by the colonel in command of the garrison. Whereupon they decided to capture or kill me, but in order not to awaken my suspicions by employing too great a number of men for this exploit, they limited the number to three hundred. It appeared that the leader of these partisans had been well briefed, for, knowing that I had too few men to guard the old gates and ancient, partly demolished, ramparts, he took his men, during a dark night, to the rampart, where the major part of them dismounted and made their way silently through the streets to the main square and the Hotel de la Poste, where I had at first stayed. However, since I had heard of the crossing of the Rhine by the enemy, I had gone every evening to the barracks, where I spent the night surrounded by my troops. It was as well that I had done so, for the German Cossacks surrounded the hotel and rifled through all the rooms. Then, furious at not finding any French officers, they set on the inn-keeper, whom they robbed and mal-treated, and whose wine they drank until both officers and soldiers were drunk.

A Belgian, a former corporal in my regiment, named Courtois, for whom I had obtained a decoration as one of my bravest sol-diers, arrived at this moment at the hotel. This man, born at Saint-Ghislain near Mons, had lost a leg in Russia the previous year, and happily I had been able to save him by securing means for him to return to France. He was so grateful for this that during my stay in Mons in the winter of 1814, he came often to visit me, and on those occasions he dressed in the uniform of the 23rd Chasseurs which he had once so honourably worn. Now, it so happened that on the night in question, Curtois, while returning to the house of one of his relatives where he had been staying, saw the enemy detachment heading in the direction of the hotel, and although the gallant corporal knew that I did not sleep there, he wanted to be sure that his colonel was in no danger, so he went to the hotel, taking with him his relative.

At the sight of the French uniform and the Legion of Honour, the Prussians shamefully grabbed the crippled man and tried to snatch the cross of the Legion from him. When he resisted, the Prussian Cossacks killed him and dragged his body into the street before continuing their drinking.

Mons was so large in comparison to my small garrison, that I had taken refuge in the barracks and having arranged my defences for the night at this spot, I had forbidden my men to go near the main square, although I had been told that the enemy were there, because I did not know their strength and feared that the local populace would combine with them; but when the townspeople heard of the murder of Courtois, their fellow countryman and one regarded with affection by all, they resolved to be revenged, and forgetting their complaints against the French, they sent a deputation, comprising the brother of the dead man and some of the leading citizens, to ask me to put myself at their head in order to drive away these "Cossacks".

I was well aware that the pillage and excess at the Hotel de La Poste inspired in every bourgeois fear for his family and his house, which motivated them to expel the Cossacks as much as the death of Curtois, and that they would have acted very differently if, instead of robbers and assassins, it had been regular troops who had entered the town. Nonetheless I thought it my duty to take advantage of the good-will of those inhabitants who were prepared to take up arms to help us. I then took part of my troop and set off for the square, while the remainder, in charge of the battalion commander, who knew the town well, I sent to lie in wait at the breach in the wall through which the Prussian Cossacks had entered.

At the first shots fired by our people at these rogues, there was a great tumult in the hotel and the square. Those who were not killed took to their heels, but many got lost in the streets and were finished off one by one. As for those who reached the place where they had left their horses tied up to trees in the promenade, they ran into the battalion commander, who greeted them with a withering fusillade. At daylight we counted in the town and in the old breach more than 200 dead, while we had not lost a single man because our adversaries, fuddled by wine and strong liquor had offered no defence. Those of them who escaped into the country were caught and killed by the peasantry, who were enraged at the death of the unfortunate Curtois, who was something of a local celebrity, and who, given the name of "Jambe de bois", had become as dear to them as General Daumesnil, another "Jambe de bois". was to the working class of Paris.

I do not cite this fighting in Mons as something to be particularly proud of, for with the national guard, I had twelve or thirteen hundred men compared to the three hundred of the Prussians; but I thought it worth recording this bizarre encounter to demonstrate the volatility of the masses, which is displayed by the fact that all the peasants and coal miners of Borinage who a month previously had come in a mass to exterminate or at least disarm the few Frenchmen remaining in Mons, had come to join us to oppose the Prussians because they had killed one of their compatriots. I greatly regretted the death of the brave Courtois, who had fallen victim to his regard for me.

The most important trophy from our victory was the three hundred horses which the enemy abandoned. They nearly all came from the region of Berg and were of very good quality so I took them into my regiment, for which this unexpected provision of remounts was extremely welcome.

I passed a further month at Mons, whose inhabitants treated us perfectly well despite the approach of the enemy armies. However their continued advance meant that the French were forced not only to abandon Brussels but the whole of Belgium, and recross the frontiers into their motherland. I was ordered to take my regimental depot to Cambrai where, with the horses which I had taken from the Prussian Cossacks I was able to remount 300 good troopers who had returned from Leipzig, and make two fine squadrons, which commanded by Major Sigaldi, were sent to the army which the Emperor was assembling in Champagne. There they upheld the honour of the 23rd chasseuers, particularly at the battle of Champaubert, where the gallant Captain Duplessis, an outstanding officer, was killed.

I have always favoured the lance, a lethal weapon in the hands of a good cavalryman. I asked for and obtained permission to distribute to my squadrons some lances which artillery officers had been unable to carry away when they left the forts on the Rhine. They were so much appreciated that several other cavalry units followed my example, and were glad to have done so.

The regimental depots were obliged to cross to the left bank of the Seine to avoid falling into the hands of the enemy, mine went to Nogent-le-Roi, an arrondissment of Dreux. We had a fair number of troopers but almost no horses. The government was making great efforts to collect some at Versailles, where it had created a central cavalry depot commanded by General Préval.

The General, like his predecessor General Bourcier, knew much more about remounts and organisation than he did about war, in which he had rarely been involved. He did his utmost to fulfil the difficult task which the Emperor had given him; but as he could not improvise horses or equipment, and as he would not send out detachments until they were fully organised, departures were not very frequent. I grumbled, but no colonel could return to his unit without the permission of the Emperor, who to conserve his resources, had forbidden the employment of more officers in any unit than was justified by the number of men they had to command. It was therefore useless for me to beg General Préval to let me go to Champagne. He fixed my departure for the end of March, at which time I would lead to the army a draft composed of mounted men from my own depot and several others.

Until this time I was authorised to live in Paris with my family, for M. Caseneuve, my second-in-comand could take care of the 200 men who were still at Nogent-le-Roi, which I could reach if necessary, in a few hours. So I went to Paris, where I spent the greater part of March, which, although I was with those I loved most, was one of the most miserable months of my life. The imperial government, to which I was attached, and which I had for so long defended at the cost of my blood, was everywhere crumbling. The armies of the enemy, spreading from Lyon, occupied a large part of France, and it was easy to see that they would soon arrive at the capital.

Chapter 33
Paris Capitulates

The Emperor's greatest antagonists are forced to admit that he excelled himself in the winter campaign which he conducted in the first three months of 1814. No previous general had ever shown such talent, or achieved so much with such feeble resources. With a few thousand men, most of whom were inexperienced conscripts, one saw him face the armies of Europe, turning up everywhere with these troops, which he led from one point to another with marvellous rapidity.

Taking advantage of all the resources of the country in order to defend it, he hurried from the Austrians to the Russians, and from the Russians to the Prussians, going from Blücher to Schwarzenberg and from him to Sacken, sometimes beaten by them, but much more often the victor. He hoped, for a time, that he might drive the foreigners, disheartened by frequent defeats, from French soil and back across the Rhine. All that was required was a new effort by the nation; but there was general war-weariness, and there was in all parts, and particularly in Paris, plotting against the Empire.

There are those who have expressed surprise that France did not rise in mass, as in 1792, to repel the invader, or did not follow the Spanish in forming, in each province, a centre of national defence.

The reason is that the enthusiasm which had improvised the armies of 1792 had been exhausted by twenty-five years of war, and the Emperor's over-use of conscription, so that in most of the departments there remained only old men and children. As for the example of Spain, it is not applicable to France, where too much influence has been allowed to Paris, so that nothing can be done unless Paris leads the way, whereas in Spain each Province was a little government and was able to create its own army, even when Madrid was occupied by the French. It was centralisation which led to the loss of France.

It is no part of the task which I have set myself, to relate the great feats performed by the French army during the campaign of 1814, to do so I would have to write volumes, and I do not feel inclined to dwell on the misfortunes of my country. I shall content myself by saying that after disputing, foot by foot, the territory between the Marne, the Aube, the Saône and the Seine, the Emperor conceived a daring plan which, if it had succeeded, would have saved France. This was to go, with his troops, by way of Saint-Dizier and Vitry towards Alsace and Lorraine, which by threatening the rear of the enemies, would make them fear being cut off from their depots and finding themselves without any route of retreat. This would decide them to withdraw to the frontier while they still had the opportunity.

However, to ensure the success of this splendid strategic movement, it required the fulfilment of two conditions which failed him. These were the loyalty of the high officers of state, and some means of preventing the enemy from seizing Paris if they ignored the movement of the Emperor towards their rear and launched an attack on the city.

Sadly, loyalty to the Emperor was so much diminished in the Senate and the legislative body, that there were leading members of these assemblies, such as Tallyrand, the Duc de Dalberg, Laisné and others, who through secret emissaries informed the allied sovereigns of the dissatisfaction among the upper-class Parisians with Napoleon, and invited them to come and attack the capital.

As for defences, it must be admitted that Napoleon had not given this sufficient thought, and they were limited to the erection of a spiked palisade at the gates on the right bank, without the provision of any positions for guns. As the garrison, formed by a very small number of troops of the line, of invalids, veterans and students from the polytechnic was insufficient to even attempt resistance, the Emperor, when he left the capital in January to go and head the troops assembled in Champagne, confided to the National Guard the defence of Paris, where he left the Empress and his son. He had called together at the Tuileries the officers of this bourgeois militia, who had responded with numerous vows and bellicose undertakings to the rousing speech which he addressed to them. The Emperor named the Empress as Regent and appointed as overall commander his brother Joseph the ex-King of Spain, the pleasantest but most unsoldierlike of men.

Napoleon, under the illusion that he had thus provided for the safety of the capital, thought that he could leave it for some days to its own devices, while he went with those troops which still remained to him to carry out the project of getting behind the enemy. He left for Lorraine about the end of March; but he had been on his way for only a few days, when he learned that the allies, instead of following him as he had hoped, had headed for Paris, driving before then the weak debris of Mortier's and Marmont's corps who, positioned on the heights of Montmartre, attempted to defend the city without any help from the National Guard except an occasional infantryman.

This alarming news opened Napoleon's eyes; he turned his troops to march towards Paris, for where he set out immediately.

On the 30th of March, the Emperor, riding post and with no escort, had just passed Moret when a brisk cannonade was heard; he held on to the hope of arriving before the allies entered the capital, where his presence would certainly have had a remarkable effect on the population, who were demanding arms. (There were one hundred thousand muskets and several million cartridges in the barracks of the Champ de Mars, but General Clarke, the Minister for War, would not allow their distribution.)

On his arrival at Fromenteau, only five leagues from Paris, the Emperor could no longer hear gunfire and he realised that the city was in the hands of the allies, which was confirmed at Villejuif. Marmont had, in fact signed a capitulation which delivered the capital to the enemy.

As danger approached, the Empress and her son, the King of Rome, had gone to Blois, where they were shortly joined by King Joseph, who abandoned the command which the Emperor had given him. The troops of the line left by the Fontainebleau gate, a route by which the Emperor was expected to arrive.

It is not possible to describe the agitation which seized the city whose inhabitants, divided by so many different interests, had been surprised by an invasion which few of them had foreseen. As for me, who had expected it, and who had seen at close quarters the horrors of war, I was most anxiously thinking of a way to ensure the safety of my wife and our young child, when the elderly Marshal Sérurier offered a shelter for all my family at Les Invalides, of which he was the governor. I was comforted by the thought that as everywhere the homes for old soldiers had always been respected by the French, the enemy would act in the same way towards ours. I therefore took my family to the Invalides and left Paris, before the entry of the allies, to report to General Préval at Versailles. I was given command of a small column made up of available cavalrymen from my own regiment and from the 9th and 12th Chasseurs.

Even if the allies had not marched on Paris, this column was due to be assembled at Rambouillet, and it is to there that I went. I found there my horses and my equipment, and I took command of the squadrons which had been allotted to me. The road was full of the carriages of those who were flying from the capital. I was not surprised by that; but I was unable to understand where the great number of troops of all arms came from, which one saw arriving from all directions in detachments, which if they had been combined would have formed a corps of sufficient size to hold up the enemy at Montmartre, and allow time for the army which was hurrying from Champagne and Brie to arrive and save Paris. The Emperor misled by his Minister for War, had given no instructions regarding the matter, and was probably unaware that he still had so great a capacity for defence at his disposal, a description of which follows, taken from Ministry of War documents.

There were at Vincennes, the military school of the Champ de Mars and the central artillery depot some four hundred cannons with ammunition and 50,000 muskets. As for men, there were the troops brought by Marshals Marmont and Mortier, which together with troops gathered from other sources including 20,000 workmen, nearly all of them old soldiers, who had volunteered to help defend the city, amounted to some 80,000.

It would have been possible for Joseph and Clarke to assemble this force in a few hours and to defend the city until the arrival of the Emperor and the army which was following him.

Joseph and Clarke had forty-eight hours warning of the enemy approach, but did nothing, and as a final act of incompetence, at the moment when the enemy troops were attacking Romainville, they sent 4000 men of the Imperial Guard to Blois, to reinforce the escort of the Empress, which was already quite big enough.

When the Emperor learned that Paris had capitulated and that the two small corps of Marmont and Mortier had left, and were retiring towards him, he sent them orders to take up positions at Essonnes, seven leagues from Paris and mid-way between that city and Fontainebleau. He went himself to this last town, where were arriving the heads of the columns coming from Saint-Dizier, an indication that he intended to march on Paris as soon as his army was gathered together.

The enemy generals have later stated that if they had been attacked by the Emperor, they would not have risked a battle, with the Seine behind them and also the great city of Paris, with its million inhabitants, which might rise in revolt at any moment during the fighting and barricade the streets and the bridges, thus cutting off their line of retreat. So they had decided to draw back and camp on the heights of Belleville, Charonne, Montmartre and the slopes of Chaumont, which dominate the right bank of the Seine and the route to Germany, when new events in Paris kept them in the city.

M. de Tallyrand, a former bishop now married, who had always appeared to be devoted to the Emperor, by whom he had been loaded with riches and made prince of Benevento, Grand Chamberlain, etc., etc., felt his pride injured when he was no longer Napoleon's confidant, and the minister directing his policy. So, after the disasters of the Russian campaign, he had put himself at the head of an underground conspiracy, which included all the malcontents from every party, but mainly the Faubourg Saint-Germain, that is to say the high aristocracy, who, after appearing at first submissive and even serving Napoleon in the time of his prosperity, had become his enemy and without openly compromising themselves, attacked, by all means, the head of government.

These people, guided by Tallyrand, the most cunning and scheming of them all, had been waiting for an occasion to overthrow Napoleon. They realised that they would never have a more favourable opportunity than that offered by the occupation of the country by a million and a half enemies, and the presence in Paris of all the crowned heads of Europe, most of whom had been grossly humiliated by Napoleon at one time or another. Napoleon, however, though greatly weakened, was not yet entirely beaten, for, apart from the army which he had with him, and with which he had performed prodigies, there was Suchet's army, between the Pyrenees and the Haute-Garonne, there were troops commanded by Marshal Soult, there were two fine divisions at Lyon, and finally, the army in Italy was still formidable, so that in spite of the occupation of Bordeaux by the English, Napoleon might still assemble considerable forces and prolong the war indefinitely, by raising a population, exasperated by the exactions of the enemy.

Tallyrand, for his part, realised that if they gave the Emperor time to bring to Paris the troops who were with him, he might beat the allies in the streets of the capital, or withdraw to some loyal provinces, where he might continue the war, until the allies were exhausted and ready to make peace. In the view of Tallyrand and his friends, it was therefore necessary to change the government. Here there arose a great difficulty, for they wanted to restore the Bourbons to the throne, in the person of Louis XVIII, while other parts of the country wanted to retain Napoleon, or at most to install his son.

The same difference of opinion existed amongst the allied sovereigns. The kings of England and Prussia were on the side of the Bourbons, while the emperor of Russia, who had never liked them, and who feared that the antipathy felt by the French nation towards these princes and the émigrés would lead to a fresh revolution, was inclined to favour Napoleon's son.

To cut short these discussions, and decide the question by making the first move, the astute Tallyrand, in an attempt to force the hand of the foreign sovereigns, arranged for a group of about twenty young men from the Faubourg Saint-Germain to appear on horseback in Louis XV square, decked with white cockades, and led by Vicomte Talon, my former comrade in arms, from whom I have these details. They went towards the mansion in the rue Saint-Florentin occupied by the Emperor Alexander, shouting at the top of their voices "Long live King Louis XVIII! Long live the Bourbons! Down with the tyrant!"

The effect produced on the curious gathering of onlookers by these cries, was at first one of astonishment, which was quickly succeeded by threats and menaces from the crowd, which shook even the boldest of the cavalcade. This first royalist demonstration having been unsuccessful, they repeated the performance at various points on the boulevards. At some places they were booed, at others applauded. As the entry procession of the allied sovereigns approached, and as the Parisians need a slogan to animate them, the one produced by Vicomte Talon and his friends rang in the ears of the Emperor Alexander throughout the whole day, which permitted Tallyrand to say to that monarch in the evening, "Your Majesty can judge for himself with what unanimity the nation desires the restoration of the Bourbons!"

From that moment, although his supporters greatly outnumbered those of Louis XVIII, as the events of the following year would show, Napoleon's cause was lost.

Epilogue

Marbot's 'Memoirs' end with the first abdication of Napoleon, so that we lose what we would gladly have had —his reminiscences of the Elba and Waterloo period; though a few letters exist giving some scanty details with regard to the Waterloo campaign. From an article by M. Cuvillier-Fleury, published in the 'Journal des Débats' shortly after the general's death, we learn that at the first Restoration he was maintained in the army, and placed in command of the 7th Hussars. As might be expected when Napoleon returned, Marbot and his regiment went back to their former allegiance, and at Waterloo they formed part of the corps under the Count of Erlon; being posted on the extreme right of the French line. On April 10 he had written:

> *I have to guard the line from Mouchin to Chéreng. It is not much trouble to do, for the English do not stir, and are as quiet at Tournay as if they were in London. I think that everything will pass of peaceably.*

Writing from Saint-Amand in the following month, he still reports all quiet; the enemy's troops deserting in heaps; men flocking *'thick as flies'* to the French regiments.

> *People think there will be no fighting. Here we think that almost certain.*

By June 13 the complexion of affairs is changed, and he writes from Pont-sur-Sambre: *'I do not think there will be a battle for another five days'*—a very accurate forecast. After the affair of June 17 at Genappe, Marbot was promoted major-general; but this appointment did not take effect. The following letter, written on June 26 from Laon, gives Marbot's fresh impressions of Waterloo:

> *I cannot get over our defeat. We were manœuvred like so many pumpkins. I was with my regiment on the right flank of the army almost throughout the battle. They assured me that Marshal Grouchy would come up at that point; and it was guarded only by my regiment*

with three guns and a battalion of infantry—not nearly enough. In-
stead of Grouchy, what arrived was Blucher's corps. You can imagine
how we were served. We were driven in, and in an instant the enemy
was on our rear. The mischief might have been repaired, but no one
gave any orders. The big generals were making bad speeches at Paris;
the small ones lose their heads, and all goes wrong. I got a lance-
wound in the side; it is pretty severe, but I thought I would stay to
set a good example. If everyone had done the same we might yet get
along; but the men are deserting, and no one stops them. Whatever
people may say, there are 50,000 men in this neighbourhood who
might be got together; but to do it we should have to make it a capi-
tal offence to quit your post, or to give leave of absence. Everybody
gives leave, and the coaches are full of officers departing. You may
judge if the soldiers stay. There will not be one left in a week, unless
they are checked by the death penalty. The Chambers can save us
if they like; but we must have severe measures and prompt action.
No food is sent to us, and so the soldiers pillage our poor France as
if they were in Russia. I am at the outposts, before Laon; we have
been made to promise not to fire, and all is quiet.

In a letter written fifteen years later to General F. de Grouchy,
Marbot enters more into detail. From this we learn that his regiment formed part of the force which was thrown back en potence
on the extreme right, fronting the stream of the Dyle, as may be
seen in any plan of the battle. The Emperor's instructions, conveyed
to him by his old comrade Labédoyere, who was then acting as
aide-de-camp to Napoleon, were, while keeping the bulk of his
force in view of the field of battle, to push forward his outposts towards Saint-Lambert and Ottignies; leaving a line of cavalry pickets a quarter of a league apart one from the other, so that when
Grouchy arrived the news might be passed along without delay.
One of these detachments reached Moustier about 1 p.m., and the
officer in command at once sent back word that the French troops
posted on the right bank of the Dyle were crossing the river—i.e.
falling back. This intelligence was forwarded to the Emperor, and
an orderly officer soon came with orders to Marbot to push as far
as possible in the direction of Wavre. Near Saint-Lambert one of his
sections fell in with some Prussian cavalry, capturing an officer and
a few men. These were promptly sent to the Emperor, and Marbot

hastened with a squadron towards Saint-Lambert. There he saw a strong column advancing and again sent intelligence to headquarters. But the reply was that it could be nothing but Grouchy; that the prisoners were doubtless some Prussian stragglers flying before his advance, and that Marbot might go forward boldly. Of course he had to obey orders; but soon had proof positive as to the nature of the advancing column. After hard fighting he had to retire, again reporting the circumstances to the Emperor. So possessed, however, was Napoleon with his own view of the case, that he merely sent back the adjutant with orders to Marbot 'to let Grouchy know.' By this time his outposts were all falling back, and soon he was closely engaged with the English left, near Frischermont, and received the wound which he mentions in the letter already quoted. A report which he drew up later in the year at the instance of Davout, then Minister of War, has unfortunately disappeared.

After Waterloo, Marbot had to leave France; and during the period of his exile, which he spent in Germany, he composed the work by which until the appearance of the present Memoirs he was best known—a criticism on General Rogniart's *Considérations sur l'Art de la Guerre.* It was this which earned the flattering reference to him, accompanying a legacy of 100,000 francs, in Napoleon's will. '*I bid Colonel Marbot,*' he says, '*continue to write in defence of the glory of the French armies, and to the confusion of calumniators and apostates.*'

In 1818 Marbot was recalled to France and placed on half-pay. He occupied his leisure by writing another book, '*On the Necessity of Increasing the Military Forces of France,*' which was well thought of. Presently his services were again in request, and in 1829 he was placed in command of the 8th Chasseurs. In the following year he became aide-de-camp to the Duke of Orleans, and a second time attained the rank of major-general. From that time till the fall of the monarchy 'of July' he was constantly employed. He received one more wound; when he was nearly sixty years old. During the Medeah expedition in Algiers he was hit by a bullet in the left knee. As he was being carried to the rear, he remarked with a smile to the Duke: '*This is your fault, sir.*' '*How so?*' naturally said the Duke. '*Did I not hear you say, before the fighting began, that if any of your staff got wounded, you could bet it would be Marbot? You see you have won!*'

On the death of the Duke in 1842, he was attached to the staff of the Count of Paris, then a child of four years old; a post which at all events may have kept the veteran out of danger. In 1848 he was placed for the last time on the retired list; and in November 1854 his honourable life came to an end. Few men of that age seem to have left a more creditable record.

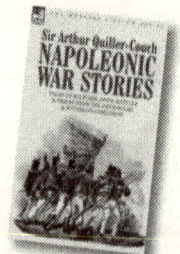

www.ingramcontent.com/pod-product-compliance
Lightning Source LLC
Chambersburg PA
CBHW030357100426
42812CB00028B/2749/J